"Gabriele Boccaccini's book is a fascinating, incisively reasoned contribution to Qumran research."

—ELAINE PAGELS
Princeton University

8/09 Free for the taking!!

Beyond the Essene Hypothesis

The Parting of the Ways between Qumran and Enochic Judaism

GABRIELE BOCCACCINI

WILLIAM B. EERDMANS PUBLISHING COMPANY
GRAND RAPIDS, MICHIGAN / CAMBRIDGE, U.K.

© 1998 Wm. B. Eerdmans Publishing Co.
255 Jefferson Ave. S.E., Grand Rapids, Michigan 49503 /
P.O. Box 163, Cambridge CB3 9PU U.K.

Printed in the United States of America

03 02 01 00 99 98   7 6 5 4 3 2 1

Library of Congress Cataloging-in-Publication Data

Boccaccini, Gabriele, 1958-
Beyond the Essene hypothesis: the parting of the ways
between Qumran and Enochic Judaism / Gabriele Boccaccini.
p.   cm.
Includes bibliographical references and index.
ISBN 0-8028-4360-3 (pbk.: alk. paper)
1. Qumran community.
2. Essenes.
3. Dead Sea scrolls — Criticism, interpretation, etc.
4. Ethiopic book of Enoch — Criticism, interpretation, etc.
I. Title.
BM175.Q6B63   1998
296.8′14 — dc21   97-41870
                                                CIP

For Paolo and Cherubina

Contents

CONTENTS

Preface

I have always been fascinated by the study of second temple Judaism.

I can hardly remember a time when I wasn't.

If you grow up in Florence, Italy, from the moment you are born you live totally immersed in the past.

My people speak of our Etruscan, Roman, and Renaissance ancestors as if they were good friends who just passed away. Their belongings are still around to remind us of their existence, and we take care of everything they left, as we do with our own belongings.

When I was barely old enough to read the Scriptures, my parish priest gravely warned me that the only way to understand Jesus' words was to study them critically in their own historical and cultural context. At that time I could not possibly understand what he meant. In my own confused way, however, I realized that this had something to do with my grandpa telling me anedoctes about the great Florentines buried in the Basilica of Santa Croce, or my mother reading books for hours when she was studying for her Ph.D. in philosophy. My mother's books, full of strange phrases whose meaning I could not yet understand, intrigued me not less than the mysterious Latin inscriptions on the funeral monuments of Santa Croce. Although I was still a child, history and philosophy had already enticed me with their magic spell.

It was more than intellectual curiosity.

In my family, stories were told about my grandfather's and father's involvements in the Italian anti-Nazi underground during World War II.

My paternal grandfather had died long before I was born, and my father, a public figure with a successful career in the opera business, privately was the most reserved person I have ever known. Stories of false identity cards fabricated with stolen letter-headed paper and "borrowed" stamps were whispered in family gatherings, alluded to as secrets that grown-ups know and hide from children. I never got the details, but it was enough for me to understand that the war had been a terrible time, when people were hungry and scared and when some members of my family were even killed. In my child's mind I could not figure out why, at that time, some bad people persecuted innocent people, women and children included, for no plausible reason, but I felt proud that my father and the grandpa I never met sided with the people who tried to help. Later I would meet some of those good people.

In Florence during the war, there was an underground organization led by a committee of Jews and Christians, including the young rabbi of Florence, Nathan Cassuto, and appointees of the Catholic archbishop of Florence, Cardinal Elia Dalla Costa. The Cardinal had never hidden his anti-Nazi attitudes, so much so that before the war when Hitler visited Florence, the Cardinal shut the windows of his residence and forbade the clergy to attend the celebrations. Many of the members of that wartime clandestine committee were arrested or sent to death at Auschwitz, but not before they had rescued hundreds of Jews and other refugees.

Immediately after the war, some of the people involved in that operation founded one of the first European associations for Jewish-Christian dialogue. The name they chose, Amicizia Ebraico-Cristiana (Jewish-Christian Friendship), tastes of personal ties, common joy, and common tears. Many years later, when I joined that association, I had the opportunity to become acquainted with don Leto Casini, an old and venerable priest and the last surviving member of that committee. Never in his adventurous life, not even when he was captured and beaten by the Nazis, had Casini lost either his trust in the goodness of humankind or his contagious sense of humor. I came to realize that good people are embarrassed to tell the good things they have done.

In the meantime, during the 1960s and 1970s, Florence had become the laboratory for one of the most daring attempts at reforming the Catholic Church according to the principles and the "spirit" of Vatican II. Cardinal Elia Dalla Costa and a former city mayor of the 1950s, Giorgio La Pira, two charismatic leaders whom Florentines regarded as saints, had prepared the way for a new generation of priests and laypeople who reclaimed the right of Catholics to read Scripture on its own terms and who called for reconciliation and justice among people from different religions and ways of life. Figures like don Lorenzo Milani, don Ernesto Balducci, Raniero La Valle, Giampaolo Meucci, and Mario Gozzini may not mean much outside Italy, but they were the heroes of my youth. A student at the University of Florence and of an idealistic nature, I vowed to devote my life to the study of the historical, cultural, and philosophical environment of first-century Palestine and to a better contemporary understanding between Christians and Jews.

I have so many people to thank for helping me make my dreams come true.

First, there was my parish priest, who taught me the rudiments of the historical method. Then there were many teachers and distinguished professors who taught me the art of being a scholar. Finally, I found Paolo Sacchi, the person who understood my deepest motivations. He became the mentor and model I had always dreamed of studying under and even imitating. The years I spent with him and the other members of the "Turin team" at the Department of Oriental Studies of the University of Turin were blessed by friendship and joy. I will never forget the experience.

Then it was Princeton and the long conversations on the lawns of the Seminary with James Charlesworth, Joel Marcus, and John Barclay and the frequent visits to the Institute for Advanced Studies where Jacob Neusner was spending a sabbatical. In the fall of 1992, I eventually settled in Ann Arbor, where the University of Michigan became my second home. The chairs, colleagues, and staff of the Department of Near Eastern Studies, of the Program on Studies in Religion, and of the Frankel Center for Judaic Studies have welcomed me with great hospitality and been very supportive. With friendship and affection, Jane Hansen has taught me the mechanism of the administration, while the wisdom and sensitivity of Astrid Beck have helped me to penetrate more deeply into the world of American university. My colleagues in biblical studies, David Noel Freedman, Ralph Williams, Jarl Fossum, and Brian Schmidt, have been an inexhaustible source of inspiration and advice. Together, we have worked at forging, and have been forged by, a remarkable group of graduate students who are now distinguished colleagues: April De Conick, Harold Ellens, Charles Gieshen, Mark Kinzer, Lynne Kogel, Phillip Munoa, and Rick Rogers. I wish I could also mention here the names of each of the thousand students who have crammed into my undergraduate classes. They were the ones who came to learn; but because of their questions, enthusiasm, and participation, it was I who learned the most.

Joy and sorrow are ingredients of everyone's life. In these last years my beloved father passed away, and my brother and my German sister-in-law have somehow managed to evade the busyness of their work as scientists in Karlsruhe and give to our family the joy of two adorable and perfectly bilingual children, Enrico and Elena. With Roman and Alyosha, the two lovely Belarusian kids we foster during the summer, Enrico and Elena have transformed our annual vacations in Italy into a joyous kindergarten. In all these events, since we first met eighteen years ago in a Hebrew class at the University of Florence, I have always had at my side my sweet wife, Aloma Bardi. She is a scholar herself in American music, and an extraordinary woman of character and integrity, and I admire and adore her with all my heart. Without her I would have accomplished nothing.

My first works on "middle Judaism" were largely dominated by methodological issues. Studying the history of research on second temple Judaism, I soon came to realize how much our understanding of the period was still affected by a cultural pattern that for confessional reasons aimed to present Christianity and Judaism as separate and independent monoliths. Centuries of religious confrontation made second temple Judaism the battlefield for the conflicting identities of Christians and Jews. Christians described the period as the "late" degenerative phase of Judaism between the Old and the New Testament; for the Jews, on the othe hand, it was the "early" stage in the evolution of Rabbinic Judaism between the Tanak and the Mishnah. The literature of the period was forced into confessionally divided corpora only to serve as weapons for theological disputes. Through the superimposition of anachronistic criteria, the original ties among ancient documents were lost.

Three points became clear to me.

First, we needed to recover the integrity of the period. A terminology that labeled the period as either the end point of Judaism before Jesus, or as the starting point of classical Rabbinic Judaism, failed to recognize its fundamental character as the transitional age ("middle Judaism") when both Christianity and Rabbinic Judaism emerged from their common "biblical" roots.

Second, we needed to recover the pluralism of the period, which was not simply a stage in the evolution of a single system of thought. The object of a history of middle Judaism had to be the identification and diachronic study of parallel Judaisms (including early Christianity) and of their complex synchronic relationships.

Third, we needed to free the documents from the cages of their corpora. A confessional criterion for collecting sources could no longer be the distinguishing criterion for understanding their content. We had to rearrange the material according to a taxonomy that respected the historical diversity within middle Judaism and the ideological ties between its various groups.

In this perspective, the history of philosophy gave me an effective model of how to infer a taxonomy of competing systems of thought based on the extant documents. What I call "systemic analysis" of middle Jewish documents is nothing more than the application of criteria commonly used by intellectual historians in the study of the history of competing philosophical positions in antiquity. It was a rather obvious step for one who was trained in Florence at the school of the philosophers and historians Eugenio Garin and Francesco Adorno. In the United States, intellectual history also has a significant and glorious tradition in the *Journal for the History of Ideas,* founded in 1940 by Arthur O. Lovejoy.

My early investigations resulted in a couple of books — *Middle Judaism: Jewish Thought, 300 BCE to 200 CE* (Minneapolis: Fortress, 1991; Italian rev. ed.: *Il medio giudaismo* [Genoa: Marietti, 1993]) and *Portraits of Middle Judaism in Scholarship and Arts: A Multimedia Catalog from Flavius Josephus to 1991* (Turin: Zamorani, 1992) — as well as in a series of articles on "middle Judaism," including "Middle Judaism and Its Contemporary Interpreters" (*Henoch* 15 [1993] 207-33), "History of Judaism: Its Periods in Antiquity" (*Judaism in Late Antiquity,* ed. Jacob Neusner [Leiden: Brill, 1995] 2:285-308), and "Multiple Judaisms" (*Bible Review* 11/1 [1995] 38-41, 46). An intense schedule of lectures has driven me coast to coast, from Barnard College and the University of Pennsylvania to the University of California at Los Angeles and Claremont Graduate School, through the University of Chicago, the Hebrew Union College, Duke University, and many other American Universities and Seminaries. In addition, it has taken me back to Europe, the Royal Irish Academy in Dublin, the Pontifical Biblical Institute in Rome, to the Society of Biblical Literature meeting in Münster, and, every two years, to the the conferences of the Italia Biblical Association at Seiano, L'Aquila, and Rocca di Papa.

While in those publications and lectures my concern was mostly to deconstruct the foundations of traditional research and to establish new criteria for analysis, this book takes an entirely constructive approach. It traces the existence of a chain of documents representative of a particular variety of Judaism ("Enochic Judaism") that played a crucial role in the distinctive development of Essene theology at Qumran. The attempt goes beyond that of disarticulating the traditional corpora; the book proposes an alternative taxonomy for the material. Some of the choices may be debatable and are offered to scholarly attention as a working hypothesis, but the questions my taxonomy raises — for example, whether and to what degree the Testaments of Twelve Patriarchs belongs to the same party that produced the Enoch books — seem much more interesting and appropriate than discussing whether the document should be part of the modern collections of the Old Testament Pseudepigrapha or the Dead Sea Scrolls.

This book on Qumran and Enochic Judaism will soon be paired with another volume to be published by Eerdmans, *Rabbinic Origins: An Intellectual History,* in which I trace the roots of a proto-Rabbinic tradition in the literature of second temple Judaism, from Daniel to the Mishnah. I have been working on these two parallel projects since I arrived in Ann Arbor in 1992. The Italian Conference on the Dead Sea Scrolls held at L'Aquila in the summer of 1995 prompted this book to be completed first. It was at L'Aquila that I first articulated the "Enochic/Essene hypothesis" as an attempt to make sense of the many relationships between the Enoch books and the sectarian literature of Qumran.

In the composition of this volume, I have greatly benefited from meetings and conversations with James Charlesworth, John Collins, Philip Davies, Ithamar Gruenwald, Anthony Saldarini, James Sanders, Lawrence Schiffman, Emanuel Tov, James VanderKam, and Ben Zion Wacholder, who were guests at the University of Michigan in two series of public lectures and graduate seminars on the Dead Sea Scrolls. Florentino García Martínez and Paolo Sacchi have reviewed the entire manuscript, and have given valuable advice and welcome words of encouragement. Mark Kinzer and Lynne Kogel have accompanied the growth of this project, step by step, as only guardian angels or good friends will do. They have done more much than helping me polish the presentation; they have been the first critics of my book. In Eerdmans I have found a publishing company that takes good care of its authors, edits their books competently, and treats them with respect.

On the one hand, the Dead Sea Scrolls will be claimed unilaterally as witnesses of either formative Christianity or formative Rabbinic Judaism, and become just one more chapter in the exercise in denial that Christians and Jews have so masterfully practiced in the attempts of each to disinherit the other. On the other hand, the Dead Sea Scrolls may become a unique opportunity to rediscover, along with our common heritage, an even more precious treasure — living brothers and sisters whom we have too long neglected. I love Alan Segal's imagery of Christians and Jews as "Rebecca's children." Yes, the struggle began in our mother's womb, and through childhood and adulthood we have viciously and remorselessly fought over the birthright. Historical research now confirms that the feeling many Christians and Jews experienced as a result of the tragedy of the Holocaust was more than human solidarity: it was the call of the blood. Our walks of life are different and will remain such, but our genetic code is largely the same: whether we like it or not, we are children of the same parents. After so many years of struggle and estrangement, the time has come, as for Jacob and Esau, to meet again, reconcile, mourn our deceased parents, and tell each other about our new identities.

I have always been fascinated by the study of second temple Judaism. I can hardly remember a time when I wasn't.

Ann Arbor, MI
26 October 1997

Gabriele Boccaccini

Abbreviations and Sigla

AB	Anchor Bible
ABD	*Anchor Bible Dictionary*
AGJU	Arbeiten zur Geschichte des antiken Judentums und des Urchristentums
ANRW	*Aufstieg und Niedergang der römischen Welt*
Arch	*Archaeology*
ASE	*Annali di Storia dell'Esegesi*
ATANT	Abhandlungen zur Theologie des Alten und Neuen Testaments
AUUHR	Acta Universitatis Upsaliensis, Historia Religionum
BA	*Biblical Archaeologist*
BARev	*Biblical Archaeology Review*
BASOR	*Bulletin of the American Schools of Oriental Research*
BASORSupSt	*Bulletin of the American Schools of Oriental Research, Supplemental Studies*
BETL	Bibliotheca ephemeridum theologicarum lovaniensium
BHT	Beiträge zur historischen Theologie
Bib	*Biblica*
BibOr	Biblica et orientalia
BJS	Brown Judaic Studies
BK	*Bibel und Kirche*
BR	*Bible Review*
BTB	*Biblical Theology Bulletin*

BZAW	Beihefte zur *Zeitschrift für die alttestamentliche Wissenschaft*
BZNW	Beihefte zur *Zeitschrift für die neutestamentliche Wissenschaft*
CBQ	*Catholic Biblical Quarterly*
CBQMS	*Catholic Biblical Quarterly* Monograph Series
ConBNT	Coniectanea biblica, New Testament
CRINT	Compendia rerum iudaicarum ad novum testamentum
CSCO	Corpus scriptorum christianorum orientalium
DJD	Discoveries in the Judaean Desert
DSD	*Dead Sea Discoveries*
DUJ	*Durham University Journal*
EncJud	*Encyclopaedia Judaica*
ErIsr	*Eretz Israel*
EstBib	*Estudios bíblicos*
FB	Forschung zur Bibel
FO	*Folia Orientalia*
FOTL	Forms of the Old Testament Literature
HAR	*Hebrew Annual Review*
Hen	*Henoch*
HeyJ	*Heythrop Journal*
HSM	Harvard Semitic Monographs
HTR	*Harvard Theological Review*
HTS	Harvard Theological Studies
HUCA	*Hebrew Union College Annual*
IEJ	*Israel Exploration Journal*
IOS	*Israel Oriental Studies*
IRT	Issues in Religion and Theology
JBL	*Journal of Biblical Literature*
JJS	*Journal of Jewish Studies*
JQR	*Jewish Quarterly Review*
JSHRZ	Jüdische Schriften aus hellenistisch-römischer Zeit
JSJ	*Journal for the Study of Judaism*
JSOT	*Journal for the Study of the Old Testament*
JSOTSup	*Journal for the Study of the Old Testament, Supplements*
JSP	*Journal for the Study of the Pseudepigrapha*

JSPSup	*Journal for the Study of the Pseudepigrapha,* Supplements
JTC	*Journal for Theology and the Church*
LD	Lectio divina
NovTSup	*Novum Testamentum,* Supplements
NTS	*New Testament Studies*
OrChr	*Oriens christianus*
OTL	Old Testament Library
OTP	J. H. Charlesworth, ed., *The Old Testament Pseudepigrapha*
PdV	*Parole di Vita*
PSV	*Parola, Spirito e Vita*
PTMS	Pittsburgh Theological Monograph Series
PVTG	Pseudepigrapha Veteris Testamenti Graece
RB	*Revue biblique*
RevQ	*Revue de Qumrân*
RH	*Revue historique*
RHR	*Revue de l'histoire des religions*
RivB	*Rivista Biblica*
RSB	*Ricerche Storico-Bibliche*
RSR	*Recherches de science religieuse*
SANT	Studien zum Alten und Neuen Testament
SAOC	Studies in Ancient Oriental Civilization
SBLDS	Society of Biblical Literature Dissertation Series
SBLEJL	SBL Early Judaism and Its Literature
SBLMS	SBL Monograph Series
SBLRBS	SBL Resources for Biblical Study
SBLSCS	SBL Septuagint and Cognate Studies
SBT	Studies in Biblical Theology
ScrHier	Scripta hierosolymitana
SJLA	Studies in Judaism in Late Antiquity
SNTSMS	Society for New Testament Studies Monograph Series
SPB	Studia postbiblica
STDJ	Studies on the Texts of the Desert of Judah
SUNT	Studien zur Umwelt des Neuen Testaments
SVTP	Studia in Veteris Testamenti pseudepigrapha
TRE	*Theologische Realenzyklopädie*
TSAJ	Texte und Studien zum Antiken Judentum

TZ	*Theologische Zeitschrift*
VC	*Vigiliae christianae*
VT	*Vetus Testamentum*
VTSup	Supplements to *Vetus Testamentum*
WBC	Word Biblical Commentary
WMANT	Wissenschaftliche Monographien zum Alten und Neuen Testament
WUNT	Wissenschaftliche Untersuchungen zum Neuen Testament
ZAW	*Zeitschrift für die alttestamentliche Wissenschaft*
ZDPV	*Zeitschrift des deutschen Palästina-Vereins*
ZNW	*Zeitschrift für die neutestamentliche Wissenschaft*
[[ ]]	Double brackets mark author's explicatory notes in quotations from ancient texts (which use square brackets for restorations and lacunae, and hooked brackets for philological emendations)

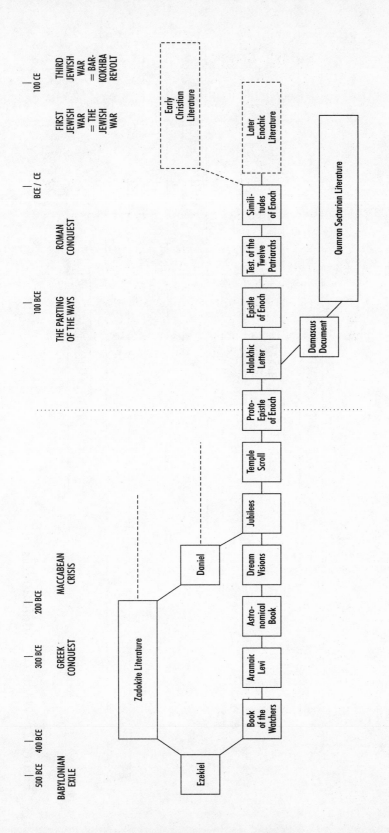

Figure 1. The "Qumran Chain" of Documents

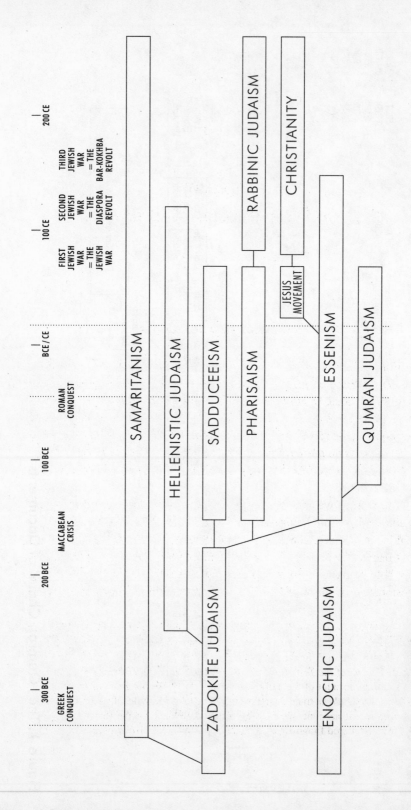

Figure 2. A Map of Middle Judaisms

Timeline markers: 300 BCE — GREEK CONQUEST · 200 BCE · MACCABEAN CRISIS · 100 BCE · ROMAN CONQUEST · BCE/CE · FIRST JEWISH WAR = THE JEWISH WAR · 100 CE · SECOND JEWISH WAR = THE DIASPORA REVOLT · THIRD JEWISH WAR = THE BAR-KOKHBA REVOLT · 200 CE

Traditions: SAMARITANISM · HELLENISTIC JUDAISM · ZADOKITE JUDAISM · SADDUCEEISM · PHARISAISM · RABBINIC JUDAISM · JESUS MOVEMENT · CHRISTIANITY · ESSENISM · ENOCHIC JUDAISM · QUMRAN JUDAISM

CHAPTER 1

Introduction:
Beyond the Essene Hypothesis

1. The Calm after the Storm

Fifty years after the discovery of the Dead Sea Scrolls, the sky looks unusually clear and calm, now that the clouds and thunder that came in the early 1990s with the fight for free access to the yet unpublished manuscripts have dispersed.[1] With the release in fall 1991 of the complete set of photographs of the scrolls and the subsequent publication of the microfiche edition,[2] there is no more room for pretended surprises or only-announced-and-never-fulfilled revelations. At last, the era of big expectations and big suspicions is over.

The stormy weather so recently passed has not prevented many remarkable results from being accomplished on the philological and technological levels. Looking back at the frontier environment in which the first editors began the process of piecing together the fragmentary texts, one cannot help being amazed by the progress that has been made concerning the restoration of the manuscripts.[3] The first, timid attempts at applying

---

1. A survey is offered by J. C. VanderKam, "Controversies about the Dead Sea Scrolls," in *The Dead Sea Scrolls Today* (Grand Rapids: Eerdmans, 1994) 187-201.

2. E. Tov with S. J. Pfann, *The Dead Sea Scrolls on Microfiche: A Comprehensive Facsimile Edition of the Texts from the Judaean Desert* (Leiden: Brill, 1993).

3. For an account of the early years, see J. T. Milik, *Ten Years of Discovery in the Wilderness of Judaea*, trans. J. Strugnell, SBT 1/26 (Naperville, Ill.: Allenson, 1959). For a more recent account, see H. Stegemann, "Methods for the Reconstruction of Scrolls from Scattered Fragments," in L. H. Schiffman, ed., *Archaeology and History*

computer science to the study of the scrolls have blossomed into a new generation of philological studies, based on the most advanced technologies.[4] The discussion about the ideological identification of the community who owned the scrolls and wrote some of them, however, has remained basically stalled at the Essene hypothesis, which since the discovery of the first manuscripts immediately presented itself to scholars as the most likely. According to this hypothesis, the Dead Sea Scrolls would be the main library of an Essene community led by Zadokite priests who in the aftermath of the Maccabean revolt retired into the wilderness in a settlement known today as Qumran.[5]

Recent years have seen a revival and proliferation of revisionistic hypotheses, in particular about the archaeology of Qumran. Some scholars have once again challenged the identification of Khirbet Qumran as the ruins of a sectarian communal center, although none of the alternative hypotheses (a fortress, a *villa rustica,* a trading center) has gained scholarly consensus.[6]

---

in the Dead Sea Scrolls: The New York University Conference in Memory of Yigael Yadin (Sheffield: Sheffield Academic Press, 1990) 189-220.

4. On the first computer applications, see R. Busa, "The Index of All Non-Biblical Dead Sea Scrolls Published up to December 1957," *RevQ* 1 (1958) 187-98. For recent developments, see B. E. Zuckerman, "Bringing the Dead Sea Scrolls to Life: A New Evaluation of Photographic and Electronic Imaging of the Dead Sea Scrolls," *DSD* 3 (1996) 178-207; D. W. Parry and S. D. Ricks, eds., *Current Research and Technological Developments on the Dead Sea Scrolls: Conference on the Texts from the Judean Desert, Jerusalem, 30 April 1995,* STDJ 20 (Leiden: Brill, 1996).

5. The first scholar to relate the scrolls to the Essenes was Eleazar L. Sukenik (*Megillot Genuzot mittok Genizah Qedumah še-Nimṣe'ah be-Midbar Yehudah: Seqirah Rišonah* [Jerusalem: Bialik Foundation, 1948]). Roland de Vaux established the connection between Qumran and the Dead Sea Scrolls as the result of a series of archaeological excavations in the 1950s. For a recent reassessment of the Essene hypothesis in the context of an updated overview of the *status quaestionis,* see VanderKam, *Dead Sea Scrolls Today,* esp. 71ff.; cf. also F. M. Cross, *The Ancient Library of Qumran,* 3rd ed. (Sheffield: Sheffield Academic Press, 1995).

6. Norman Golb (*Who Wrote the Dead Sea Scrolls?* [New York: Scribner, 1995]) argues that Qumran was a fortress and the scrolls were carried from some private libraries of Jerusalem before the siege of the city in 68-70 CE. In a way, Golb's hypothesis repeats the theory of K. H. Rengstorf (*Ḥirbet Qumrân and the Problem of the Library of the Dead Sea Caves* [Leiden: Brill, 1963]), who claimed that the scrolls belonged originally to the library of the temple in Jerusalem. Lena Cansdale (*Qumran and the Essenes: A Re-Evaluation of the Evidence* [Tübingen: Mohr, 1997]; cf. A. D. Crown and L. Cansdale, "Qumran: Was It an Essene Settlement?" *BARev* 20/5 [1994] 24-35, 73-78) maintains that

Other scholars have taken a less radical approach. They do not question that Qumran was a religious communal center related directly to the scrolls. They argue, however, that the site should be understood as a facility center for the larger Essene movement, not the headquarters of an autonomous Essene community. According to Hartmut Stegemann, Qumran was a place for temporary retreat, "a study center for all members," a combination book factory and library intended for the use of the entire Essene sect.[7] Edward M. Cook has a similar but slightly different theory about what Qumran was in relationship to the larger Essene movement. He speaks of Qumran as a ritual purification center, "an outpost or annex for the Jerusalem branch of [Essene] sectarians, . . . housing a small permanent staff as well as providing for a constant stream of incoming unclean members and outgoing clean ones."[8]

Although not compelling enough to revolutionize the course of mainstream research, these revisionistic arguments have been sufficiently documented to open new horizons of possibilities and to force scholars to reassess the archaeology of Qumran with an open mind. At the very least, this revisionism serves as a healthy reminder that many crucial questions remain unanswered and the final archaeological report is still to be written.[9]

Qumran was a stopping place along a major commercial route. Robert Donceel and Pauline Donceel-Voûte ("The Archaeology of Khirbet Qumran," in M. O. Wise, et al., eds., *Methods of Investigation of the Dead Sea Scrolls and the Khirbet Qumran Site: Present Realities and Future Prospects* [New York: New York Academy of Sciences, 1994] 1-38) speak of Qumran as a *villa rustica*. These hypotheses are more sophisticated versions of earlier objections raised in the 1950s and 1960s. For a useful overview of the earliest hypotheses about the ideological identification of the scrolls, see G. Vermes, *The Dead Sea Scrolls: Qumran in Perspective* (repr. Philadelphia: Fortress, 1981).

7. H. Stegemann, "The Qumran Essenes: Local Members of the Main Jewish Union in Late Second Temple Times," in J. Trebolle Barrera and L. Vegas Montaner, eds., *The Madrid Qumran Congress: Proceedings of the International Congress on the Dead Sea Scrolls, Madrid, 18-21 March, 1991,* STDJ 11/1-2 (Leiden: Brill, 1992) 1.83-166 (quotation on p. 161). See also idem, *Die Essener, Qumran, Johannes der Taufer und Jesus: Ein Sachbuch* (Freiburg: Herder, 1993).

8. E. M. Cook, "Qumran: A Ritual Purification Center," *BARev* 22/6 (1996) 39, 48-51, 73-75.

9. De Vaux died in 1971, having published the results of his excavations but not a detailed final report. A summary of his notes has only recently come out: J.-B. Humbert and A. Chambon, *Fouilles de Khirbet Qumrân et de Ain Feshkha,* 1 (Göttingen: Vandenhoeck & Ruprecht; Fribourg: Presses Universitaires, 1994).

Recent years have also seen the development of alternative theories about the origins and ideological roots of the community of the Dead Sea Scrolls. Both Ben Zion Wacholder and Shemaryahu Talmon locate the origins of the community in anti-Zadokite circles of the second temple before the Maccabean uprising. Wacholder contends that "the roots of Qumran . . . are . . . the invisible turbulence hidden behind the seeming serenity of the third century BCE" in a movement that directly challenged mainstream Zadokite Judaism and the centrality of the Mosaic torah.10 "Authors of texts like the Heavenly Jerusalem, the Aramaic Testament of Levi, the book of Jubilees, 11QTorah, and CD refused to recognize the legitimacy of the second temple." 11 Similarly, Talmon views "the community of the renewed covenant," which he does not identify with the Essene movement, "as the third- or second-century[-BCE] crystallization of a major socio-religious movement which arose in early post-exilic Judaism. The movement, . . . prophetically inspired and inclined to apocalypticism, . . . runs parallel to that of the competing rationalist stream which . . . will ultimately crystallize in Rabbinic or normative Judaism." 12

Whereas Wacholder and Talmon see Qumran as the ultimate result of an opposition party, Lawrence H. Schiffman describes a schism that gradually turned the once normative Zadokite tradition into a sectarian phenomenon. That the Temple Scroll (11QT) and the Halakhic Letter (4QMMT) show striking similarities to the halakhah which rabbinic literature attributes to the Sadducees is for Schiffman evidence that "the origins and roots of the halakhic tradition [of the Dead Sea sect] lie in the Sadducean Zadokite priesthood." Only when it became clear that the Hasmonean succession was permanent, "the Qumran Zadokites gradually developed the sectarian mentality of the despised, rejected, and abandoned outcast."13

---

10. B. Z. Wacholder, *The Dawn of Qumran: The Sectarian Torah and the Teacher of Righteousness* (Cincinnati: Hebrew Union College Press, 1983) 226.

11. Idem, "Ezekiel and Ezekielianism as Progenitors of Essenianism," in D. Dimant and U. Rappaport, eds., *The Dead Sea Scrolls: Forty Years of Research,* STDJ 10 (Leiden: Brill, 1992) 186-96 (quotation on p. 191).

12. S. Talmon, "The Community of the Renewed Covenant: Between Judaism and Christianity," in E. C. Ulrich and J. C. VanderKam, eds., *The Community of the Renewed Covenant: The Notre Dame Symposium on the Dead Sea Scrolls* (Notre Dame: University of Notre Dame Press, 1994) 3-24 (quotation on p. 22).

13. L. H. Schiffman, *Reclaiming the Dead Sea Scrolls: The History of Judaism, the Background of Christianity, the Lost Library of Qumran* (Philadelphia and Jerusa-

These studies on Qumran origins have played an important role in shifting the emphasis from the community of the Dead Sea Scrolls to the broader context of second temple Jewish thought and convincing even the staunchest champions of the Essene hypothesis that, in order to be maintained, it needs some radical reorientation. By contrast, the success of fanciful theories about the Christian origins of the scrolls displayed in the media has resulted in an unfortunate waste of time and energy.[14]

The Essene hypothesis can be overcome only by moving forward and not backward, beyond and not against the accomplishments of fifty years of scholarship. This goal cannot be reached without a comprehensive reassessment of the pluralistic development of Judaic thought in the second temple period, particularly in the transitional age of "middle Judaism."[15]

---

lem: Jewish Publication Society, 1994) 88-89; cf. idem, "Origin and Early History of the Qumran Sect," *BA* 58/1 (1995) 37-48. The first attempt to identify the Qumranites and the Sadducees was made by R. North, "The Qumran Sadducees," *CBQ* 17 (1955) 164-88.

14. In the 1950s Jacob L. Teicher maintained the Christian origin of the scrolls and Edmund Wilson was the journalist who popularized the theory. See J. L. Teicher, "The Dead Sea Scrolls: Documents of the Jewish Christian Sect of Ebionites," *JJS* 2 (1951) 67-99; idem, "The Damascus Fragments and the Origin of the Jewish Christian Sect," *JJS* 2 (1951) 115-43; idem, "The Teaching of the Pre-Pauline Church in the Dead Sea Scrolls," *JJS* 4 (1953) 1-13; cf. E. Wilson, "A Reporter at Large," *The New Yorker* 31/13 (14 May 1955) 45-121; idem, *The Scrolls from the Dead Sea* (New York: Oxford University Press, 1955). Barbara E. Thiering and Robert H. Eisenman have recently revived the Christian hypothesis; their journalistic counterparts are Michael Baigent and Richard Leigh. See B. E. Thiering, *Redating the Teacher of Righteousness* (Sydney: Theological Explorations, 1979); idem, *The Gospels and Qumran: A New Hypothesis* (Sydney: Theological Explorations, 1981); idem, *The Qumran Origins of the Christian Church* (Sydney, Theological Explorations, 1983); idem, *Jesus and the Riddle of the Dead Sea Scrolls: Unlocking the Secrets of His Life Story* (San Francisco: Harper, 1992); R. H. Eisenman, *Maccabees, Zadokites, Christians, and Qumran: A New Hypothesis of Qumran Origins*, SPB 34 (Leiden: Brill, 1983); idem, *James the Just in the Habakkuk Pesher* (Leiden: Brill, 1986); cf. M. Baigent and R. Leigh, *The Dead Sea Scrolls Deception* (New York: Summit Books, 1991). A brilliant review and criticism of the Christian hypothesis is in O. Betz and R. Riesner, *Jesus, Qumran and the Vatican: Clarifications,* trans. J. Bowden (New York: Crossroad, 1994).

15. In place of stressing the final point ("late Judaism") in light of Christianity, or the starting point ("early Judaism") in light of Rabbinic Judaism, "middle Judaism" refers to the pluralistic age of 300 BCE to 200 CE as a time that does not belong to either Christianity or Rabbinic Judaism but rather is the formative period of *both*. "Middle

In this perspective, the most promising scholarly works are those of Philip R. Davies, who sees Essenism as the parent movement of the Dead Sea sect, and Florentino García Martínez, whose "Groningen hypothesis" also implies "a split within the actual Essene movement" and locates "the ideological roots of the Qumran community . . . within the Palestinian apocalyptic tradition."[16] Johann Maier also agrees and describes the Qumran community as a group that gradually parted from its original Essene setting and turned out to be, in the first century CE, a rather insignificant clique.[17]

Davies and García Martínez do not question the existence of an autonomous religious community at Qumran, nor its connection with the Essene movement, but point to the need of fully exploring the complexity of Judaic thought, which Flavius Josephus simplified in his threefold description of Jewish sectarianism. As Qumran specialists widely recognize, the major shortcoming of the Essene hypothesis is its tendency to equate Qumran with the Essenes, though Qumran represented only one part of a larger and complex Essene movement. "The question of the relations of the Qumran group with [the Essenes] is inescapable. Every theory which

Judaism" means the time between the common heritage of "ancient postexilic Judaism" and the parting of the ways of their separate existences. See G. Boccaccini, *Middle Judaism: Jewish Thought, 300 BCE to 200 CE* (Minneapolis: Fortress, 1991); idem, *Portraits of Middle Judaism in Scholarship and Arts: A Multimedia Catalog from Flavius Josephus to 1991* (Turin: Zamorani, 1992); idem, "History of Judaism: Its Periods in Antiquity," in J. Neusner, ed., *Judaism in Late Antiquity,* 2 vols. (Leiden: Brill, 1996) 2.285-308. The same terminology is adopted by P. Sacchi, *Storia del Secondo Tempio: Israele tra VI secolo a.C. e I secolo d.C.* (Turin: Società Editrice Internazionale, 1994).

16. See P. R. Davies, *Sects and Scrolls: Essays on Qumran and Related Topics* (Atlanta: Scholars Press, 1996); idem, "The Prehistory of the Qumran Community," in Dimant and Rappaport, eds., *Dead Sea Scrolls,* 116-25; idem, *Behind the Essenes: History and Ideology in the Dead Sea Scrolls,* BJS 94 (Atlanta: Scholars Press, 1987). See F. García Martínez and J. Trebolle Barrera, *The People of the Dead Sea Scrolls,* trans. W. G. E. Watson (Leiden: Brill, 1995); F. García Martínez and A. S. van der Woude, "A Groningen Hypothesis of Qumran Origins and Early History," *RevQ* 14 (1990) 521-41; idem, "Qumran Origins and Early History: A Groningen Hypothesis," *FO* 25 (1989) 113-36; F. García Martínez, "Essénisme Qumrânien: Origines, caractéristiques, héritage," in B. Chiesa, ed., *Correnti culturali e movimenti religiosi del Giudaismo* (Rome: Carucci, 1987) 37-57.

17. J. Maier, *Zwischen den Testamenten: Geschichte und Religion in der Zeit des zweiten Tempels* (Würzburg: Echter, 1990).

reduces the whole to one of its parts, even if it is the best known part, is flawed and deficient."[18]

Even today, for many scholars, and certainly for the general public of nonspecialists, the people of Qumran are not only members of an Essene community — they *are* the Essenes. The indistinctiveness of the Essene movement and the absence of a recognized Essene literature lead scholars to use Qumranic texts to describe Essene attitudes. As a result, the terms "Essene" and "Qumranic" have become virtually interchangeable.

In addition, the Dead Sea Scrolls corpus has delimited a field for itself, with its own research tools, journals, bibliographies, professional societies, and audience. The consequence has been one of isolating the Qumran specialist from the other specialists in second temple Judaism, exactly as has happened to New Testament scholars. While the study of the Dead Sea Scrolls certainly requires a specific training and expertise, the boundaries set around the newly born field of specialization may have generated an illusion of self-sufficiency; the research would greatly benefit from interdisciplinary approaches. James H. Charlesworth's call for overcoming the fragmentation of modern studies in second temple Judaism has never been so topical: "We scholars together must seek ways to move beyond the isolation that tends to characterize the study of the Apocrypha, Pseudepigrapha and Qumran scrolls."[19]

Davies and García Martínez have made a move in the right direction, out of the cage of Josephus's precious yet so cumbersome testimony and out of the boundaries set by modern scholarship. Their approach has the great merit of having introduced a fundamental distinction between Essene origins and Qumran origins, a distinction that allows scholars to make more sense of the often conflicting evidence. The history of the Qumran community may not coincide with the history of the Essene movement. The

18. F. García Martínez, "The Origins of the Essene Movement and of the Qumran Sect," in García Martínez and Trebolle Barrera, *People of the Dead Sea Scrolls,* 77-96 (quotation on p. 79).

19. J. H. Charlesworth, "Qumran in Relation to the Apocrypha, Rabbinic Judaism, and Nascent Christianity: Impacts on University Teaching of Jewish Civilization in the Hellenistic-Roman Period," in S. Talmon, ed., *Jewish Civilization in the Hellenistic-Roman Period* (Philadelphia: Trinity Press International, 1991) 168-80 (quotation on p. 180); cf. G. Boccaccini, "Middle Judaism: Judaism between the Third Century BCE and the Second Century CE as a Historiographical Unit," in *Middle Judaism,* 7-25.

goal of giving a satisfactory answer to the identity of the Essene movement and its relationship with the Qumran community is, however, far from being accomplished. "While some excellent work has been done on the individual documents, as yet the opportunity to perceive a history of [the Essene] movement in these texts has not been taken. This may be partly because it was not suspected that such a history was there. . . . It is about time we put [the Essenes] back on the centre of the Jewish stage."[20] Davies's words are echoed by García Martínez and Adam S. van der Woude at the end of their presentation of the Groningen hypothesis. "The history of the ideas of the religious movement that ultimately gave birth to the Qumran group and their relation with the rest of post-exilic Judaism still need to be written, as well as the development of those ideas once the group settled at Qumran. The texts are there, writings belonging to the apocalyptic tradition, to the Essene movement and to the Qumran sect, and . . . this intellectual history can indeed be written from these sources."[21] While the agenda is clearly set, the problem of contemporary research is exactly its apparent inability to develop a methodology capable of identifying, from the extant documents, the diverse varieties of middle Judaism. This methodological weakness makes it difficult to write such an "intellectual history" and makes us waver between the extremes of complete skepticism about or total confidence in the Essene hypothesis. In the face of the uncertainties inherent in any other alternative hypothesis, we are continuously pushed back toward Josephus's threefold taxonomy and the comfortable self-sufficiency of Qumran studies.

2. Historiographical Analysis and Systemic Analysis

The method of systemic analysis of middle Judaic documents may give us the means to overcome this vicious circle.[22] It enables us to compare and

20. Davies, *Behind the Essenes,* 134.

21. García Martínez and van der Woude, "Groningen Hypothesis of Qumran Origins," 541.

22. G. Boccaccini, "Middle Judaism and Its Contemporary Interpreters (1986-1992): Methodological Foundations for the Study of Judaisms, 300 BCE–200 CE," *Hen* 15 (1993) 207-33. For the foundations of a methodology that privileges "holistic comparison" to the search for parallels, cf. J. Neusner, *The Ecology of Religion: From Writing to*

group documents, regardless of their traditional corpora, exclusively on the basis of their ideological structure. By forming chains of ideologically and chronologically connected documents, systemic analysis gives us the way to identify and describe Judaisms autonomously from what ancient historians, such as Josephus and others, have recorded about the plurality of middle Judaic thought.

Contrary to the recent past, contemporary scholars are extremely cautious about ascribing a document to any of the groups recorded in ancient historiography. We are aware that the trends of middle Jewish thought are much more complex than those presented by ancient sources. Many documents simply do not fit in the framework provided by ancient historiography.

Although the discrepancy between what ancient historiography says and what extant documents let us say about the nature, history, and ideology of middle Judaisms is a well-known phenomenon, not all the implications have been articulated. Documents are not only pieces of evidence that help us assess the validity of ideological structures offered by ancient historiography, but are also in themselves evidence of ideological structures. They are scattered elements of a puzzle that we have to reconstruct patiently.

Historiographical analysis and systemic analysis do not lead necessarily to the same picture, and one must be careful not to mix the results of these two methods of analysis prematurely. It is like an archaeologist who is asked to reconstruct the structure of an ancient building, of which significant ruins remain. Before starting the work of reconstruction on the basis of the description, no matter how detailed, given by ancient historiography, it is wise to assess the ruins and the structure that the ruins themselves suggest. Sometimes there is a perfect correspondence; sometimes archaeological evidence does not fit the data of ancient historiography. In any case, archaeological analysis and historiographical analysis can help one another only if each science works *iuxta propria principia,* keeping its autonomous rules and methods.

Religion in the Study of Judaism (Nashville: Abingdon, 1989); idem, *The Systemic Analysis of Judaism,* BJS 137 (Atlanta: Scholars Press, 1988); S. Talmon, "The Comparative Method in Biblical Interpretation," in J. E. Emerton, ed., *Congress Volume: Göttingen, 1977,* VTSup 29 (Leiden: Brill, 1978) 320-52; E. P. Sanders, "The Holistic Comparison of Patterns of Religion," in *Paul and Palestinian Judaism* (Philadelphia: Fortress, 1977) 12-24; S. Sandmel, "Parallelomania," *JBL* 81 (1962) 1-13.

In the archaeology of ideas, as well as in the archaeology of buildings and manufactured products, one must keep the two sets of information distinct in order to compare them successfully. As archaeological analysis and historiographical analysis are complementary, so are systemic analysis and historiographical analysis; they need each other. Both historiographical analysis and systemic analysis search for ideological lines of thought characteristic of diverse Judaisms. Historiographical analysis verifies the historical reliability of ancient and subsequent records on middle Judaisms. Systemic analysis studies, groups, and maps out the ideological remains of middle Judaisms: the documents.

Historiographical analysis is limited by the quantity of surviving records, by their state of preservation, and by the historical probability or accident of their survival. Through historiographical analysis, we have the description and names of a certain number of middle Judaisms, notably the Pharisees, the Sadducees, the Essenes, and the Christians; but a precise framework of relationships between them and the extant documents is not given in ancient historiography. In addition, ancient sources may have misrepresented, neglected, or even failed to record some Judaisms whose documents have survived. Conversely, ancient historiography may reveal the existence of Judaisms that time has deprived of any literary evidence.

Systemic analysis also is limited by the quantity of surviving documents, by their state of preservation, and by the historical probability or accident of their survival. Through systemic analysis, we group the documents according to their different systems of thought, thus identifying and describing a certain number of middle Judaisms. But documents are often silent about the historical and sociological context of the group behind the author(s). Sometimes we do not even know what these systems of thought called themselves or what outsiders called them during ancient times. In addition, a large quantity of documents surviving from one group may make the ideological system of that group seem more prevalent than actually was the case, and therefore modern interpreters may overestimate it, while they underestimate other systems because of the lack or loss of their documents.

In brief: historiographical analysis leads to the identification of a certain number of named, but often not source-supported, Judaisms; systemic analysis leads to the identification of a certain number of source-supported, but often unnamed, Judaisms. Both methodologies have the means and legitimacy to identify and describe Judaisms apart from one another. The results may not finally lead to the same conclusion. Often, the status of research does not allow us to harmonize the data, and we are tantalized by the discrepancy between what ancient historiography says and what the extant documents let us say. But sometimes the critical analysis of ideological documents corresponds to the critical analysis of the records of ancient historiography. Then, on the one hand, we have an ideological system identified throughout its documents and, on the other hand, a certain amount of critically assessed historiographical data referring to it. When such a correspondence occurs, systemic analysis and historiographical analysis converge to give a comprehensive view of that specific Judaism. In some cases, we may even be lucky enough to put together an ancient name and a certain number of unlabeled documents, and say with some confidence whether they are Sadducean, Pharisaic, Essene, Christian, or belong to yet another variety of middle Judaism.

3. Moving Forward: From the Essene Hypothesis to the Enochic/Essene Hypothesis

Is this the case with Qumran? Is there any relationship between what ancient historiography says about the Essenes and the Judaisms witnessed by the Dead Sea Scrolls? Before even considering such a possibility, one would be wise to inquire about the respective ideological structures revealed by ancient historiography and by the documents. I make this inquiry in the first two sections of this book. In part one ("Historiographical Analysis") I examine the records of ancient historiography on the Essenes; in part two ("Systemic Analysis") I offer a study of the documents found at Qumran and other closely related documents. I initially keep the two levels of analysis completely separate; only in part three ("Comparative Analysis") do I compare the findings. I then articulate the hypothesis that what the ancient historians called Essenism encompasses not only the Qumran community but also what modern scholars have identified, on the basis of its extant documents, as Enochic Judaism. I present the consequences of this hypothesis for the relationship between Qumran and Essenism, as well as for the understanding of the history of

Enochic Judaism in its major ramifications. I call my hypothesis the Enochic/Essene hypothesis in order to distinguish it from the classical Essene hypothesis.[23]

That 1 Enoch is the core of an ancient and distinct variety of second temple Judaism is a conviction that more and more scholars now share, and that has received a recent boost by the translation into English of Paolo Sacchi's studies on Enochic Judaism.[24] What we call 1 (Ethiopic) Enoch is not a single document, but a collection of five independent books. The chronological order, different from the literary order, is as follows: the Book of the Watchers (chs. 6–36), the Astronomical Book (chs. 72–82), the Dream Visions (chs. 83–90), the Epistle of Enoch (chs. 91–105), and the Similitudes of Enoch (chs. 37–71). An introduction (chs. 1–5) and some appendixes (chs. 106-7, 108) complete the collection. The Enochic documents were written by different authors over a vast span of time, possibly from the fourth century BCE through the very beginning of the first century CE,[25] yet they are closely related to one another through a consistent internal system of literary connections, metaphors, allusions, and quotations. It was certainly a complex and dynamic trend of thought, with its own developments and deepenings, and therefore cannot be fit entirely into a unitary scheme or a univocal definition. Its generative idea, however, can be identified in a particular conception of evil, understood as an autonomous reality antecedent to humanity's ability to choose, the result of "a contamination that has spoiled [human] nature," an evil that "was produced before

23. I first presented this hypothesis in a paper ("Configurazione storica della comunità di Qumran") offered at the VI Conference of New Testament Studies organized by the Italian Biblical Association (Qumran e le origini cristiane, L'Aquila, 14-16 September 1995). A revised and enlarged version of the paper is published in the proceedings of the conference. See G. Boccaccini, "E se l'essenismo fosse il movimento enochiano? Una nuova ipotesi circa i rapporti tra Qumran e gli esseni," *RSB* 7/2 (1997) 49-67.

24. P. Sacchi, *Jewish Apocalyptic and Its History,* trans. W. J. Short, JSPSup 20 (Sheffield: Sheffield Academic Press, 1997); cf. G. Boccaccini, "Jewish Apocalyptic Tradition: The Contribution of Italian Scholarship," in J. J. Collins and J. H. Charlesworth, eds., *Mysteries and Revelations: Apocalyptic Studies since the Uppsala Colloquium,* JSPSup 9 (Sheffield: JSOT Press, 1991) 33-50. A presentation of Enochic Judaism for the nonspecialist is provided by M. Barker, *The Lost Prophet: The Book of Enoch and Its Influence on Christianity* (Nashville: Abingdon, 1988).

25. Sacchi, *Jewish Apocalyptic;* G. W. E. Nickelsburg, "Enoch, First Book of," *ABD* 2.508-16.

the beginning of history."[26] That this apocalyptic idea was the motivating power behind a distinct party in second temple Judaism is testified by the Enochic documents, which were continuously reassembled over time into a single collection, in spite of the often strong theological differences between one book and another, and by the synchronic production of other documents that appear to share and support the same system of thought. We do not know what this party was called or what it may have called itself in ancient times. Since 1 Enoch is the major literary accomplishment of this party, it is not unsuitable to use the term "Enochic Judaism."

Having identified Enochic Judaism as a variety of second temple Judaism, of which 1 Enoch was the constitutive, not the only, document, I need to make some caveats for the sake of methodology. First, despite the fact that 1 Enoch is the major source of Enochic traditions, a history of Enochic Judaism does not coincide with a history of the oral and literary traditions associated with Enoch.[27] On the one hand, Enochic Judaism produced or inspired documents in which the figure of Enoch was not central (Jubilees, Testaments of the Twelve Patriarchs), or was even missing (4 Ezra). 2 Enoch is a case in point. In the first section of the document the protagonist is the revealer, Enoch, while the final section has no revealer and the leading figure becomes Melchizedek. The changing of protagonist does not disturb the ideological continuity.[28] On the other hand, the mere reference to the figure of Enoch does not make a document representative of Enochic Judaism. Thus Sirach, Philo, and Josephus mention Enoch yet strenuously oppose the principles of Enochic Judaism.[29]

Second, despite the fact that 1 Enoch is an apocalypse, a history of Enochic Judaism does not coincide with a history of Jewish apocalypses. The documents of Enochic Judaism are neither all nor only apocalypses;

---

26. P. Sacchi, "Riflessioni sull'essenza dell'apocalittica: peccato d'origine e libertà dell'uomo," *Hen* 5 (1983) 31-58 (quotation on p. 57).

27. For a history of Enochic traditions, see J. C. VanderKam, *Enoch: A Man for All Generations* (Columbia: University of South Carolina Press, 1995); idem, *Enoch and the Growth of an Apocalyptic Tradition,* CBQMS 16 (Washington, D.C.: Catholic Biblical Association of America, 1984); L. Rosso-Ubigli, "La fortuna di Enoc nel giudaismo antico," *ASE* 1 (1984) 153-63; P. Grelot, "La légende d'Hénoch dans les apocryphes et dans la Bible: Origine et signification," *RSR* 46 (1958) 5-26, 181-220.

28. P. Sacchi, "Historical Introduction to the Book of the Secrets of Enoch (Slavonic Enoch)," in *Jewish Apocalyptic,* 233-49.

29. VanderKam, *Enoch: A Man for All Generations,* 104-7, 148-53.

some of the major apocalypses, such as Daniel, Revelation, or 2 Baruch, belong to different, if not opposing, parties.[30]

Third, despite the fact that 1 Enoch is one of the most significant testimonies to the apocalyptic worldview, a history of Enochic Judaism does not coincide with a history of Jewish apocalypticism. With his work, John J. Collins has introduced an essential "distinction between apocalypticism as a worldview and apocalypse as a literary form."[31] While apocalypticism can be defined as the worldview of the apocalypses, "the apocalyptic worldview could find expression in other genres besides apocalypses."[32] Credit goes to Sacchi for having added to this distinction another essential distinction: between apocalypticism as a worldview and apocalyptic as an ideological party. The fact that two documents share, or are influenced by, the same worldview does not mean that they belong to the same party. The same worldview can assume a different meaning in different contexts.

The distinction in modern European history between nationalism and nationalistic parties applies to Collins's apocalypticism and Sacchi's apocalyptic. On the one hand, nationalism is a worldview that affects different, even opposite, parties; we have a leftist nationalism as well as a rightist nationalism. Likewise, as Collins also sharply notices, apocalypticism was not a party. "In the last two centuries [before] the common era . . . apocalypticism constituted a distinctive worldview within Judaism. . . . It is impossible to say how widely [it] was shared. . . . But neither was it peculiar to a particular sect or the product of a single movement."[33] On the other hand, the presence of

---

30. The author of Revelation states explicitly that his work belongs to yet another party of middle Judaism: Christianity. A comparison between Daniel and the contemporaneous Dream Visions (1 En 83–90) shows that they were not produced in the same circles; see G. Boccaccini, "Daniel and the Dream Visions: The Genre of Apocalyptic and the Apocalyptic Tradition," in *Middle Judaism,* 126-60; idem, "E' Daniele un testo apocalittico? Una (ri)definizione del pensiero del Libro di Daniele in rapporto al Libro dei Sogni e all'apocalittica," *Hen* 9 (1987) 267-302; J. J. Collins, *Apocalypticism in the Dead Sea Scrolls* (London and New York: Routledge, 1997) 153. An analysis of the relationship between 2 Baruch and 4 Ezra leads to an analogous conclusion; see G. Boccaccini, "Testi apocalittici coevi all'Apocalissi di Giovanni," *RSB* 7/2 (1995) 151-61.

31. Collins, *Apocalypticism in the Dead Sea Scrolls,* 8.

32. Ibid.; cf. idem, "Genre, Ideology and Social Movements in Jewish Apocalypticism," in Collins and Charlesworth, eds., *Mysteries and Revelations,* 11-32.

33. Collins, *Apocalypticism in the Dead Sea Scrolls,* 7-8.

organized nationalistic parties in modern Europe does not give to these parties the monopoly of nationalism, which continues to inspire even their opponents and competitors, nor does it prevent the nationalistic parties from being influenced by other worldviews. Likewise, as Sacchi demonstrated, the presence of an organized apocalyptic party, Enochic Judaism, did not give this party a monopoly on apocalypticism, which continued to inspire even its opponents and competitors; nor did it prevent the same party from being influenced by other worldviews.

Everybody would agree that writing a history of French nationalism and its influence on French political and cultural life differs from writing the history of the French nationalistic party. A history of French nationalism would include the leader of the nationalistic party, Jean-Marie Le Pen, as well as his opponents, Jacques Chirac and François Mitterand. Despite their ideological differences, all of them can be said to share or to be influenced by the same nationalistic worldview. On the contrary, a history of the French nationalistic party would not include the socialist, Mitterand, and the conservative, Chirac. In such a history, one would even find the paradoxical statement that the nationalistic Mitterand, in spite of his nationalism, was ideologically antinationalistic, perhaps one of the most fiercely antinationalistic politicians of modern France.

What Collins has masterfully done is to write a history of Jewish apocalypticism that correctly includes 1 Enoch as well as its opponents, Daniel and Revelation. Despite their ideological differences, all of them can be said to share, or to be influenced by, the same apocalyptic worldview.[34] What Sacchi has masterfully done is to write a history of the Jewish apocalyptic party, Enochic Judaism,[35] that correctly does not include the "covenantal" Daniel and the Christian Revelation.[36] In Sacchi's history of the Enochic apocalyptic party, one even finds the paradoxical statement that the apocalyptic Daniel, in spite of its apocalypticism, was ideologically antiapocalyptic, thus anti-Enochic.[37]

---

34. J. J. Collins, *The Apocalyptic Imagination* (New York: Crossroad, 1984). For an earlier attempt, see D. S. Russell, *The Method and Message of Jewish Apocalyptic,* OTL (Philadelphia: Westminster, 1964).

35. Sacchi, *Jewish Apocalyptic,* 26: "I have used the term 'apocalyptic' to indicate all the works that reflect the problematic of the Enochic tradition, the basic structure of its thought, which endures through the centuries."

36. On the "covenantal" theology of Daniel, see ch. 4, pp. 81-86, below.

37. Sacchi, *Jewish Apocalpytic,* 23. Cf. Boccaccini, *Middle Judaism,* 160.

Collins and García Martínez have argued about the influence of apoc-alypticism on the Dead Sea Scrolls.[38] While covering most of the same material, I deal here with a different topic, the relationship between Enochic Judaism and the Qumran community. My claim is that Enochic Judaism is the modern name for the mainstream body of the Essene party, from which the Qumran community parted as a radical, dissident, and marginal offspring. Subsequently, Enochic/Essene Judaism polemically rejected the ideas of the Qumran Essenes, continued to exist side by side with its radical progeny, contributed to the birth of the parties of John the Baptist and Jesus, and even survived Qumran for some time after the destruction of the temple in 70 CE.

In presenting this theory, I do not claim a new reading of the Dead Sea Scrolls, nor do I promise any revelation based on previously unknown material. I confidently rely on the results of two generations of distin-guished philologists and archaeologists who have devoted their lives to understanding the scrolls. In my reading of the original texts I am in debt particularly to the work of the team of scholars of the Princeton Theological Seminary Dead Sea Scrolls Project led by James H. Charlesworth, and to the skill of García Martínez, whose translation of the scrolls, first published in Spanish in 1992, has blossomed in these last years, from the 1994 English edition (rev. in 1996) and the 1994-95 annotated Dutch edition coedited with van der Woude, to the superb 1996 Italian edition coedited with Corrado Martone with notes and addenda.[39]

---

38. Collins, *Apocalypticism in the Dead Sea Scrolls;* F. García Martínez, *Qumran and Apocalyptic: Studies on the Aramaic Texts from Qumran,* STDJ 9 (Leiden: Brill, 1992). For some earlier attempts to address the same issue, see J. Carmignac, "Qu'est-ce que l'apocalyptique? Son emploi à Qumrân," *RevQ* 10 (1979) 3-33; H. Stegemann "Die Bedeutung der Qumranfunde für die Erforschung der Apokalyptik," in D. Hellholm, ed., *Apocalypticism in the Mediterrenean World and in the Near East: Proceedings of the International Colloquium on Apocalypticism, Uppsala, August 12-17, 1979* (Tübingen: Mohr, 1983) 495-530; F. García Martínez, "Les traditions apoc-alyptiques à Qumrân," in C. Kappler, ed., *Apocalypses et voyages dans l'au-delà* (Paris: Cerf, 1987) 201-35; J. J. Collins, "Was the Dead Sea Sect an Apocalyptic Community?" in Schiffman, ed., *Archaeology and History,* 25-51; H. H. Rowley, *Jewish Apocalyptic and the Dead Sea Scrolls* (London: Athlone, 1957).

39. See J. H. Charlesworth, ed., *The Princeton Theological Seminary Dead Sea Scrolls Project,* 12 vols. (Tübingen: Mohr; Louisville: Westminster/John Knox, 1994-); F. García Martínez, *Textos de Qumrán* (Madrid, 1992; 4th ed., 1994); idem, *The Dead Sea Scrolls Translated: The Qumran Texts in English,* trans. W. G. E. Watson, 2nd ed. (Leiden: Brill; Grand Rapids: Eerdmans, 1996); F. García Martínez and A. S. van der

As a scholar of intellectual history, I have given preference to an interdisciplinary approach that in the study of ancient Jewish literature may overcome too rigid a separation among the different fields of scholarly research.[40] The goal is to address a specific, basic, and inescapable question for the comprehension of middle Judaic thought, that is, the historical, ideological, and literary identification of the Essene movement and its relationship with the Qumran community. It is this desire for intellectual understanding that, under the clear skies of a waning storm, has made me dare tread the uncharted zone beyond the Essene hypothesis.

Woude, *De Rollen van de Dode Zee: Ingeleid en in het Nederlands vertaald,* 2 vols. (Kampen: Kok Pharos, 1994-95); F. García Martínez and C. Martone, *Testi di Qumran* (Brescia: Paideia, 1996).

40. On the philosophical and methodological foundations of intellectual history as a branch of historical enterprise, see M. G. Murphey, *Philosophical Foundations of Historical Knowledge* (Albany, N.Y.: SUNY Press, 1994); D. R. Kelley, ed., *The History of Ideas: Canon and Variations* (Rochester, N.Y.: University of Rochester Press, 1990); E. Garin, *La filosofia come sapere storico* (Bari: Laterza, 1959).

PART I

HISTORIOGRAPHICAL ANALYSIS

CHAPTER 2

The Essenes in Ancient Historiography

1. First-Century Jewish and Non-Jewish Sources

The Jewish-Alexandrian philosopher and exegete Philo, the Jewish historian and politician Flavius Josephus, and the Roman geographer and curiosity-collector Pliny the Elder are the earliest witnesses to the Essenes, or, better, the earliest ones whose writings have come down to us. It seems likely that the Greek orator and philosopher Dio of Prusa (Dio Cocceianus, later called Chrysostom) also wrote something about the Essenes, but all we have is a passage (*Dio* 3.2) from his biographer, Synesius of Cyrene (c. 370-413 CE). After the first century CE, historical sources (Hegesippus, Hippolytus of Rome, Epiphanius of Salamis, *Constitutiones Apostolorum,* Jerome, Philaster of Brescia, Nilus of Ancyra, Isidore of Seville, Michael of Antioch, Solinus, Josippon, Dionysios Bar Salibi, etc.) show an increasing confusion regarding the identity of the Essene movement as soon as they depart from the first-century authors on whom they all depend.[1] In

1. On the historical records on the Essenes, see R. Bergmeier, *Die Essener-Berichte des Flavius Josephus: Quellenstudien zu den Essenertexten im Werk des Judischen Historiographen* (Kampen: Kok Pharos, 1993); G. Vermes and M. D. Goodman, *The Essenes: According to the Classical Sources* (Sheffield: JSOT Press, 1989); T. S. Beall, *Josephus' Description of the Essenes Illustrated by the Dead Sea Scrolls,* SNTSMS 58 (Cambridge: Cambridge University Press, 1988); M. Stern, *Greek and Latin Authors on Jews and Judaism,* 3 vols. (Jerusalem: Israel Academy of Sciences and Humanities, 1974-84); E. Schürer, "The Essenes According to Philo, Josephus and Pliny," in *The History of the Jewish People in the Age of Jesus Christ,* rev. G. Vermes,

some cases, however, in particular in the works of Hippolytus, who appears to be familiar with the same source(s) used by Josephus,[2] interesting original details may be accurate derivatives from ancient narratives.

It is beyond the scope of this chapter to offer a comprehensive analysis of all that the ancient sources say about the Essenes. A synthesis would imply a degree of compatibility among our sources that we simply cannot take for granted. While the first-century narratives of Philo and Josephus, on one hand, and Pliny and Dio, on the other hand, present clear affinities in language and content, it remains to be verified whether and to what extent the descriptions offered by Jewish authors fit the analogous narratives by non-Jewish authors. Did they describe the same community, namely, the same group of Essenes? Or did they describe two different groups of Essenes, or two different stages in the life of the same group? To what extent can we borrow details from different authors and inlay them as bits of a comprehensive mosaic of the Essene movement?

In order to compare and contrast the descriptions offered by Jewish and non-Jewish authors, I restrict myself to those elements that they have in common. As programmatically stated in the introduction, in this chapter I make no reference to the Dead Sea Scrolls or to the archaeology of the scrolls. I consider only the archaeological data that pertain to the historical narratives studied here. Let these ancient witnesses speak for themselves and be understood, each on its own terms.

2. Location, Extent, and Antiquity of the Essenes

The first features noticed by both Jewish and non-Jewish witnesses are the Jewish and voluntary character of the Essene movement and its antiquity. The

---

et al., 3 vols. (Edinburgh: T. & T. Clark, 1973-87) 2.562-74; A. Adam, *Antike Berichte über die Essener* (Berlin: De Gruyter, 1961; 2nd ed. 1972).

2. For a discussion of the relationships between Josephus and Hippolytus, see A. I. Baumgarten, "Josephus and Hippolytus on the Pharisees," *HUCA* 55 (1982) 1-25; C. Burchard, "Die Essener bei Hippolyt," *JSJ* 8 (1977) 1-41; M. Smith, "The Description of the Essenes in Josephus and the Philosophoumena," *HUCA* 29 (1958) 273-313; M. Black, "The Account of the Essenes in Hippolytus and Josephus," in W. D. Davies and D. Daube, eds., *The Background of the New Testament and Its Eschatology* (Cambridge: Cambridge University Press, 1956) 172-75.

Essenes were a free association of individuals, who lived so close to one another and so differently from outsiders that Pliny describes them as a *gens* (*Nat. Hist.* 5.73) and Josephus as a *genos* (*J.W.* 2.113; *Ant.* 13.172; 15.371), a term that, notably, he does not apply to the other two Jewish sects, the Pharisees and Sadducees. If the term *genos* sounds inappropriate to Philo, it is only because he wants to stress that Essene membership was by choice, not by birth; it was a special option for zealous members of the Jewish people. "Our lawgiver encouraged the multitude of his disciples to live in community: they are called Essenes. . . . Their enlistment is not due to race, the word 'race' [Gk. *genos*] being unsuitable where volunteers are concerned, but is due to zeal [Gk. *dia zēlon*] for the cause of virtue and an ardent love of men" (*Apol.* 2; cf. *Vit. Cont.* 1 and *Omn. Prob. Lib.* 85, where the fellow members are called *homozēloi,* "people of equal zeal"). Significantly, when Josephus speaks of the relationship between the Essenes and other Jews, his terminology is the same as Philo's. The term *genos* is now related to the Jewish people, to which it properly belongs: "[the Essenes] are Jews by race [Gk. *genos*], but, in addition, they are more closely united among themselves by mutual affection than are the others" (*J.W.* 2.119). As in Philo, it is a verb of zeal, *zēloō* (*J.W.* 2.137), that describes the attitude of those Jews who are eager to join the Essene communities.[3]

Although Pliny and Dio do not explicitly say that the Essenes were Jews, or Jews only, this is implicit in their descriptions of the social and physical geography of Judaea. Pliny agrees that the Essenes are a *gens* only in a special sense, their continuous "rebirth" being owed only to "the throng of newcomers." With much admiration Pliny also emphasizes that nothing else but a personal choice leads to membership: "those whom, wearied by the fluctuations of fortune, life leads to adopt their customs, stream in great number" (*Nat. Hist.* 5.73).

Both Jewish and non-Jewish sources speak of the Essenes as an ancient and venerable movement. Philo says that "over the course of time, many kings of diverse character and inclinations have risen against this land [[= Palestine]] . . . but none of them, neither the most cruel, nor the unprincipled and false, was ever able to lay a charge against the society known as Essenes, or Saints" (*Omn. Prob. Lib.* 88-91; cf. *Apol.* 18). The reference to "many kings" who ruled one after the other implies the flow

---

3. The reference to the "zeal" of the Essenes may be responsible for the confused presentation in Hippolytus of Zealots and Sicarii as factions of the Essenes (*Ref.* 26).

of several generations. In his history of the Jewish people, Josephus first introduces the Essenes as an established group at the time of Jonathan Maccabee (161-143 BCE): "At this time there were three sects of the Jews . . . the third was the Essenes" (*Ant.* 13.171-72). Nothing is said in this context about their origins. In a text dealing with the early first century CE, Josephus acknowledges initially that the "three philosophies" of Essenes, Pharisees, and Sadducees are "from the most ancient times of the fathers' traditions" (Gk. *ek tou pany archaiou tōn patriōn; Ant.* 18.11), and then singles out the Essenes' practice of righteousness for going back "from a remote age" (Gk. *ek palaiou*): "nothing similar ever existed among any others, neither Greeks nor barbarians, even for a short time [Gk. *mēd' eis oligon*]" (*Ant.* 18.20). An indirect indication of the antiquity of the Essene philosophy is found in Josephus's tendency to explain parallels between (some) Essene beliefs and Greek philosophy in terms of a one-way borrowing of the latter from the former. In *Ant.* 15.371 he identifies "the Essenes as a race that employs the same daily regime as was revealed to the Greeks by Pythagoras." Hippolytus makes explicit that Josephus's comparison in *J.W.* 2.154-58 between Essene and Greek doctrines of the immortality of the soul is also to be understood in light of the general principle that the Greek philosophers, including Pythagoras, "derived their doctrines from no other source than from Jewish legislation" (*Ref.* 27). Philo agrees that, ultimately, at the roots of the Essene movement are the teachings of Moses: "Our lawgiver encouraged the multitude of his disciples to live in community: these are called the Essenes" (*Apol.* 1). The most bombastic but also the least specific author, Pliny, takes pleasure in amazing his readers by saying of the Essenes: "for thousands of centuries a people has existed that is eternal"; yet he is the first to cast doubt on his own words, "unbelievable though this may seem" (Lat. *incredibile dictu*).

(a) *In contrast to non-Jewish authors,* Philo and Josephus present Essenism as a much more widespread phenomenon in Palestine. They claim that the membership of the movement exceeded four thousand: "There are more than four thousand men [Gk. *andres*] who behave in this way" (*Ant.* 18.20; cf. Philo, *Omn. Prob. Lib.* 75: "over four thousand"). These statistics are remarkable when compared with the relatively small Jewish population of the time and with the size of the other Jewish groups. According to Josephus, the Pharisees numbered more than six thousand members (*Ant.* 17.42), while the Sadducees were a much smaller movement (*Ant.* 18.17).

The statistics are even more impressive when one considers that Philo and Josephus speak of "adult males" (Gk. *andres*) only, who voluntarily joined the group. "There are no children of tender years among the Essenes, nor even adolescents or young men . . . but they are men [Gk. *andres*] of ripe years already inclining to old age" (Philo, *Apol.* 3).

Philo and Josephus also witness that the Essenes did not live all together in one place but had many communities in Palestine. "They dwell in many cities [Gk. *poleis*, accusative] of Judaea, and in many villages [Gk. *kōmas*, accusative], in great and populous groups [Gk. *homilous*]" (Philo, *Apol.* 1). Generally, it is said that in the treatise *Quod omnis probus liber sit (That Every Good Man Is Free)*, Philo contradicts himself by suggesting that the Essenes "live in villages, fleeing the cities." But this translation may not faithfully reflect the original. "Fleeing the *poleis* [accusative] because of the ungodliness customary among citizens, they live *kōmēdon* [adverb]; for they know that, as noxious air breeds epidemics there, so does the contact [Gk. *prosbolē*] afflict the soul with incurable ills" (*Omn. Prob. Lib.* 76). Here Philo is talking of *poleis* as political and social communities rather than as places. The Essenes separate themselves from the city community and live not "in villages" (Gk. *kōmas*, accusative) but "village-wise" (Gk. *kōmēdon*, adverb), that is, in communities or districts, in order to avoid any "contact" (Gk. *prosbolē*) with the impious way of life of those who belong to the city community. In a way that is consistent with both the Philonic passages, Josephus uses the Greek verb *metoikeō* ("to found a colony") to describe the Essene settlements. "There is not one town [Gk. *polis*] of them only, but in every town [Gk. *polis*] several of them form a colony [Gk. *metoikeō*]" (*J.W.* 2.124; cf. Hippolytus, *Ref.* 20). Philo and Josephus therefore agree that the Essenes formed large groups (Gk. *homiloi*) in Jewish towns and villages, and there lived in their own quarters, as if they were foreign settlers. The Essenes shared the same place, within the same walls, but not the same laws with the other town inhabitants, whom they did not regard as fellow citizens.

Exactly as in the case of colonists, the adoption of a way of life that embraced separation meant neither isolationism nor indifference to political and social affairs. In his work Josephus names four individuals "who were of the sect of the Essenes": Judas under Aristobulos I (*Ant.* 13.311-13), Menaemus under Herod the Great (*Ant.* 15.373-79), Simon under Archelaus (*Ant.* 17.345-48; *J.W.* 2.112-13), and John during the Jewish war (*J.W.* 2.567; 3.9-21). Notably, they are all introduced in an urban, not rural or isolated, environment. Judas was preaching to a group of disciples in the temple of Jerusalem when "he saw Aristobulos passing by." Menaemus also happened "once to see Herod when he was a child and going to school," and when after some years Herod "was king and in the height of his dominion, he sent for Menaemus," and the two met for a second time. Simon was one of the diviners whom Archelaus sent for in order to interpret a dream. In all these cases the Essene involvement in political affairs is at the top level. Judas, Menaemus, and Simon prophesied the duration of the king's power, in the case of Menaemus and Simon at the king's request and in his presence, face-to-face. Even more striking is the political career of John the Essene. While Judas, Menaemus, and Simon were basically prophets and religious teachers, John was one of the six generals to whom the defense of Palestine was entrusted in the first year of the Jewish war, when the leadership of the revolt was still in the hands of the Jewish aristocracy of Jerusalem. John acted in both military and civil capacities as the commander of the district of Thamna, including Lydda, Joppa, and Emmaus, exactly as Josephus was in charge of Galilee and Gamala. The fact that, in this phase of the revolt, John the Essene was counted at the same rank as a personage like Josephus, with all his noble family connections, is further evidence that the Essenes were not outcasts from Jewish society. A few months later, in the spring of 67 CE, the Jews, still confident from their victory over Cestius, sent three of their best and more daring generals, "who were the chiefs of them all, both for strength and sagacity," among them John the Essene, to launch an attack on Askalon. The expedition turned into catastrophe; the Jewish army, strong in numbers and enthusiasm but poorly equipped and inexperienced, was overwhelmed by the superior military organization of the Roman garrison, and John himself died in battle.

The reference to the bravery the Essenes demonstrated during "our war against the Romans," facing torture and death before "blaspheming their legislator or eating what was forbidden to them" (*J.W.* 2.152-53), also points to the fact that Essene participation in the Jewish war was not an isolated phenomenon.[4] That the Essenes were anything but an isolated fringe group is confirmed by Philo, who, at the beginning of his treatise *De vita contemplativa (On the Contemplative Life),* contrasts the "active

---

4. L. L. Grabbe, *Judaism from Cyrus to Hadrian,* 2 vols. (Minneapolis: Fortress, 1992); E. M. Smallwood, *The Jews under Roman Rule: From Pompey to Diocletian* (Leiden: Brill, 1976).

life" practiced with great zeal and success by the Essenes to the "contemplative life" in which the Egyptian Therapeutae excelled (*Vit. Cont.* 1–2).

Finally, Josephus stresses that the Essenes were not only geographically dispersed in Palestine but also ideologically divided; he mentions a "second order" with different attitudes toward marriage (*J.W.* 2.160). If, as seems likely, the Therapeutae were not a separate movement but a branch of Egyptian Essenes, we would have from Philo a further glimpse at the pluralism and geographical extent of the movement. Many of the customs of the Therapeutae are indeed strikingly similar to those of the Palestinian Essenes. Philo even attributes to the Palestinian Essenes the same name, *therapeutai* (*Omn. Prob. Lib.* 12). In addition, the beginning of his treatise *De Vita Contemplativa* sounds more like the prologue to the description of a different group of Essenes than an introduction to a completely unrelated phenomenon. "I have spoken of Essenes who followed with zeal and constant diligence the active life, and so excelled in all, or to put it more moderately, in most particulars. And, therefore, I will presently, following the due sequence of my treatise, say whatever is meant to be said about them [[= those Essenes?]] who have embraced contemplation. . . . They are called Therapeutae and Therapeutridae" (*Vit. Cont.* 1-2). Philo, however, makes clear that the Egyptian Therapeutae had different customs from their Palestinian cousins. They lived isolated, "having left their homes and emigrated to a certain spot most suitable, which is situated above the Mareotic Lake, on a low hill" (*Vit. Cont.* 22), and were totally devoted to contemplation (*Vit. Cont.* 1–2). Any parallelism between the Palestinian Essenes and the Egyptian Therapeutae requires great caution; if the Therapeutae were Essenes, they formed a completely autonomous group.[5]

Neither Philo nor Josephus speaks explicitly of an Essene settlement in Jerusalem, even though Josephus's narratives about individual members of the Essenes, such as Judas and Menaemus, show that Jerusalem was far from being off limits for the Essenes during both the Hasmonean and the Herodian periods. The most remarkable clue to the presence of an Essene

---

5. J. Riaud, "Les Thérapeutes d'Alexandrie dans la tradition et dans la recherche critique jusqu'aux découvertes de Qumran," in *ANRW* 2.20.2 (1987) 1189-1295; O. Betz, "Essener und Therapeuten," *TRE* 10 (1982) 386-91; Schürer, "The Therapeutae," in *History,* 2.591-97; M. M. Elizarova, *The Community of the Therapeutae* {Russian} (Moscow: Akademia Nauk, 1972); G. Vermes, "Essenes and Therapeutae," *RevQ* 3 (1962) 495-504 (repr. in G. Vermes, *Post-Biblical Jewish Studies,* SJLA 8 [Leiden: Brill, 1975] 30-36); idem, "Essenes-Therapeutae-Qumran," *DUJ* 21 (1960) 97-115.

settlement in Jerusalem, however, is a passage in which Josephus does not deal with the Essenes but with a more prosaic subject, the walls of Jerusalem. When describing the southwestern part of the city, he incidentally mentions that the wall "stretched down through the place called Bethso to the gate of the Essenes" (*J.W.* 5.145). Archaeological excavations have recently confirmed Josephus's narrative and strengthened the credibility of his testimony.[6] Archaeology has also revealed a network of ritual baths outside the wall and a likely connection between the obscure Greek "Bethso" and the Hebrew *bt ṣw'h* ("house of waste"). From Josephus we know that the Essenes had a complex ritual for the evacuation of excrement, which was considered a defiling act and therefore forbidden on the seventh day. "On the other days, they dig a hole deep with their mattocks. . . . They squat there, covered by their mantles so as not to offend the rays of God. Then they push back the excavated soil into the hole. For this operation they choose the loneliest places . . . and are accustomed to wash themselves afterwards as though defiled" (*J.W.* 2.149).

The hypothesis that the latrines and the gate lay in a quarter inhabited by the Essenes has already produced a vast bibliography.[7] Scholars are intrigued in particular by the fact that according to the Christian tradition,[8]

---

6. B. Pixner, D. Chen, and S. Margalit, "Mount Zion: The Gate of the Essenes Re-excavated," *ZDPV* 105 (1989) 85-95, and plates 8-16. Cf. also B. Pixner, "The History of the Essene Gate Area," *ZDPV* 105 (1989) 96-104; R. Riesner, "Josephus' Gate of the Essenes in Modern Discussion," *ZDPV* 105 (1989) 105-9.

7. R. Riesner, "Essene Gate," *ABD* 2.618-19; idem, "Jesus, the Primitive Community, and the Essene Quarter of Jerusalem," in J. H. Charlesworth, ed., *Jesus and the Dead Sea Scrolls* (New York: Doubleday, 1992) 198-234; M. Delcor, "A propos de l'emplacement de la porte des Esséniens selon Josèphe et de ses implications historiques, essénienne et chrétienne. Examen d'une théorie"; B. Pixner, "The Jerusalem Essenes, Barnabas and the Letter to the Hebrews"; and R. Reisner, "Das Jerusalemer Essenerviertel antwort auf einige Einwände," in Z. J. Kapera, ed., *Intertestamental Essays in Honour of Józef Tadeusz Milik* (Cracow: Enigma, 1992) 25-44, 167-78, and 179-86, respectively; B. Pixner, "Das Essenerquartier in Jerusalem," in R. Riesner, ed., *Wege des Messias und Stätten der Urkirche* (Giessen: Brunnen, 1991) 180-209; R. Riesner, "Essener und Urkirche in Jerusalem," *BK* 40 (1985) 64-76; B. Pixner, "An Essene Quarter on Mount Zion?" in G. C. Bottini, ed., *Studi archeologici in onore di Bellarmino Bagatti OFM,* Studia Hierosolymitana 1 (Jerusalem: Franciscan Printing Press, 1976) 245-85.

8. D. Baldi, *Enchiridion locorum sanctorum: Documenta S. Evangelii loca respicientia,* 3rd ed. (Jerusalem: Franciscan Printing Press, 1982) 471-531, 737-52; B. Bagatti and E. Testa, *Corpus scriptorum de ecclesia matre* 4 (Jerusalem: Franciscan Printing Press, 1982) 169-87.

the same area of Jerusalem was the setting for the earliest stages of the Christian movement. Even without this significant link with Christian origins, the excavations related to the "gate of the Essenes" and to "the place called Bethso" are of the greatest importance. The evidence is circumstantial, yet it is the only occurrence in which archaeological findings can be used to support the existence of an Essene settlement in a Judaean city.

(b) *In contrast to Jewish authors,* who point to the great complexity and extent of the Essene movement, Pliny and Dio of Prusa speak of the Essenes as a single isolated community and connect them with a single well-defined area near the Dead Sea. Both give precise geographical coordinates. Pliny says that "the people of the Essenes live to the west [of the Dead Sea], having put the necessary distance between themselves and the insalubrious shore." That the Essene settlement was located somewhere northwest of the Dead Sea can be inferred from the fact that Pliny's description proceeds southward. Having mentioned Jerusalem and Herodium, Pliny describes the Jordan River and the Dead Sea (*Nat. Hist.* 5.70-72). Then he locates the Essenes on its western shore, somewhere north of Engedi and Masada. "Below them [Lat. *infra eos*] was the town of Engada [Lat. *Engedi*]. . . . From there, one comes to the fortress of Masada, situated on a rock, and itself near the lake of Asphalt" (*Nat. Hist.* 5.73).[9] More specifically, Dio of Prusa claims that "the Essenes . . . form an entire and prosperous city [Gk. *polis*] near the Dead Sea, in the center of Palestine, not far from Sodom." Unfortunately, this is all we know from Synesius of Cyrene. In spite of its brevity, Dio's testimony is particularly remarkable inasmuch as it openly contradicts Josephus, for whom, as we have seen, "there is not one town [Gk. *polis*] of them only" (*J.W.* 2.124). Epiphanius offers another interesting piece of evidence. As did other later Christian authors, he mistook the Essenes for a Samaritan sect, yet he located a *genos* of Jews with a strikingly similar name, the Ossaioi, in the vicinity of the Dead Sea (*Haer.* 19.1.1-4, 10). It is likely that this piece of information came from a source similar to that available to Pliny and Dio. The changing of the name may have been the way Epiphanius sought to harmonize his conflicting sources.

Archaeologists have excavated a settlement, so-called Khirbet Qum-

---

9. C. Burchard, "Pline et les Esséniens: A propos d'un article récent," *RB* 69 (1962) 533-69; E.-M. Laperrousaz, "Infra hos Engadda," *RB* 69 (1962) 369-80.

ran, on the northwest bank of the Dead Sea. Despite attempts to prove the contrary, no other site in this region corresponds as well to Pliny's and Dio's portrait.[10] The archaeology of Qumran has given strong evidence to the reliability of their testimony, including the fact that the Essenes described by non-Jewish authors lived among themselves without sharing the same territory with other people. Even the pottery from Qumran shows clear signs of uniqueness; it "suggests that the inhabitants practiced a deliberate and selective policy of isolation, manufacturing ceramic products to suit their own special needs and requirements."[11] Of great interest is also the presence of a large cemetery; both the careful ordering of the graves and their orientation with the head toward the south are unparalleled in ancient Israel. The interpretation of Roland de Vaux, who directed the excavations in the 1950s, that the site was a sectarian settlement, "still makes the most sense."[12]

A major disagreement between archaeological and literary sources concerns the antiquity of the settlement, which archaeology dates between the second century BCE and the first century CE, a span of only two or three centuries compared to Pliny's "thousands of centuries." One should notice, however, that Pliny's statement refers to the Essenes as a *gens,* not necessarily to their settlement near the Dead Sea. At any rate, "thousands of centuries" is too vague and bombastic to have any historical reliability. According to all ancient Jewish chronologies, the origin of the Essenes would then precede even the time of creation. The phrase serves only to turn the chronologically indefinite notion of the antiquity of the group that Pliny shared with Jewish sources into an ingenious trick to capture the imagination of his Roman readers.

10. M. Broshi, "The Archaeology of Qumran — A Reconsideration," in D. Dimant and U. Rappaport, eds., *The Dead Sea Scrolls: Forty Years of Research,* STDJ 10 (Leiden: Brill, 1992) 103-15; P. R. Davies, *Qumran* (Grand Rapids: Eerdmans, 1982); E.-M. Laperrousaz, *Qoumrân, l'établissement essénien des bords de la Mer Morte, histoire et archéologie du site* (Paris: Picard, 1976); R. de Vaux, *Archaeology and the Dead Sea Scrolls,* rev. ed. (London: Oxford University Press, 1973).

11. J. Magness, "The Community at Qumran in Light of Its Pottery," in M. O. Wise, et al., eds., *Methods of Investigation of the Dead Sea Scrolls and the Khirbet Qumran Site: Present Realities and Future Prospects* (New York: New York Academy of Sciences, 1994) 39-50 (quotation at p. 47). For a revisionistic approach that denies the uniqueness of Qumran, see R. Donceel and P. Donceel-Voûte, "The Archaeology of Khirbet Qumran," in ibid., 1-38.

12. J. Magness, "Not a Country Villa," *BARev* 22/6 (1996) 38, 40-47, 72-73.

3. Communal Ownership

The second element shared by Jewish and non-Jewish witnesses is the uniqueness and distinctiveness of the Essene way of life, based on communal organization and the sharing of goods. In particular, ancient sources were impressed by a way of life in which money was not necessary. For Pliny, the Essenes lived "without money" (Lat. *sine pecunia*). Josephus claims that among the Essenes economic transactions were regulated neither by money nor by exchange, but by common ownership. "They neither buy nor sell anything among themselves; but each one gives what he has to whoever needs it, and receives freely in return whatever he himself requires. And they can even receive freely from whomsoever they like without giving anything in exchange" (*J.W.* 2.127). "They hold their possessions in common, and the wealthy person does not benefit any more from his household possessions than the man who owns nothing at all" (*Ant.* 18.20). Philo's assertions agree with Josephus: "None of them can endure to possess anything of his own; neither house, slave, field, nor flocks, nor anything which feeds and procures wealth. . . . It is agreed that whatever belongs to each belongs to all, and conversely, whatever belongs to all belongs to each" (*Apol.* 4, 12). Among the Essenes, therefore, everything was in common.

(a) *In contrast to non-Jewish authors,* Philo and Josephus speak of the Essenes as people who lived their otherness in a normal environment, "being useful to themselves and to their neighbors" (Philo, *Omn. Prob. Lib.* 76). According to Josephus, the Essenes "live among themselves" (Gk. *eph' heautōn zōntes; Ant.* 18.21) in a special way. Josephus (like Hippolytus) describes the typical day of the Essenes:

> Before sunrise they speak no profane word but recite certain ancestral prayers. After these prayers the superiors dismiss them. . . . Then, after working without interruption until the fifth hour, they reassemble in the same place [Josephus: *chōrion;* Hippolytus: *topos*] and, girded with linen loincloths [Hippolytus: + to conceal their private parts], bathe themselves in cold water. After this purification they assemble in a special building [Josephus: *eis idion oikēma;* Hippolytus: *eis en oikēma*] to which no one is admitted who is not of the same faith; they themselves only enter the refectory [Gk. *deipnētērion*] if they are pure, as though into a holy precinct. When they are quietly seated, the baker serves out

the loaves of bread in order, and the cook serves only one bowlful of one dish to each man. Before the meal the priest says a prayer and no one is permitted to taste the food before the prayer; and after they have eaten the meal they recite another prayer. . . . Afterwards they lay aside the [Hippolytus: + linen] garments which they have worn for the meal, since they are sacred garments, and [Hippolytus: + having resumed the clothes in the vestibule (Gk. *proodos*)] apply themselves again to work until the evening. Then they return and take their dinner in the same manner. (*J.W.* 2.128-32; cf. Hippolytus, *Ref.* 21)

The ordinary weekday of an Essene was therefore divided into five parts: morning prayers, work, lunch, work, dinner. The seventh day was honored with particular sacredness, and work was forbidden; however, the reference to the care with which food was prepared in advance suggests that the practice of communal meals was not discontinued. "On the seventh day, they are forbidden, more rigorously than any other Jew, to attend their work. Not only do they prepare their food on the day before to avoid lighting a fire on that day, but they dare not even move an object, or go to stool [Hippolytus: some would not even rise from a couch]" (*J.W.* 2.147). Philo adds that during the seventh day, more time was devoted to religious instruction. "They continually instruct themselves in the [ancestral] laws but especially every seventh day; for the seventh day is thought holy. On that day they abstain from other work and proceed to the holy places [Gk. *topoi*] called synagogues, where they sit in appointed places, according to their age, the young men below the old, attentive and well-behaved" (*Omn. Prob. Lib.* 81).

That the communal meals, with their complex rituals of purification and prayers, were the center of Essene life is confirmed by the rigid exclusion of nonmembers (Josephus, *J.W.* 2.129). Even the postulants had to wait until the completion of the three-year process of admission. During the first year they were not even allowed to enter the meeting place of the Essenes. "For one year the postulant waits outside [Gk. *exō*]" (*J.W.* 2.137), or as Hippolytus says more specifically, "for the space of one year they set before them the same sort of food, while they continue to live in a different house [Gk. *oikos*] outside [Gk. *exō*] the Essenes' own place of meeting [Gk. *synodos*]" (*Ref.* 23). The postulant had to wait "two more years [in which] his character is tested, and if he appears worthy he is received into the company permanently. But before touching the common food he makes solemn vows before his brethren" (Josephus, *J.W.* 2.137-39).

Participation in the communal meals was the ultimate goal of the entire probationary period of the postulants.

Philo also emphasizes that in the Essene experience the "communal meals" (Gk. *syssitia; Omn. Prob. Lib.* 86, 91; *Apol.* 5) were the highest expression of their "communal life" (Gk. *koinōnia*). The Essenes "dwell together, in brotherhoods, having adopted the form of associations and the custom of eating in common" (*Apol.* 5). "Daily they share the same way of life, the same table [Gk. *homotrapezoi*], and even the same tastes. . . . They have a common table [Gk. *koinē trapeza*]" (*Apol.* 11). "Food [is] held in common, for they have adopted the practice of eating together, . . . sharing the same roof, the same way of life, and the same table [Gk. *homotrapezon*]" (*Apol.* 86).

Ancient sources agree that the sacred and, for nonmembers, inaccessible meeting place of the Essenes was basically a dining hall. It was a "place" (Philo, Hippolytus: *topos;* Josephus: *chōrion*) that could be called an "assembly" (Philo: *synagogē;* Hippolytus: *synodos*) with regard to its function, or, with regard to its architecture, a "building" (Josephus, Hippolytus: *oikēma*), including a "vestibule" (Hippolytus: *proodos*) where the Essenes changed their clothes and a "refectory" (Josephus, Hippolytus: *deipnētērion*) where the Essenes consumed food.

Although the communal life of the Essenes was highly demanding, it was limited to some times of the day and did not consume the individual completely. "After the [morning] prayers the superiors dismiss them so that each man attends the craft with which he is familiar" (Josephus, *J.W.* 2.128-29; cf. Hippolytus: "each going to whatever employment they please," *Ref.* 21). Philo confirms that there was no communal work. Although the ideal of the Essenes was to "employ their whole activity for the common good, nevertheless they all follow different occupations and apply themselves with zeal. . . . There are farmers among them expert in the art of sowing and cultivation of plants, shepherds leading every sort of flock, and beekeepers. Other are craftsmen in diverse trades. . . . They never defer until the morrow whatever serves to procure for them blameless revenue" (*Apol.* 5–6, 8). Philo reveals that some jobs were considered unsuitable: "they have not the smallest idea, nor even a dream, of wholesale, retail, or marine commerce, rejecting everything that might excite them to cupidity" (*Omn. Prob. Lib.* 78). Josephus agrees that agriculture was the Essenes' main and ideal occupation: "they are excellent men and wholly given up to agricultural labour" (*Ant.* 18.19). But the general picture that emerges from our sources is that of people who worked outside their brotherhoods, practicing the ordinary jobs of the time and receiving revenues, exactly as everybody else did. "Some Essenes work in the fields, and others practice various crafts contributing to peace" (*Omn. Prob. Lib.* 76).

Because the Essene communities were not the employers of their members and were not economically self-sufficient, Essenes used to spend much of their time working among non-Essenes. It is possible that this was not the only time that Essenes were with nonmembers. Interestingly, our sources make no mention of where the Essenes actually dwelt and spent the night. It is not said from where in the morning they assembled in the same meeting place. The Essenes gathered for prayers and communal meals; we do not have any evidence whatsoever that the meetinghouses of the Essenes were also dormitories. Neither are we told that the community owned any facility for lodging. On the contrary, Philo and Josephus speak of private houses that were to be shared. "No one has a private house that is not shared with all. For as well as living in communities, their homes are open to members of the sect arriving from elsewhere" (Philo, *Omn. Prob. Lib.* 85). "Everything they have is at the disposal of members of the sect arriving from elsewhere as though it were their own, and they enter into the house of people whom they have never seen before as though they were intimate friends" (Josephus, *J.W.* 2.124). These passages reveal, first, that the Essenes had private houses, and, second, that the practice of sharing them was perhaps a general rule but was applied in particular on behalf of occasional visitors from elsewhere, which is to say, only if and when necessary. A local community had no difficulty providing meals in its refectory to fellow members coming from other cities, but manifestly could only count on the hospitality of its own members in order to offer them an accommodation for the night. The reference to private houses also leaves open the possibility that the Essenes continued to dwell under the same roof with their own families, including wives and children.

The public dimension of the Essene life is apparent even in the way in which their most secret practices were performed. Their holy places were barred to strangers but were somewhere that was not too far from the ears of outsiders, who could testify to the majesty of ceremonies that their eyes might never have seen. "No shouting or disturbance ever defiles the house. . . . To those outside, this silence of the men inside seems a great mystery; but the cause of it is their invariable sobriety and the fact that their food and drink are so measured out that they are satisfied and no more" (Josephus, *J.W.* 2.132-33).

It is within this context that we must understand the economic communism of the Essenes. They "despise riches" (*J.W.* 2.122) and live a simple and frugal life. "They do not hoard silver and gold, and do not acquire vast domains with the intention of drawing revenue from them, but they procure for themselves only what is necessary to life. Almost alone among all humankind, they live without goods and without property; and this by preference, and not as a result of a reverse of fortune. They think themselves thus very rich, rightly considering frugality and contentment to be real superabundance" (Philo, *Omn. Prob. Lib.* 76-77).

When an Essene joined the community, he was asked to share his property, as among brothers. "For it is a law that those entering the sect transfer their property to the order; consequently, among them there appears neither abject poverty nor superabundance of wealth, but the possessions of each are mingled together, and there is, as among brothers, one property common to all" (Josephus, *J.W.* 2.122). Philo clarifies that "they put everything together into the public stock and enjoy the benefit of them all in common" (*Apol.* 10.4).

Since people continued to work outside the community and earn "blameless revenue," sharing property was not a once-in-a-lifetime act but a continuous process. "There is but one purse for them all and a common expenditure . . . whatever they receive as salary for their day's work is not kept to themselves, but it is deposited before them all, in their midst, to be put to the common employment of those who wish to make use of it" (*Omn. Prob. Lib.* 86). Josephus also says that "to collect the revenues and the produce of the earth they select excellent men" (*Ant.* 18.22).

The "one purse" was used for the communal meals and clothes, for the sick and the elderly. "Thanks to the common purse, they have whatever is needed to treat [the sick]. . . . The aged also are surrounded with respect and care" (Philo, *Omn. Prob. Lib.* 87). "If any of them falls ill he is treated at the expense of the community, and is surrounded by the care and attention of them all. As for the aged, even if they have no children they are as fathers not only of many children but of very good ones" (*Apol.* 13). That the mechanism of redistribution of goods targeted, besides the general expenses of the community, only people with special needs, such as the sick, the aged, and the guests, means that the reference to "one purse" and "a common expenditure" must be taken more as a hyperbole than a reality. In an economy in which money and wages played only a limited role and people lived by the products of their own hands within an extended family, the ordinary members of the community could, and were expected to, take care of themselves without the control and assistance of the superiors. Only those people who were unable to work and produce needed assistance and money. The sociological context in which the sharing of goods was practiced made inevitable that the individual retained a certain control over his own properties.

This view is confirmed by the way in which charity was regulated. "They are allowed on their own discretion to help those worthy of help whenever it is asked for, and to offer food for the needy, but they have no right to subsidize members of their own family without the authority of the superiors" (Josephus, *J.W.* 2.134). This passage is enlightening. First, it shows that the Essenes continued to feel responsible to support their relatives economically; the leadership of the community limited itself to authorizations and did not oppose this practice. Second, that the Essenes were allowed to help the needy "on their own discretion" implies that they must have had the private means to do so.[13]

In short, the ideal of the Essenes was the communal usage of their properties as if there were no private property, and the sharing of goods for the needs of the community and of the poorest members, as among brothers. The Essenes continued to work, to earn money, to be economically independent, to live by their own goods and in their own homes, possibly with their own relatives,[14] and to have some control over their own property. These limitations to the general principle of "everything in common" have been clearly recognized by Hartmut Stegemann, who describes "the realistic background" of the Essene way of life in the Palestinian communities: "What is actually meant by 'everything in common'? If somebody became a full member of the Essenes, he surely was expected to continue to stay at his home, to harvest his garden, his fields, or his vineyards, and to live by those products together with his family."[15]

13. See J. C. VanderKam, *The Dead Sea Scrolls Today* (Grand Rapids: Eerdmans, 1994) 83.

14. On the problem of the relations of the Essenes with their relatives, including wives and children, see the section on "Marriage and Celibacy" on pp. 38-46 below.

15. H. Stegemann, "The Qumran Essenes — Local Members of the Main Jewish Union in Late Second Temple Times," in J. Trebolle Barrera and L. Vegas Montaner, eds., *The Madrid Qumran Congress: Proceedings of the International Congress on the Dead Sea Scrolls, Madrid, 18-21 March, 1991,* STDJ 11/1-2 (Leiden: Brill, 1992) 1.83-166 (quotation on p. 113).

(b) *In contrast to Jewish authors,* Pliny and Dio depict a single community that had more radical rules of separation. The geographical isolation of the group, which is said "to enjoy for company only the palm trees" (Lat. *socia palmarum*), reflects a practice of communal life of individuals "whom, wearied by the fluctuations of fortune, life leads to adopt their customs" (Lat. *quos vita fessos ad mores eorum fortuna fluctibus agit*). The result was the creation of an alternative society. According to Dio the Essenes were a *polis,* a "town," not just a brotherhood. As a result, the contacts with the outside were strictly limited and de facto abolished on the individual level.

In this different sociological context, Pliny's statement that the community was "without money" (Lat. *sine pecunia*) does not reflect an ideal life of sharing and communion, but states a reality in which all economic bonds of the individual with the outside were cut off, except through the mediation of the communal institutions. The isolation of the Dead Sea community and its distance from the economic centers of the region made it impossible for its members to work daily outside the community. The Essenes of Pliny and Dio not only shared their goods but also lived together in an economically self-sufficient community.

Despite attempts to dismiss the evidence of archaeological data, the most reasonable hypothesis remains that the ruins of Qumran are those of a community center in which a Jewish group practiced some kind of self-sufficient communal life. Also, in this case, archaeological remains have demonstrated that Pliny's and Dio's narratives are more than pieces of literature. No private houses have been found at Qumran, no evidence of private ownership. On the contrary, everything points to the conclusion that the people of Qumran wanted their economy to be as self-sufficient as possible.[16] At Khirbet Qumran several workshops, a pottery, an installation for the production of date honey, and a stable for animals have been identified, and a farm has been excavated at Ain Feshkha, two miles south of Qumran. In addition, storage areas for grain have been found below the plateau on which the Qumran buildings sit. This evidence suggests that the Qumran community had a developed economy and sophisticated organizational skills; it provided communal work and earned its living by the work of its members.[17]

16. See W. R. Farmer, "The Economic Basis of the Qumran Community," *TZ* 11 (1955) 297-308; L. M. Pákozdy, "Der wirtschaftliche Hintergrund der Gemeinschaft von Qumran," in H. Bardtke, ed., *Qumran-Probleme* (Berlin: Akademie-Verlag, 1963) 267-91.

17. See de Vaux, *Archaeology;* Davies, *Qumran.*

The finding of numerous coins does not contradict the self-sufficiency of the Qumran community and the poverty of its members.[18] An ostracon found in February 1996 by James F. Strange at Qumran provides a list of supplies brought from Jericho by a newcomer and thus confirms that the people who joined the community of the Dead Sea actually transferred their property to the community (Heb. *yḥd*).[19] The treasury, which was the result of such private donations, was necessary for the relations of the community with the outside and allowed the members to regulate their internal economy without money. The people of Qumran worked for the community without receiving wages, having no necessity of money for their own needs, since everything was provided *sine pecunia* by the community.

4. Marriage and Celibacy

The third element shared by both Jewish and non-Jewish witnesses is that the Essenes had a particular attitude toward marriage that immediately distinguished them from other Jews. They were men without women, living in celibacy (Pliny). They banned marriage (Philo, Josephus).

(a) *In contrast to non-Jewish authors,* Philo and Josephus describe a less radical refusal of marriage. Modern scholars have often spoken of Essene celibacy.[20] If we want to continue using this phrase, we must be

18. De Vaux argues that the hundreds of coins found at Qumran come exclusively from the administration buildings, not from the living quarters of the community, and were handed over for communal usage (*Archaeology,* 129).

19. F. M. Cross and E. Eshel, "Ostraca from Khirbet Qumrân," *IEJ* 47 (1997) 17-28.

20. On the attitude of the Essenes toward marriage, see J. M. Baumgarten, "The Qumran-Essene Restraints on Marriage," in L. H. Schiffman, ed., *Archaeology and History in the Dead Sea Scrolls: The New York University Conference in Memory of Yigael Yadin* (Sheffield: Sheffield Academic Press, 1990) 13-24; J. Coppens, "Le célibat essénien," in M. Delcor, ed., *Qumrân: Sa piété, sa théologie et son milieu,* BETL 46 (Paris: Duculot, 1978) 295-304; Y. Yadin "L'attitude essénienne envers la polygamie et le divorce," *RB* 79 (1972) 98-99; A. Guillaumont, "A propos du célibat des Esséniens," in A. Caquot and M. Philonenko, eds., *Hommages à A. Dupont-Sommer* (Paris: Adrien-Maisonneuve, 1971) 395-404; A. Marx, "Les racines du célibat essénien," *RevQ* 7 (1971) 323-42; H. Hübner, "Zölibat in Qumran?" *NTS*

clear that Essene refusal of marriage was something different from the modern category of "celibacy." It was not related to the idea of perpetual virginity and sterility; a "celibate" Essene might not be an unmarried and childless man.

The best key to understanding the nature of Essene "celibacy" is given by Philo's statement that the Essene communities were composed exclusively of "men of ripe years already inclining to old age who are no longer carried away by the flux of the body nor drawn by the passions, but enjoy true and unparalleled liberty. . . . There are therefore no children of tender years among the Essenes, not even adolescents or young men, since at this age the character, because of its immaturity, is inconstant and attracted to novelty" (*Apol.* 2-3).

The Essene communities were therefore made up of adult males, who at a certain point in their existence, at an older age than that considered suitable for marriage, decided to join a group with special laws. When Philo claims that the Essenes "banned marriage [Gk. *gamos*] at the same time as they ordered the practice of perfect continence; indeed, no Essene takes a woman [Gk. *agetai gynaika*]" (*Apol.* 14), he refers to the way of life of the group, which banned marriage and sexuality. This does not rule out that members of the Essenes, before joining the group, were married and had children, nor does Philo imply that the Essenes had to cut off any social relationship with their families. A few lines before the Philonic text presents the case of childless Essenes as a clear and unfortunate exception, "even if they have no children," claiming that "even" they "are as fathers . . . of many sons who care for them spontaneously rather than as a result of natural necessity" (*Apol.* 13). For the majority of Essenes, who apparently were not childless, it seems likely to infer that the children were expected to provide some care for their aging and ailing parents. The Essene "celibacy" therefore was not the condemnation of the matrimonial institution by unmarried men and virgins, but the abandoning of marital life and sexuality by individuals who may have experienced marriage and fatherhood.

Josephus confirms this interpretation. On one hand, he claims that "as the Essenes renounce pleasure as an evil, and regard continence and

---

17 (1971) 153-67; H. R. Moehring, "Josephus on the Marriage Customs of the Essenes," in A. P. Wikgren, ed., *Early Christian Origins* (Chicago: Quadrangle, 1961) 120-27.

resistance to the passion as a virtue, they disdain marriage [Gk. *gamos*] for themselves" (*J.W.* 2.120). On the other hand, Josephus clarifies that "it is not that they abolish marriage [Gk. *gamos*], or the propagation of the species resulting from it" (*J.W.* 2.120-21). Compared to Philo, Josephus is neither contradictory nor ambiguous in his testimony. Celibacy was one of the rules of the Essene communities, not a prerequisite; neither Philo nor Josephus states that only unmarried men and virgins were allowed to join the community while married men with children were banned.

Against this background, one can explain why Josephus uses *gametas eisagesthai* ("to take wives") instead of the usual *gynaikas eisagesthai* ("to take women") in *Ant.* 18.21. His point may not be that "the Essenes take no women [in their homes]" but that "they do not take [their] wives [in the community] . . . but live among themselves."[21]

That the central point was not marriage but the admission of women in the same community is confirmed by Hippolytus's interesting addition in a passage that otherwise parallels perfectly Josephus's narrative. "They renounce matrimony. . . . They do not forbid marriage but they themselves refrain from matrimony. *Women, however, even though they may be disposed to adhere to the same course of life, they do not admit,* for in no way whatsoever have they confidence in women" (*Ref.* 18).

In order to understand better the Essene attitude, it is convenient to recall the nature of marriage in antiquity. Matrimony was essentially a contract between a man and a woman based on sexual obligations (procreation) and social obligations (living together, mutual caring, raising children). The Essenes discontinued sexual obligations while they subordinated social obligations to a more binding relationship (communal membership in the community) from which women were excluded. That the Essenes "had no right to subsidize members of their own family without the authority of the superiors," while no authorization was required to help the needy (Josephus, *J.W.* 2.134), reveals that the relationship between the members and their families (including wives and children?) was a delicate matter that the leadership of the community wanted to control and regulate in detail. Although not forbidden, family ties were

---

21. Thus Stegemann also interprets the passage: "this statement does not say that the Essenes had no wives, but only that their wives were not admitted as full members of their community" ("Qumran Essenes," 126).

potentially disruptive and therefore had to remain strictly subordinated to the community.

Unfortunately, neither Philo nor Josephus clarifies the theology underlying Essene misogyny. The Essenes clearly considered marriage incompatible with communal life. According to Philo, "marriage is the sole or principal obstacle threatening to dissolve the bonds of communal life" (*Apol.* 14), and Josephus describes it as a way of life "leading to discord" (*Ant.* 18.21). But the only explanation they offer is a series of antiwoman stereotypes. "Women are selfish, excessively jealous, skillful in ensnaring the morals of a spouse and in seducing him by endless charms. . . . The husband, bound by his wife's spell, or anxious for his children from natural necessity, is no more the same toward others, but unknown to himself he becomes a different man, a slave instead of a freeman" (*Apol.* 14-17). According to Josephus, the Essenes "are on their guard against the licentiousness of women and are convinced that none of them is faithful to one man" (*J.W.* 2.121), and Hippolytus adds that "in no way whatsoever have [the Essenes] confidence in women" (*Ref.* 18). Our sources clearly describe a phenomenon of rejection of marital life and distrust in the compatibility of women with communal life, but the absence of any theological justification leaves the reader in suspense about the real foundations of these Essene attitudes.

Josephus and Hippolytus also testify to the existence of a dispute within the Essene movement over the issue of marriage. The passage throws some light on the deepest reasons motivating the Essene attitude toward women; it reveals that a woman's purity was much more at stake than her morality.

> There exists another order [Gk. *tagma*] of Essenes who, although in agreement with the others on the way of life, usages, and customs, are separated from them on the subject of marriage [Gk. *kata gamon*]. Indeed, they believe that people who do not marry cut off a very important part of life, namely, the propagation of the species; and all the more so that if everyone adopted the same opinion the race[22] would very quickly disappear. Nevertheless, they test [Gk. *dokimazō*] their wives

22. Josephus's text is ambiguous: the term *genos* could refer to the "human," the "Jewish," or the "Essene race." The parallel passage in Hippolytus (*Ref.* 28) reads: "the entire race of humans" (Gk. *to pan genos anthrōpōn*).

41

[Gk. *gametas*] for three years. Then, after they have purified themselves three times and thus proved themselves capable of bearing children, they took [Gk. *agontai*] them. And when they are pregnant they have no intercourse with them, thereby showing that they do not marry for pleasure but because it is necessary to have children. The women [Gk. *gynaikes*] bathe wrapped in linen, whereas the men [Gk. *andres*] wear a loincloth [Gk. *perizōma*]. Such are the customs of this order. (Josephus, *J.W.* 2.160-61; cf. Hippolytus, *Ref.* 28)

As in *Ant.* 18.21, the reference to *gametas* ("wives") instead of *gynaikes* ("women") might betray that Josephus and Hippolytus (or better, their common source) had in mind not only the testing of the Essenes' "betrothed women" but also of their "actual wives." The ancient testimony of Dionysios Bar Salibi points to the same conclusion, which seems to fit the customs of the second order of Essenes: "For three years [the Essenes, or 'pure'] would leave their wives without intercourse; and [then] once they had become pregnant they did not come near them again, [thus] demonstrating that not out of lust did they do this, but so as to establish children" (*Against the Jews* 1).[23]

The gender-related language (women/men, Gk. *gynaikes/andres*) re-emerges in Josephus and Hippolytus only regarding the rituals and the purificatory baths; obviously, wearing different clothing depended not on the family status of the candidate but on the gender. The probation period required for the Essenes' "wives" paralleled that required for men, as indicated by the same time interval ("three years") and by the identical terminology. "Those [men] desiring to enter the sect do not obtain immediate admittance. The postulant waits outside for one year . . . and he is given . . . the loincloth [Gk. *perizōma*]. . . . Having proved his continence during this time, he draws closer to the way of life and participates in the purificatory baths. . . . His character is tested [Gk. *dokimazō*] for another two years, and if he appears worthy he is received into the company permanently. But before touching the common food he makes solemn vows before his brethren" (Josephus, *J.W.* 2.137-39). As the comparison makes clear, the same verb

23. See S. P. Brock, "Some Syriac Accounts of the Jewish Sects," in R. H. Fischer, ed., *A Tribute to Arthur Vööbus: Studies in Early Christian Literature and Its Environment, Primarily in the Syrian East* (Chicago: Lutheran School of Theology at Chicago, 1977) 265-76.

(dokimazō) is used for men and women, and the bathing of women is equated with the purification baths in which men wear a loincloth (Gk. *perizōma*).

The reference to the same rituals means that this group of Essenes admitted and recognized their wives as part of the community. The three-year testing was a formal admission process, after which we may assume that, analogously to what happened to male candidates, if "[she] appears worthy, [she] is received into the company permanently" (cf. *J.W.* 2.137-39). However, since no mention is made of the final step of men's probation, the solemn vows, and participation to common meals, it seems unlikely that wives were granted full membership even by the second order of Essenes.[24] The feminine role was probably limited to what was considered a masculine duty, procreation, yet the only one that could not be accomplished without women and sex. The only other rituals that wives were required to undergo were the three periods of purification, that is, three menstrual cycles, in order to prove the regularity of the menses and thus their fecundity, according to the common wisdom of the time (cf. Philo, *Spec. Leg.* 3.33).

The most interesting element in Josephus's narrative is the link it reveals between admission and purification. The second order of Essenes allowed some women to undertake the admission rituals. The ultimate goal, however, was not to make them part of the community but to make them cohabit as wives with their husbands for the propagation of the race. Participation in the community was a secondary, perhaps even unwelcome, yet inescapable effect. Even the second order of Essenes would probably never have opened the doors of their community to women if the admission rituals were not believed to be the only effective means to produce the desired goal: purification.

Moral instruction alone was obviously not enough. Women had to undergo a process of purification, despite the fact that this process brought them somehow within the horizons of the Essene communal life. This point the first order of Essenes could not accept; their insistence on the wickedness of women and on the danger of their presence for the community implies that they considered a woman's purification unlikely, or even impossible. Purity concerns, more than moral concerns, were involved in the attitude of both orders of Essenes toward marriage.[25]

24. Stegemann, "Qumran Essenes," 129.
25. Guillaumont, "Célibat des Esséniens"; G. W. Buchanan, "The Role of Purity in the Structure of the Essene Sect," *RevQ* 4 (1963-64) 402-5.

At any rate, the debate between the two orders of Essenes was not between virgin and married Essenes, but between Essenes who disagreed whether marital life and procreation could and should be part of the communal life or be completely banned and replaced by the new communal bonds. The difference was not that some Essenes had wives and children and others did not; probably the majority of Essenes of both orders had wives and children and to some extent continued to take care of them. The difference is that the first order of Essenes discontinued the sexual obligations of matrimony when joining the community, while the second order believed that, provided certain rituals occurred, women could reach a sufficient degree of purity that made marriage and procreation compatible with communal life.

(b) *In contrast to Jewish authors,* Pliny describes a community that followed a way of life certainly opposed to that of the "second order" of Essenes but equally distant from mainstream Essenism. Sexuality and procreation were totally banned. "They are a unique people . . . without women and renouncing sex entirely . . . into which no one is born" (Lat. *gens sola . . . sine ulla femina, omni venere abdicata . . . in qua nemo nascitur*). The survival of the group is totally based on the newcomers, an amazing phenomenon that Pliny boasts to the admiration of his readers: "Owing to the throng of newcomers, this people is daily reborn in equal number [Lat. *in diem ex aequo convenarum turba renascitur*]. . . . Thus, unbelievable though this may seem, for thousands of centuries a people has existed that is eternal yet into which no one is born [Lat. *gens aeterna est, in qua nemo nascitur*]" (*Nat. Hist.* 5.73).

Pliny says nothing about the family status of the newcomers, whether they were widowers, virgins, or, more likely, married men who, like the Egyptian Therapeutae, "flee without turning back, having abandoned brethren, children, wives, parents, all the throng of their kindred, all their friendship with companions, yea, their countries in which they were born and bred" (Philo, *Vit. Cont.* 18). We cannot infer from Pliny that the Essenes living near the Dead Sea were unmarried; they may have been married at one time, as were the majority of the Essenes living in Palestinian towns. The isolation of the group, however, marked an even deeper separation between them and their families. They not only discontinued the sexual obligations of marriage, but also no longer shared the same roof with their wives or fulfilled the social obligations of marital life.

Although Pliny's emphasis is on survival without women and sex

44

(renascitur versus *nemo nascitur),* the phrase *sine ulla femina* suggests that no woman whatsoever lived among the Essenes. If at stake had been only marriage, as for the first order of Essenes, Pliny could have said *sine ulla uxore* ("without wives"). Pliny's language implies the absence of women, unlike the Therapeutic settlement in Egypt where men and women lived side by side in celibacy, joined the same table, and sang God's praises together (Philo, *Vit. Cont.* 32-33, 68-69, 83-89). Pliny would hardly have failed to mention such an extraordinary and picturesque phenomenon, if he had been aware of it. If there were women in the community of the Dead Sea, their role was negligible.

Archaeological evidence is somewhat puzzling about the presence of women at Qumran. The existence of a large cemetery containing about eleven hundred remains of adult males, close to Qumran, confirms that the community who lived there was predominantly male and that some kind of separation between men and women was in force.[26] But graves of women and children have been found on the periphery of the main graveyard and in two small separated cemeteries, consisting of about one hundred graves altogether. Since the same pottery has been recovered everywhere, these graves were apparently also dug by the same people. How should one explain this phenomenon? One hypothesis is the presence of refugees or travelers, or even relatives, mothers, sisters, possibly wives and children, who wanted to remain as close as possible to their loved ones, or who came to visit them or chose to be reunited to them in death. Another possibility, which cannot be dismissed on the basis of archaeology, is that, as among the Therapeutae, some women lived there in celibacy and to a certain extent took part in the life of the community.[27] However, the archaeology of the communal center at Qumran has shown no trace of the existence of a structure resembling the Therapeutae's "common sanctuary . . . [with] a double enclosure, divided into one chamber for the men and another for the women . . . [with] a wall which runs midway up the buildings . . . built

26. R. Hachlili, "Burial Practices at Qumran," *RevQ* 62 (1994) 247-64; N. Haas and N. Nathan, "Anthropological Survey on the Human Skeletal Remains from Qumran," *RevQ* 6 (1968) 345-52; S. H. Steckoll, "Preliminary Excavation Report on the Qumran Cemetery," *RevQ* 6 (1968) 323-36. For a revisionistic approach that denies the connection between the Essenes and the cemetery, see Z. J. Kapera, "Some Remarks on the Qumran Cemetery," in Wise, et al., eds., *Methods of Investigation*, 97-113.

27. L. B. Elder, "The Women Question and Female Ascetics among Essenes," *BA* 57/4 (1994) 220-34.

up together like a breastwork from the floor to a height of three or four cubits, but that part which extends above up to the roof is left open for two reasons: namely, to safeguard the modesty which is proper to woman's nature, and, at the same time, to facilitate on the part of those who sit within the auditory the apprehension of what is said" (Philo, *Vit. Cont.* 32-33). In the area of Qumran there may have been a place for temporary or permanent, official or unofficial, sheltering of women and children, but the structure of the communal center and cemetery strongly suggests that women at Qumran were a negligible and marginal minority, not a well-organized and equal group like the Egyptian Therapeutridae.

In any case, one can exclude the notion that at Qumran there was room for family life. The most compelling element in the Qumran cemetery is not the separation between men and women, or the paucity of female graves, but the fact that the dead, men and women as well, with the exclusion of small children found with their mothers, were buried individually each in one grave — no family burial whatsoever. This practice is unique to Qumran and shows a disregard for family ties unparalleled in contemporary Jewish cemeteries.[28] However one interprets the presence of women buried at Qumran, this was not the cemetery of an ordinary settlement of Jewish families. Rather, this was the cemetery of a community whose members, predominantly male, possibly with the association of some women, lived in continence, having abolished not only marriage but also any vestige of family life.

5. Summary: The Palestinian Communities and the Community of the Dead Sea

Philo and Josephus, on the one hand, and Pliny and Dio, on the other hand, describe two different things: a network of Essene communities in Palestine and a single Essene settlement near the Dead Sea. It is unlikely that the discrepancy is chronological, recording two different stages in the history of the Essene movement. The community of the Dead Sea cannot belong to an earlier or later phase of the Palestinian Essene movement. Such a traumatic conversion from plurality to unicity, or vice versa, is historically

28. Hachlili, "Burial Practices at Qumran."

groundless. It is hard to believe that the Essene movement could have had the will and the skill to lead such a massive migration of people from or to the Dead Sea and that such an undertaking remained unnoticed in ancient sources. Archaeological and literary sources concur that the Palestinian communities and the Dead Sea community were contemporaneous. The only logical conclusion is that Essenism was a widespread movement of communities in Palestine, whose complexity was well known by Jewish authors, such as Philo and Josephus. Near the Dead Sea, however, there must have been an Essene settlement with such peculiar characteristics as to draw the attention and curiosity of non-Jewish authors, such as Pliny and Dio.

Comparing the descriptions of Jewish and non-Jewish sources, we can infer some interesting elements. First, whatever its etymology,[29] the name "Essenes" (Lat. *Esseni;* Gk. *Essēnoi,* or its variant *Essaioi,* which Philo connects with *Hosoi,* "saints," and Epiphanius corrupted into *Ossaioi*) denoted the members of both the Palestinian communities and the settlement near the Dead Sea. This means that the ancients perceived the existence of a common ground between these groups. Unfortunately, no ancient author explains the relationship between the community of the Dead Sea and the other Essene communities. No ancient author deals contemporaneously with both phenomena. Jewish sources describe the Essene communities in Palestine, but fail to mention any special community near the Dead Sea. Non-Jewish sources describe a community near the Dead Sea, but fail to mention the existence of other communities elsewhere in Palestine.[30] The common name, however, demonstrates that the two groups were related, even though we are not told how or to what extent. From

29. On the etymology of "Essenes" see J. Kampen, "A Reconsideration of the Name Essene in Greco-Jewish Literature in Light of Recent Perceptions of the Qumran Sect," *HUCA* 57 (1986) 61-81; S. Goranson, "Essenes: Etymology from *'šh,*" *RevQ* 11 (1984) 483-98; B. Vellas, "Zur Etymologie des Namens Essaioi," *ZAW* 81 (1969) 94-100; G. Vermes, "The Etymology of Essenes," *RevQ* 2 (1960) 427-43.

30. See the analogous conclusion in Stegemann: "While Philo Alexandrinus and Josephus Flavius spoke of the Essenes as living together with other Jews in most of the towns and villages of Palestine, saying nothing of any special Essene settlements in the Judaean desert, Pliny, on the other hand, had heard only about Essenes living in splendid isolation on the western shore of the Dead Sea north of En Gedi. He knew nothing about Essenes in towns and villages all over the country" ("Qumran Essenes," 84).

archaeology, we understand that the harsh environment and the limited facilities of the Qumran settlement could sustain only a minority of the four thousand Essenes; obviously, the majority of Essenes lived elsewhere.

Second, all the elements recorded by non-Jewish authors about the community of the Dead Sea have parallels in the narratives of Jewish authors with regard to the Essene communities in Palestine. The difference always lies in a higher degree of intensity with which the community of the Dead Sea lived those common elements: separation that turned into isolation, sharing of goods that turned into abolition of private property, rejection of marital life that turned into abandoning family ties.

The opposite is not true. The descriptions of Jewish authors contain some information about the Essenes that have no parallel in non-Jewish authors. Without additional evidence, we cannot assume that the features of the Essene communities in Palestine applied also, or in the same way, to the community of the Dead Sea.

Third, radicalization means a higher degree of separation and, consequently, a higher degree of distinctiveness. Otherness was exactly what made non-Jewish sources, and still makes modern archaeologists, interested in the community of the Dead Sea. Compared with the archaeology of Qumran, the archaeology of urban Essenes is barren: a gate, some latrines, a few buildings. Without the testimony of Josephus, those ruins would not present any distinctiveness. Neither an artifact nor a type of construction provides any evidence of belonging to a particular group of Jews. By contrast, the people who lived at Qumran created a distinctive architecture, a communal center that in shape and proportions is unparalleled in Jewish archaeology, and a cemetery with unique burial practices. Thanks to Pliny's and Dio's descriptions we know that some Essenes made that complex of buildings; but even without their descriptions, we would have noticed that a particular group planned the settlement. Perhaps it is not accidental that a greater amount of archaeological data is available on the community of the Dead Sea, while archaeological data regarding other Essene communities are difficult to detect. The separate society that the Essenes of Qumran tried to build has produced more distinctive archaeological remains than those left by the Essenes of the towns, who did not require their otherness to reshape the world around them.

Finally, the different choice made by Jewish and non-Jewish authors cannot be meaningless for our inquiry about the internal structure and balance of power within the Essene movement. Pliny and Dio were in search of sensational elements. Whether they were unaware of the existence of other Essene communities, or simply more interested in captivating their readers with an exotic story, as outsiders they found the community of the Dead Sea more intriguing and selected it as the only representative of the Essene movement. Philo and Josephus were interested in a presentation of Jewish thought. Whether they were unaware of the existence of the Dead Sea community, or consciously avoided any references to it, as insiders they chose the Palestinian communities as the best representatives of the Essene movement. Non-Jewish authors chose what modern archaeology confirms was more peculiar and distinctive; Jewish authors chose what they believed was theologically and sociologically more important and representative. Philo and Josephus might have been ill informed or even biased, but the Dead Sea community was much less important for them than for ancient non-Jewish historians and modern archaeologists.

In short, historiographical analysis leads to the overall conclusion that the community of the Dead Sea, described by Pliny and Dio, was a radical and minority group within the larger Essene movement, described by Philo and Josephus.

PART II

SYSTEMIC ANALYSIS

CHAPTER 3

The Prehistory of the Sect

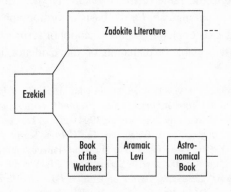

1. The "Qumran Library"

Ever since the discovery of the Dead Sea Scrolls, there has been a lot of discussion about the nature of the "Qumran library."[1] The presence of

1. D. Dimant, "The Qumran Manuscripts: Contents and Significance," in D. Dimant and L. H. Schiffman, eds., *Time To Prepare the Way in the Wilderness: Papers on the Qumran Scrolls by Fellows of the Institute for Advanced Studies of the Hebrew University, Jerusalem, 1989-1990*, STDJ 16 (Leiden: Brill, 1995) 23-58; Y. Shavit, "The 'Qumran Library' in the Light of the Attitude toward Books and Libraries in the

interrelated texts, marked by strong sectarian features, immediately suggested that the manuscripts were associated with a single community. But the presence of "biblical" material also made it apparent that not all the manuscripts could have been composed by the same group, a situation that suggested the presence of a plurality of communities behind the scrolls. How can we reconcile this conflicting evidence?

Results from paleography, radiocarbon analysis, and other scientific tests (like the measurement of the shrinkage temperature of fibers of skin or leather) demonstrate that the scrolls were all copied in the same time period, between the third century BCE and the first half of the first century CE.[2] Many elements concur in support of the view that they were originally part of a single collection. Identical copies of the same documents have been found in different caves. Certain manuscripts coming from different caves and having the most diverse features, sectarian and nonsectarian, show a handwriting that is to be attributed to the same scribe. A distinctive way of writing has also made it possible to distinguish, on the basis of orthography, between "imported texts" and texts copied by a single school of scribes.[3]

The most reasonable explanation of the evidence is to distinguish

---

Second Temple Period," in M. O. Wise, et al., eds., *Methods of Investigation of the Dead Sea Scrolls and the Khirbet Qumran Site: Present Realities and Future Prospects* (New York: New York Academy of Sciences, 1994) 299-317.

2. For paleography see S. A. Birnbaum, *The Hebrew Script, Part One: The Text* (Leiden: Brill, 1971), *Part Two: The Plates* (London: Palaeographia, 1954-57); F. M. Cross, "The Development of the Jewish Scripts," in G. E. Wright, ed., *The Bible and the Ancient Near East: Essays in Honor of William Foxwell Albright* (Garden City, N.Y.: Doubleday, 1961) 133-202; N. Avigad, "The Palaeography of the Dead Sea Scrolls and Related Documents," in C. Rabin and Y. Yadin, eds., *Aspects of the Dead Sea Scrolls* (Jerusalem: Magnes and Hebrew University Press, 1958) 56-87; S. A. Birnbaum, *The Qumrân (Dead Sea) Scrolls and Palaeography,* BASORSupSt 13-14 (New Haven: American Schools of Oriental Research, 1952). For radiocarbon analysis see D. Pardee, et al., "Report and Discussion Concerning Radiocarbon Dating of Fourteen Dead Sea Scrolls," in Wise, et al., eds., *Methods of Investigation,* 441-53; G. Bonani, et al., "Radiocarbon Dating of the Dead Sea Scrolls," *Atiqot* 20 (1991) 27-32; J. A. Fitzmyer, "The Date of the Qumran Scrolls," *America* 104 (1961) 780-81. For other tests see D. Burton, J. B. Poole, and R. Reed, "A New Approach to the Dating of the Dead Sea Scrolls," *Nature* 184 (1959) 533-34.

3. E. Tov, "Hebrew Biblical Manuscripts from the Judaean Desert: Their Contribution to Textual Criticism," *JJS* 39 (1988) 5-37; idem, "The Orthography and Language of the Hebrew Scrolls Found at Qumran and the Origin of These Scrolls," *Textus* 13 (1986) 31-57.

authorship from ownership. The geographical, chronological, and literary boundaries that unite the documents suggest common ownership, not common authorship. It is common ownership that turns any collection of books, ancient or modern, into a "library." As for the identity of the owners of the library, archaeological discoveries have made a strong case for demonstrating the similarity between artifacts found in Khirbet Qumran and the nearby caves. Despite the many revisionistic attempts to disprove the connection between the manuscripts and the ruins of Qumran, the simplest and most likely conclusion is that the owners of the scrolls were the people living at Qumran.[4]

What kind of library was the "Qumran library"? On one hand, the complete absence of secular and non-Jewish works reveals that the Dead Sea Scrolls were not part of a "library" in the Hellenistic sense. Unlike the ancient library of Alexandria,[5] the collection was not intended to be a comprehensive store of the knowledge of the period, but rather a particular selection of Jewish religious texts. On the other hand, the presence of several copies of the same work excludes the possibility that the collection constituted an individual's library. The Dead Sea Scrolls were a collection of Jewish religious documents belonging to a single group who dwelt at Qumran.[6]

Claiming that the "library" belonged to a single group and therefore must reflect a single theology is, however, once again to confuse ownership with authorship. While it is likely that one group owned all the manuscripts, evidence is compelling that the same group did not author the scrolls. Since a single community owned, yet did not author, all the texts, not merely one theology but several theologies are represented in the Dead Sea Scrolls.[7]

John J. Collins gives us a starting point of analysis: "No one, to my

---

4. For a discussion of revisionistic hypotheses, see Ch. 1 above. E.-M. Laperrousaz, "La datation d'objects provenant de Qumrân, en particulier par la méthod utilisant des propriétés du Carbone 14," in M. Delcor, ed., *Qumrân: Sa piété, sa théologie et son milieu*, BETL 46 (Paris: Duculot, 1978) 55-60.

5. M. El-Abbadi, *Life and Fate of the Ancient Library of Alexandria* (Paris: Unesco/UNDP, 1990; 2nd ed. 1992); E. A. Parsons, *The Alexandrian Library, Glory of the Hellenistic World: Its Rise, Antiquities, and Destructions* (New York: Elsevier, 1952); cf. J. H. Ellens, "The Ancient Library of Alexandria: The West's Most Important Repository of Learning," *BR* 13/1 (1997) 18-29, 46.

6. F. García Martínez and A. S. van der Woude, "A Groningen Hypothesis of Qumran Origins and Early History," *RevQ* 14 (1990) 521-41.

7. J. H. Charlesworth, "The Theologies in the Dead Sea Scrolls," in H. Ringgren, *The Faith of Qumran: Theology of the Dead Sea Scrolls*, trans. E. T. Sanders, rev. ed. (New York: Crossroad, 1995) xv-xxi.

knowledge, has ever claimed that everything found at Qumran was produced there, or was the product of the same sect. . . . Nevertheless it remains true that there is a core group of interrelated texts, with overlapping terminology and common subject matter, which show that the Qumran corpus is not just a random sample of the Jewish literature of the time."[8] The essential problem consists in finding the correct criteria to classify the material, in particular to distinguish between the documents authored by the community of the Dead Sea Scrolls and those simply owned, preserved, and copied by the group.[9]

Anachronistic criteria, like the threefold distinction among (a) biblical texts, (b) Old Testament Apocrypha and Pseudepigrapha, and (c) hitherto unknown material, have been applied too often, with the result of imposing upon ancient sources later canonical assumptions. The first modern collections of Dead Sea Scrolls were selections of previously unknown "sectarian" documents, a practical yet hardly scientific criterion. The biblical, apocryphal, and pseudepigraphic texts from Qumran became footnotes in the editions of the already established corpora of the Hebrew Bible, Apocrypha, and Pseudepigrapha. In one case only, the Damascus Document, whose sectarian features seemed too obvious to be overlooked, the overlapping was solved by removing the document from the corpus of the Pseudepigrapha, in which it had been previously included, and moving it into the Dead Sea Scrolls.[10] In other cases,

8. J. J. Collins, "Messiahs in Context: Method in the Study of Messianism in the Dead Sea Scrolls," in Wise, et al., eds., *Methods of Investigation,* 213-29 (quotation on pp. 213-14).

9. For an attempt to distinguish between sectarian and nonsectarian material in the scrolls, see D. Dimant, "Qumran Sectarian Literature," in M. E. Stone, ed., *Jewish Writings of the Second Temple Period,* CRINT 2/2 (Assen: Van Gorcum; Philadelphia: Fortress, 1984) 483-550; C. A. Newsom, " 'Sectually Explicit' Literature from Qumran," in W. H. Propp, H. Halpern, and D. N. Freedman, eds., *The Hebrew Bible and Its Interpreters* (Winona Lake, Ind.: Eisenbrauns, 1990) 167-87; E. G. Chazon, "Is *Divrei ha-me'orot* a Sectarian Prayer?" in D. Dimant and U. Rappaport, eds., *The Dead Sea Scrolls: Forty Years of Research,* STDJ 10 (Leiden: Brill, 1992) 3-17.

10. After the publication of the *editio princeps* (S. Schechter, *Fragments of a Zadokite Work* [Cambridge: University Press, 1910]), it was natural to see the Damascus Document in the collections of OT Pseudepigrapha by R. H. Charles, ed., *The Apocrypha and Pseudepigrapha of the Old Testament,* 2 vols. (Oxford: Clarendon, 1913) 2.785-834; and P. Riessler, *Altjüdisches Schrifttum ausserhalb der Bibel* (Augsburg: Filser, 1928) 920-41. After the 1950s, the Damascus Document does not appear in any of the collections of OT Pseudepigrapha.

notably 1 Enoch and Jubilees, the recognition of sectarian features was not considered sufficient to justify such a dramatic change, and the documents remained in their traditional corpus. The Dead Sea Scrolls were, and still are in the common opinion, the documents discovered at Qumran minus those belonging to other corpora. The Dead Sea Scrolls have become a scholarly and marketing label for a selected body of sectarian texts.

Studies in the Jewish and Christian canons have shown the anachronism of our canonical criterion when applied to second temple Judaism.[11] We just do not have any evidence that these categories were either known or acknowledged by the people who wrote the scrolls. How can we assume, for example, that, for the people of the Dead Sea Scrolls, 1 Enoch or the Temple Scroll belonged to a different category than Genesis or Isaiah? In particular, how can we assume that a document is sectarian simply because we formerly did not know of its existence?

The most recent editions of the scrolls are struggling to overcome this "original sin" of Dead Sea Scrolls research. Older standard collections, like Vermes's, have gradually expanded their material, edition after edition, and are now being replaced by new, more inclusive collections. Both the García Martínez and the Charlesworth editions, although still limited for practical reasons to "nonbiblical" material, have abolished the most misleading distinction among apocryphal, pseudepigraphic, and sectarian literature, and are consciously and effectively promoting a more comprehensive approach to all the materials discovered in the caves.

This change of attitude in contemporary scholarship is apparent in the attempt to classify the Dead Sea Scrolls according to more "neutral" criteria and to avoid anachronistic assumptions. A taxonomic consensus is emerging in the most recent publications that groups the texts ideologically in three categories:

(a) A core group of rather homogeneous texts, distinctive in style and ideology, that appear to be the product of a single community with a strong sense of self-identity. By convention we refer to these docu-

---

11. J. A. Sanders, "Canon," *ABD* 1.837-52; R. T. Beckwith, *The Old Testament Canon of the New Testament Church and Its Background in Early Judaism* (Grand Rapids: Eerdmans, 1985); S. Z. Leiman, *The Canonization of Hebrew Scripture: The Talmudic and Midrashic Evidence* (Hamden, Conn.: Archon, 1976).

ments as the sectarian literature of the community of the Dead Sea Scrolls. In this case, ownership is equivalent to authorship.

(b) A group of texts that have only some sectarian features, and yet are compatible with the complex of ideas characteristic of the sectarian works. These documents may belong either to the formative period of the "community of the Dead Sea Scrolls" or to a parent or sister group directly related to it, chronologically and ideologically. In this case, the evidence must be weighed carefully; ownership may or may not be equivalent to authorship.

(c) A series of texts in which sectarian elements are marginal or totally absent, the most obvious examples being, of course, the "biblical" scrolls. In this case, ownership is certainly not equivalent to authorship.

Systemic analysis shows that this threefold ideological distinction is not synchronic but diachronic. The more ancient the documents are, the less sectarian. The Dead Sea Scrolls testify to the evolution of a defined community from its ancient roots (c) to its formative age (b) to its emergence as a distinct entity (a). It was not by random circumstances that this community owned a certain number of documents that they did not author. On the contrary, they consciously selected only those which represented their past and their formative age, while eliminating any synchronic document written by rival groups. The Qumran library grew up not by chance or accident but through a deliberate and coherent process of selection and preservation. The Dead Sea Scrolls are the remnants of the organized library of a sectarian group. In this sense, the scrolls provide the key not only for recognizing the existence of a defined community but also for charting a rather comprehensive map of its origins and development in the broader context of second temple Judaism.

As I stated programmatically in the introduction, this section of the book (chs. 3–5) does not refer to the historical narratives concerning the Essenes. I consider only the archaeological and paleographical data that refer to the scrolls and to the other ancient documents here studied. Let these ancient texts speak for themselves and each document be understood on its own terms.

2. The Sectarian Texts of the Community of the Dead Sea Scrolls

Scholars widely recognize that the trait that most distinguishes (some of) the Dead Sea Scrolls from the rest of second temple Jewish literature is the presence of a particular doctrine of evil, based on a unique combination of cosmic dualism, individual predestination, and the equation of evil and impurity. Only the presence of such a complex of ideas makes a Qumran text a sectarian text. Scholars have definitively abandoned the assumption that previously unknown documents are necessarily sectarian documents; the principle that the burden of proof always falls on whoever wants to posit sectarian provenance has become the working rule of contemporary research.[12] As a result, the group of recognized sectarian documents has been subject to a radical process of restructuring that reminds me of what has happened to many American cities. While neighborhoods have developed far beyond the traditional city boundaries, downtown centers have dramatically shrunk, before expanding again on more solid foundations. An analogous process of restructuring has prevented the literature of the Qumran community from collapsing and vanishing, and has restored a nucleus of recognized sectarian documents that includes, at the least, the Rule of the Community (1QS) and related documents (1QSa and 1QSb), the Thanksgiving Hymns (1QH), the War Scroll (1QM), the Songs of the Sabbath Sacrifice (4Q400-407), and the biblical commentaries known as the *pesharim* (esp. 1QpHab and 4QpNah). All these documents appear to have been composed between the end of the second century BCE and the first half of the first century CE. All of them share the same system of thought. All of them are the product of the same sociological background.

The proportion of sectarian texts is rather small within the Dead Sea Scrolls,[13] but not less than the proportion of the New Testament documents within the Christian Bible. Arguing on the basis of the limited number of sectarian documents that the community of the Dead Sea Scrolls has vanished, as does Norman Golb,[14] is to miss the nature and scope of this literature, which,

---

12. Newsom, " 'Sectually Explicit' Literature."

13. L. H. Schiffman calculates that 33 percent of the Qumran manuscripts are sectarian texts; see *Reclaiming the Dead Sea Scrolls* (Philadelphia and Jerusalem: Jewish Publication Society, 1994) 34.

14. N. Golb, "The Dead Sea Scrolls," *American Scholar* 58 (1989) 177-207 (esp. 189-90).

like the New Testament, is not to be measured by its quantity. The sectarian texts were not intended to outnumber the traditions of the fathers; on the contrary, their goal was to give the hermeneutical key to understand the documents of the past, of which they claimed to be the fulfillment. In this sense, the sectarian literature of Qumran accomplishes, without overdoing, its task; it covers the basic aspects of the religious life of the community and gives more than a sufficient depiction of a consistent system of thought.[15]

(a) *Cosmic dualism.* The first, and most obvious, tenet of the Qumran system of thought is cosmic dualism (see esp. 1QS 3:13–4:26; 1QH 9[= 1]:5-38; 5[= 13]:1-12; 1QM 13). Since the discovery of the scrolls, many detailed studies have been devoted to this subject.[16]

The people of Qumran divide the entire universe into two radically distinctive parties, led by two "spirits." On the "good" side, the "prince of light" (Heb. *sr 'wrym*/Michael/Melki-zedek; cf. 1QM 13:10; 17:6-8) leads a "lot" *(gwrl)* of sons of light (angels and humans). On the "evil" side, the "angel of darkness" *(ml'k ḥwšk/* Belial/Melki-reshaʿ) leads a "lot" *(gwrl)* of sons of darkness (angels and humans). Eternal and irreconcilable enmity divides the two parties: light *('wr)* versus darkness *(ḥwšk),* truth *('mt)* and righteousness *(ṣdq)* versus deceit *('wl).* The opposition is so radical that it defines two distinct lexical camps, within each of which the associated terms are interchangeable. Light stands for everything true,

---

15. García Martínez and van der Woude, "Groningen Hypothesis," 533.

16. G. Widengren et al., eds., *Apocalyptique iranienne et dualisme qoumrânien* (Paris: Adrien Maisonneuve, 1995); R. Bergmeier, "Prädestination und Dualismus. Die veränderte Lage im Schrifttum aus Qumran," in *Glaube als Gabe nach Johannes* (Stuttgart: Kohlhammer, 1980) 63-116; P. von der Osten-Sacken, *Gott und Belial. Traditionsgeschichtliche Untersuchungen zum Dualismus in den Texten aus Qumran,* SUNT 6 (Göttingen: Vandenhoeck & Ruprecht, 1969); J. H. Charlesworth, "A Critical Comparison of the Dualism in 1QS 3:13–4:26 and the 'Dualism' Contained in the Gospel of John," *NTS* 15 (1968-69) 389-418 (repr. in J. H. Charlesworth, ed., *John and the Dead Sea Scrolls* [New York: Crossroad, 1991] 76-106); H. Ringgren, "Dualism," in *The Faith of Qumran: Theology of the Dead Sea Scrolls,* trans. E. T. Sanders, rev. ed. (New York: Crossroad, 1995) 68-80; M. Treves, "The Two Spirits in the Rule of the Community," *RevQ* 3 (1961) 449-52; P. Wernberg-Møller, "A Reconsideration of the Two Spirits in the Rule of the Community 1Q Serek III,13–IV,26," *RevQ* 3 (1961) 413-41; H. W. Huppenbauer, *Der Mensch zwischen zwei Welten. Der Dualismus der Texte von Qumran (Höhle I) und der Damaskusfragmente; ein Beitrag zur Vorgeschichte des Evangeliums,* ATANT 34 (Zurich: Zwingli, 1959). Cf. U. Bianchi, "The Category of Dualism in the Historical Study of Religion," *Temenos* 16 (1980) 10-25.

good, and righteous. Darkness stands for everything deceitful, unrighteous, and evil. "In a spring of light emanates the nature of truth and from a well of darkness emerges the nature of deceit. In the hand of the prince of lights is dominion over all the sons of righteousness; they walk on paths of light. And in the hand of the angel of darkness is total dominion over the sons of deceit; they walk on paths of darkness" (1QS 3:20-21).

The Qumran dualism is, however, not absolute. There is no balance of power; the struggle between good and evil is not a contest between equals. Three elements stand firmly against the idea that good and evil are on an equal level.

First, the supreme and only God and Creator is not an impartial referee; God sides openly with the good party, which is as much God's party as Michael's. "The God of Israel and the angel of his truth assist all the sons of light" (1QS 3:24-25; cf. 1QM 13:5: "They are the lot of darkness and the lot of God is for everlasting light"). Belial may be as strong as his counterpart, Michael, but God is infinitely stronger. By entering the field, God shifts the balance of power in favor of Michael's party.

Second, not only is Belial less powerful than God, but Belial lacks autonomy. In the sectarian texts of Qumran, Belial is not a rebellious angel, a heroic Titan who challenges his creator in spite of his inferiority. On the contrary, Belial obeys his creator; God made Belial evil from the instant Belial was created. Belial did not rebel; he was commanded to sin. "And you [[= God]] created Belial for the pit, angel of hatred; his [dom]inion is darkness, his counsel is for evil and wickedness" (1QM 13:11).[17]

Although Belial is the one who is exposed to blame, God bears the ultimate responsibility for evil. God is the source of the dualistic structure of the universe. God created *(br')* the two fundamental powers of the universe, the good spirit and the evil spirit. Belial's evil will is an outcome of God's good will. "From the God of knowledge stems all there is and all there shall be. Before they existed he made all their plans and when they came into being they will execute all their works in compliance with his instructions, according to his glorious design without altering anything. In his hand are the laws of all things and he supports them in all their needs. . . . [God] created [Heb. *br'*] the spirits of light and of darkness and on them established all his deeds"

17. J. J. Collins: "Belial and the sons of darkness are not portrayed as rebellious forces. . . . Rather they are playing out a role that was allotted to them in creation" (*Apocalypticism in the Dead Sea Scrolls* [London and New York: Routledge, 1997], 103).

(1QS 3:15-17, 25). An uncompromising emphasis on God's omnipotence led the sectarians to attribute the origin of all things, even evil, to the only God.

Third, the dualistic structure of the universe will not last forever. At the end of days, at the appointed time, God will destroy evil and establish eternal peace. "There will be a battle, and savage destruction before the God of Israel, for this will be the day determined by him since ancient times for the war of extermination against the sons of darkness" (1QM 1:9-10). The evil party will vanish and the good party will have peace and sovereignty forever. "For God's lot there will be everlasting redemption and destruction for all the wicked peoples" (1QM 15:1-2).

Beyond the terrifying imagery of struggle, war, and destruction, the overall message that the sectarian scrolls deliver is consoling. The universe is not out of God's control, nor is it devastated and spoiled by a long and tenacious rebellion. The reason for its dualistic configuration lies ultimately in God's inscrutable and unquestionable will. With regard to human beings, it is enough to say that God created the good to be loved and the evil to be hated. "God loved one of them [[= the good spirit]] for all eternal ages and in all his deeds he takes pleasure forever; of the other one [[= the evil spirit]] he detests his advice and hates all his paths forever" (1QS 3:26–4:1).

(b) *Predeterminism.* The emphasis placed on God's omnipotence is the only guarantee that the universe will not be torn apart by its dualistic structure. This emphasis overshadows the autonomy of human history and the freedom of human will. At the beginning of creation, God has fixed the times of history. "What will I be able to say which is not known? What will I be able to declare which has not been told? Everything has been engraved in your presence with the stylus of remembrance for all the incessant periods in the eras of the number of everlasting years in all their predetermined times, and nothing will be hidden, nothing will remain away from your presence" (1QH 9[= 1]:23-25). From the beginning to "the day of the great battle" (1QM 13:14) all human events have been preordained by God since ancient time. Everything is predetermined; events have to happen and would happen at their "appointed time" (Heb. *mw'd*).[18]

18. For a discussion of historical determinism at Qumran, see J. J. Collins, "The Periods of History and the Expectation of the End," in ibid., 52-70; R. V. Huggins, "A Canonical Book of Periods at Qumran?" *RevQ* 15 (1992) 421-36; D. Dimant, "The Pesher on the Periods (4Q180) and 4Q181," *IOS* 9 (1979) 77-102; J. Licht, "The Theory of Ages of the Judaean Desert Sect and of Other Calculations of Periods" {Hebrew}, *ErIsr* 8 (1967) 63-70.

While historical determinism was a widely accepted concept in middle Judaism, what is distinctive in the sectarian documents of Qumran are the implications of cosmic dualism on the individual level.[19] God "created the human [Heb. *'nwš*] to rule the world and placed [*yṣm*] within him two spirits so that he would walk with them until the appointed time [*mw'd*] of his visitation: they are the spirits of truth and deceit. . . . In these [two spirits] are the natures of all the sons of man, and in their (two) divisions all their hosts of their generations have a share; in their ways they walk, and the entire task of their works (falls) within their divisions according to a man's share, whether much or little, in all the times of eternity" (1QS 3:17-19; 4:15-16).

The destiny of each individual is not simply affected by cosmic dualism but entirely depends on it.[20] It is God's dualistic creation that determines the party to which each individual belongs. Everything depends on the allotted quantity of evil versus good spirits, the individual having no control whatsoever on God's decision.[21]

The Qumranites believe in the possibility of recognizing "a man's share" by examining his moral behavior or even his physical features. 4Q186 refers to three individuals whose spiritual features are discovered through physical examination:[22] of the first, "his spirit has six (parts) in the house of light and three in the pit of darkness"; of the second, "his spirit has eight parts in the house [of darkness] and one in the house of light"; of the third, "his spirit has eight parts [in the house of light] and one [in the house of darkness]" (cf. 4Q561).

The text is enlightening. Not only is no individual totally good or totally evil, but there is no balance between the two forces. The uneven number of spirits ("nine") makes a tie impossible. In this way one could

19. On historical determinism in second temple Judaism, see P. Sacchi, "Prede-terminismo e problema del male," in *Storia del Secondo Tempio* (Turin: Società Editrice Internazionale, 1994) 302-29; G. Maier, *Mensch und freier Wille*, WUNT 12 (Tübingen: Mohr, 1971). On Qumran's cosmic dualism and individual predestination, see E. H. Merrill, *Qumran and Predestination: A Theological Study of the Thanksgiving Hymns*, STDJ 8 (Leiden: Brill, 1975); A. Lange, *Weisheit und Prädestination*, STDJ 18 (Leiden: Brill, 1995); R. Bergmeier, "Prädestination und Dualismus."

20. Merrill, *Qumran and Predestination*.

21. H. Lichtenberger, *Studien zum Menschenbild in Texten aus Qumran*, SUNT 15 (Göttingen: Vandenhoeck & Ruprecht, 1980).

22. J. M. Allegro, "An Astrological Cryptic Document from Qumran," *JSS* 9 (1964) 291-94.

justify the sins of the righteous without contradicting the general theory of cosmic dualism and individual predestination. The sins of the righteous are caused by the portion of evil that is within the righteous person's heart. No sin, however, can separate a son of light from the good lot, because the quantity of good spirits remains predominant in his or her heart. For the chosen, committing a sin is like losing a battle; it does not mean losing the war. God will never deny assistance to the members of Michael's party. "Due to the angel of darkness all the sons of justice stray, and all their sins, their iniquities, their failings and their mutinous deeds are under his dominion in compliance with the mysteries of God, until his moment; and all their punishments and their periods of grief are caused by the dominion of his enmity; and all the spirits of their lot cause the sons of light to fall. However, the God of Israel and the angel of his truth assist all the sons of light" (1QS 3:21-25).

The sectarians firmly believe not only that God created the prince of darkness and the angel of light, or the good and evil spirits, but that the righteous and the wicked are individually predestined "from the womb" and forever. "I know that every spirit is fashioned by your hand, [and all its travail] you have established even before creating him. How can anyone change your words? You, you alone, have created the just man. . . . But the wicked you have created for the time of wrath, from the womb you have predestined them for the day of annihilation" (1QH 7[= 15]:17-21).

No one can change his or her own lot. The side on which each individual stands does not depend on human free will but has been already preordained by God. Human beings are saved because they are righteous, but they are righteous because they have been chosen. What they are does not depend on what they have done or will do. On the contrary, what they have done and will do depends on what they are, and what they are is totally out of human control, because it has been preordained by God. God's omnipotence deprives human beings of their freedom and leaves them with a phantom of choice. "The freedom given to man is not to choose where to go but to discover where he is."[23] For the members of the community, this is not a matter of regret but of joy; they are the beloved ones and nothing can separate them from God's love.

(c) *Impurity and evil.* The third element in the unique sectarian doctrine of evil is the identification of impurity with evil. "For the *yahad,*

23. Dimant, "Qumran Sectarian Literature," 538.

one cannot distinguish between cultic and moral impurity," a concept that Jacob Neusner singles out as "entirely without parallel."[24]

The identification of impurity with evil has dramatic consequences. On the one hand, sin makes human beings ontologically impure. It is this aspect that strikes Neusner. "The *yaḥad*'s laws treat committing a sin not as a metaphor for becoming unclean, but as an actual source of uncleanness. . . . It is not *as if* [the sinner] were unclean, as with the biblical metaphor. He is *actually* unclean and requires a rite of purification."[25] On the other hand, impurity makes human beings sinful. The implications are even more devastating, as Paolo Sacchi and Florentino García Martínez have articulated.[26] Because impurity is a constituent part of this world, humans are inescapably evil. "[Man is] a creature of clay . . . [who] is in sin from his maternal womb, and in guilty iniquity right to old age" (1QH 12[= 4]:29-30). Impurity and evil belong to the very nature of humankind. "I belong to evil humankind, to the assembly of wicked flesh; my failings, my transgressions, my sins . . . with the depravities of my heart belong to the assembly of worms and of those who walk in darkness" (1QS 11:9-10). "I am a creature of clay, fashioned with water, foundation of shame, source of impurity, oven of iniquity, building of sin, spirit of mistake, astray, without knowledge, terrified by your just judgments" (1QH 9[= 1]:21-23). All human beings are by nature impure; therefore they are by nature evil, unless they are justified by God's choice.

The identification of evil with impurity leads to the identification of atonement with purification. No one can be forgiven without being purified, and no one can be purified without being forgiven. God's justi-

---

24. J. Neusner, *The Idea of Purity in Ancient Judaism,* SJLA 1 (Leiden: Brill, 1973) 54.

25. Ibid., 54.

26. F. García Martínez, "The Problem of Purity: The Qumran Solution," in F. García Martínez and J. Trebolle Barrera, *The People of the Dead Sea Scrolls,* trans. W. G. E. Watson (Leiden: Brill, 1995) 139-57; P. Sacchi, "Il sacro e il profano, l'impuro e il puro," in *Storia del Secondo Tempio,* 415-53; cf. M. Newton, "The Concept of Purity in the Qumran Community," in *The Concept of Purity at Qumran and in the Letters of Paul,* SNTSMS 53 (Cambridge: Cambridge University Press, 1985) 10-51; A. Vivian, *I campi lessicali della separazione nell'ebraico biblico, di Qumran e della Mishna* (Florence: Istituto di Linguistica e di Lingue Orientali, 1978); P. Garnet, *Salvation and Atonement in the Qumran Scrolls,* WUNT 2/3 (Tübingen: Mohr, 1977); W. Paschen, *Rein und Unrein,* SANT 24 (Munich: Kösel, 1970).

fication is at the same time an act of atonement and an act of purification. The difference between the righteous and the wicked is that the righteous receive purification and atonement for their sins while the wicked do not. Salvation, for which God has predestined the sons of light, is the result of an act of justification. "You [God] atone for sin and cle[anse man] of his fault by your justice. . . . You created the just and the wicked" (1QH 12[= 4]:37-38).

(d) *A community apart.* The sectarian documents reflect the sociology of a single community in which all the members of the group live together in physical and geographical isolation from the rest of humankind. This community is the place of God's justification, the only place in which the chosen receive forgiveness and purification. "For, by the spirit of the true counsel concerning the paths of man all his sins are atoned so that he can look at the light of life. And by the spirit of holiness which links him with his truth he is cleansed of all his sins. And by the spirit of uprightness and of humility his sin is atoned. And by the compliance of his soul with all the laws of God his flesh is cleansed by being sprinkled with cleansing waters and being made holy with the waters of repentance" (1QS 3:6-9).

The concept of impurity was decisive in fostering the self-understanding of the community that claimed to be the only righteous and pure remnant of evil and impure humankind. "You have chosen a people in the period of your favour, because you have remembered the covenant. You established them, isolating them for yourself in order to make them holy among all the peoples. And you have renewed your covenant with them in the vision of your glory, and in the words of your holy spirit, by the works of your hand" (1Q34 [1QPrFêtes], frag. 3, 2:5-7). The "Penal Code" of the Community Rule (1QS 6:24–7:25) transfers all the requirements of purity, which in the Mosaic torah are attached to the temple, to the sphere of the community, which saw itself as a substitute for the temple.[27] The community "shall be . . . a holy house for Israel and the foundation of the holy of holies for Aaron, true witnesses for the judgment and chosen by the will (of God) to atone for the earth and to render the wicked their retribution. . . . It will be the most holy dwelling for Aaron with total knowledge of the covenant of justice and in order to offer a pleasant aroma; and it will be a house of perfection and truth in Israel. . . . And these will be accepted in

27. B. E. Gartner, *The Temple and the Community in Qumran and the New Testament,* SNTSMS 1 (Cambridge: Cambridge University Press, 1965).

order to atone for the earth and to decide the judgment of the wicked" (1QS 8:5-10; cf. 4Q174 [4QFlor]).

From the perspective in which salvation is understood not as a process but as a status, the capability of the members of the community to maintain the state of purity is the ultimate proof of their being saved. They believe that they are called, already in this world, to live in segregation a mystical life of communion and worship with the holy angels, who belong to the same good party. "I thank you, Lord, because you saved my life from the pit. . . . And I know that there is hope for someone you fashioned out of clay to be an everlasting community. The corrupt spirit you have purified from the great sin so that he can take his place with the host of the holy ones, and can enter in communion with the congregation of the sons of heaven" (1QH 11[= 3]:19-22; cf. 14[= 6]:13; 1QS 11:7-8; 1QM 7:6; 1QSa 2:8-9).

Extra ecclesiam nulla salus: outside the community God's justification is impossible. The cosmic dualism between good and evil has its historical manifestation in the opposition between outsiders and insiders. With their exclusive and intolerant theology, the Qumran sectarians are the first example of an underground trend of thought that would often resurface in the history of Christianity and Rabbinic Judaism.[28] The outside world is the dominion of Belial — the kingdom of impurity and evil; and any contact with the outside, with "the men of the pit," is barred "until the day of vengeance" (1QS 10:19). The one who does not join the community "will not become clean by the acts of atonement, nor shall he be purified by the cleansing waters, nor shall he made holy by the seas or rivers, nor shall he be purified by all the water of ablutions. Defiled, defiled, shall he be" (1QS 3:4-5).

This complex of ideas, coherently expressed in several Dead Sea Scrolls, is entirely unparalleled within second temple Judaism and therefore must be recognized as the ideology of the community who owned the scrolls. At the end of our journey through the Qumran texts we will explore the roots and dynamics of this system of thought, which, far from being rigid and monolithic, is the result of intellectual development as well as of polemical attitudes of flesh-and-blood people reacting to particular historical circumstances.

28. A. Haynal, M. Molnar, and G. de Puymège, *Fanaticism: A Historical and Psychoanalytical Study,* trans. L. Butler Koseoglu (New York: Schocken Books, 1983).

3. Pre-Maccabean Texts in the Qumran Library: Enochic and Zadokite Documents

The Dead Sea Scrolls contain a large number of documents that were composed before the Maccabean period. While we are accustomed to calling this literature "biblical," "apocryphal," and "pseudepigraphic," we should more properly, and less anachronistically, use the terms "Zadokite" and "Enochic."

(a) The Zadokite literature has a very complex history. It includes most of the so-called biblical texts, with the exception of the later Esther and Daniel, and also apocryphal texts such as the Epistle of Jeremiah, Tobit, and Sirach. From modern research in the Hebrew Bible/Old Testament we know that this literature was originally produced by different varieties of ancient Judaism, but during the Persian and early Hellenistic periods it was collected, edited, and transmitted by the religious authorities of the temple of Jerusalem, the high priesthood of the house of Zadok.[29] An analysis of the Dead Sea Scrolls demonstrates that during middle Judaism the Zadokite literature was not textually fixed but was still subjected, to some extent, to a process of growth that resulted in a plurality of texts and textual forms. None of the texts of Zadokite Judaism preserved at Qumran, however, presents evidence of explicit editing or interpolation that one could attribute specifically to the community of the Dead Sea Scrolls. The texts of Zadokite Judaism were quoted as authoritative in the sectarian scrolls, and these texts were preserved with respect and devotion in those forms in which they were then known: proto-Masoretic, proto-Samaritan, proto-Septuagintal, and others.[30]

---

29. On the role of the house of Zadok in the early second temple period, see P. Sacchi, "Il periodo sadocita," in *Storia del Secondo Tempio,* 83-186; J. L. Berquist, *Judaism in Persia's Shadow: A Social and Historical Approach* (Minneapolis: Fortress, 1995); M. Smith, *Palestinian Parties and Politics That Shaped the Old Testament* (New York: Columbia University Press, 1971).

30. E. Tov, "Groups of Biblical Texts Found at Qumran," in Dimant and Schiffman, eds., *Time to Prepare,* 85-102; E. C. Ulrich, "Pluriformity in the Biblical Text, Text Groups, and Questions of Canon," in J. Trebolle Barrera and L. Vegas Montaner, eds., *The Madrid Qumran Congress: Proceedings of the International Congress on the Dead Sea Scrolls, Madrid, 18-21 March, 1991,* STDJ 11/1-2 (Leiden: Brill, 1992) 1.23-41; E. Tov, "Hebrew Biblical Manuscripts from the Judaean Desert: Their Contribution to Textual Criticism," in S. Talmon, ed., *Jewish Civilization in the Hellenistic-Roman Period* (Philadelphia: Trinity Press International, 1991) 107-37.

I have used the phrase "explicit" editing or interpolation advisedly. The fluidity of the tradition allowed textual freedom, but, as attested by the presence of pseudo-Zadokite documents as well as of the targumim and *pesharim*, the community of the Dead Sea Scrolls had no compelling need to change the ancient Zadokite texts in order to infer their sectarian ideas.

The only possible example of an explicit sectarian interpolation in a text of Zadokite Judaism is Sir 15:14b, and, paradoxically, it does not come from the Qumran library but from some manuscripts of the lost Hebrew Sirach text discovered at the end of the last century in the Cairo Genizah, actually the attic storeroom of the ancient synagogue of Fustat (Old Cairo).[31] As in the case of the Damascus Document, a copy of which was also found in the Cairo Genizah, the Qumran fragments of Sirach (2QSir) have proved that the medieval scribes employed as the basis for their manuscripts a text virtually identical to that known at Qumran.[32] The Sirach Hebrew text discovered in the Cairo Genizah contains a significant addition unknown in the Greek and in all the other ancient versions: "In the beginning [God] created man — *and placed him in the power of his abductor* [Heb. *ḥwtpw*] — and made him subject to his own will [*yṣrw*]" (Sir 15:14). This is a clear interpolation that breaks the rhythm of the verse and whose intent is through parallelism to give a negative connotation to the term *yeṣer,* which originally was a neutral term. The community of the Dead Sea Scrolls would have the strongest interest in modifying a text that contained the most explicit reference in Zadokite literature to the freedom of human choice. Conceptually, the gloss turns the original meaning of the

31. On Sirach as a Zadokite document, see E. Rivkin, "Ben Sira and Aaronide Hegemony," in *A Hidden Revolution: The Pharisees' Search for the Kingdom Within* (Nashville: Abingdon, 1978) 191-207. The first announcement of the identification of Sirach fragments in the Genizah manuscripts was made by S. Schechter, "A Fragment of the Original Texts of Ecclesiasticus," *Expositor,* 5th series, 4 (1896) 1-15. For the Hebrew text of Sirach, see Z. Ben-Hayyim, ed., *The Historical Dictionary of the Hebrew Language: The Book of Ben Sira: Text, Concordance, and an Analysis of the Vocabulary* (Jerusalem: Academy of the Hebrew Language and The Shrine of the Book, 1973); F. Vattioni, *Ecclesiastico: Testo ebraico con apparato critico e versioni greca, latina e siriaca* (Naples: Istituto Orientale di Napoli, 1968).

32. T. Muraoka and J. F. Elwolde, eds., *The Hebrew of the Dead Sea Scrolls and Ben Sira,* STDJ 26 (Leiden: Brill, 1997); M. Gilbert, "The Book of Ben Sira: Implications for Jewish and Christian Traditons," in Talmon, ed., *Jewish Civilization,* 81-91; A. A. Di Lella, *The Hebrew Text of Sirach: A Text-Critical and Historical Study* (The Hague: Mouton, 1966).

passage from a eulogy on human free will into a statement of God's moral predestination in line with the dualistic anthropology of the community of the Dead Sea Scrolls, "which explains *yeṣer* in terms of a principle of evil which dominates a man."[33] Although the evidence is not conclusive, a growing number of scholars agree that the interpolation in Sir 15:14b and possibly other additions to the Hebrew Sirach originated at Qumran.[34]

(b) The case of the Enochic literature is parallel and analogous to that of the Zadokite literature. Before the publication of the Qumran fragments, it was customary to date 1 Enoch around and after the Maccabean crisis, even though the composite nature of the document, in particular regarding the Book of the Watchers, led some scholars to perceive a much older prehistory.[35] Milik's edition of the Aramaic fragments in 1976 made clear that the earliest parts of 1 Enoch (chs. 6–36, the Book of the Watchers; and chs. 73–82, the Astronomical Book) were pre-Maccabean.[36] The paleographic analysis showed that copies of these documents went back to the end of the third or the beginning of the second century BCE. The actual composition might have occurred even earlier. The Aramaic fragments also demonstrated that the Ethiopic version represents a text virtually identical to that of the Book of the Watchers, while the Ethiopic Astronomical Book is only an abbreviated, and rather confused, condensation of the original Aramaic composition. The pre-Maccabean dating of the earliest parts of

33. R. E. Murphy, *"Yēṣer* in the Qumran Literature," *Bib* 39 (1958) 334-44 (quotation on p. 335); cf. J. Hadot, *Penchant mauvais et volonté libre dans la Sagesse de Ben Sira* (Brussels: Presses Universitaires, 1970) 94; G. Boccaccini, "Human Freedom and the Omnipotence of God," in *Middle Judaism: Jewish Thought, 300 BCE to 200 CE* (Minneapolis: Fortress, 1991) 105-9. See also J. J. Collins: "The original Sirach had no place for a demonic spoiler" (*Apocalypticism in the Dead Sea Scrolls,* 35).

34. Cf. Gilbert, "Book of Ben Sira"; cf. also M. Philonenko, "Sur une interpolation essénisante dans le Siracide (6,15-16)," *Orientalia Suecana* 33-35 (1984-86) 317-21. Di Lella warns that the gloss in Sir 15:14b might be a medieval retroversion from the Syriac text of 4:19b (*Hebrew Text of Sirach,* 119-25).

35. For a date around the Maccabean crisis, see H. H. Rowley, *Jewish Apocalyptic and the Dead Sea Scrolls* (London: Athlone, 1957). Among those who perceived an older prehistory, see D. Dimant, "The Fallen Angels in the Dead Sea Scrolls and in the Apocryphal and Pseudepigraphic Books Related to Them" (diss., Hebrew University of Jerusalem, 1974); G. Beer, "Das Buch Henoch," in E. Kautzsch, ed., *Die Apokryphen und Pseudepigraphen des Altes Testaments,* 2 vols. (Tübingen: Mohr, 1900) 2.224-26.

36. J. T. Milik with M. Black, *The Books of Enoch: Aramaic Fragments of Qumrân Cave 4* (Oxford: Clarendon, 1976).

1 Enoch also led scholars to recognize the antiquity of another ancient text that was produced by the same Enochic circles, the Aramaic Levi.[37] This document, several copies of which were preserved among the Dead Sea Scrolls, was already known through some medieval Greek manuscripts.[38]

The high number of Enochic manuscripts found at Qumran suggests that the community of the Dead Sea Scrolls considered the Enochic texts to be as authoritative as the Zadokite documents and preserved them with equal respect and devotion. As in the case of the Zadokite literature, there is no evidence whatsoever that the ancient texts of the Enochic literature were submitted to explicit sectarian editing or interpolation.

(c) The importance of the Enochic literature lies in the fact that it testifies to the existence, during the Zadokite period, of a nonconformist priestly tradition. Zadokite Judaism was a society that clearly defined the lines of cosmic and social structure. The Priestly narrative tells that through creation God turned the primeval disorder into the divine order by organizing the whole cosmos according to the principle of division: light from darkness, the waters above from the waters below, water from dry land (Gen 1:1–2:4a). The refrain "God saw that it was good" repeats that everything was made according to God's will, until the climactic conclusion of the sixth day when "God saw that it was very good" (Gen 1:31).

The disruptive forces of the universe, evil and impurity, are not unleashed but caged within precise boundaries. As long as human beings dare not trespass the boundaries established by God, evil and impurity are controllable. Obedience to the moral laws allows one to avoid evil, which was primarily understood as a punishment from God for human transgressions, while following the purity laws brings impurity under control. The primeval history, as edited in the Zadokite torah (Gen 1–11), warns that any attempt to cross the boundary between humanity and the divine always results in disaster. Human beings have responsibility for, and the capability of, maintaining the distinction between good and evil, holy and profane, pure and impure. They can blame only themselves for their physical and moral failures.

In the Zadokite worldview, the Jerusalem temple — their temple —

---

37. M. E. Stone, "Enoch, Aramaic Levi, and Sectarian Origins," *JSJ* 19 (1988) 159-70.

38. On Aramaic Levi, see the detailed study by R. A. Kugler, *From Patriarchs to Priest: The Levi-Priestly Tradition from Aramaic Levi to Testament of Levi,* SBLEJL 9 (Atlanta: Scholars Press, 1996).

separated from the profane world around it, was a visual representation of the cosmos itself. As God's realm, heaven, is separate from the human realm, the earth, so the earthly dwelling of God produces around the temple a series of concentric circles of greater degrees of holiness separating the profane world from the most holy mountain of Jerusalem. The internal structure of the temple, with its series of concentric courts around the holy of holies, was intended to replicate the structure of the cosmos and the structure of the earth.[39]

The Zadokite priests, who controlled the temple up to the Maccabean period, claimed to be the custodians of the good and uncorrupted order created by God. "The high priest . . . and his priestly kinsmen served as the human community that established and maintained connection between the various orders of being. Their labor in the temple preserved all other orders of being from collapse. Upon them, the people of Israel, the land of Israel, and, ultimately, the entire cosmos and its population all depended."[40] It was incumbent on the priesthood to be morally irreproachable and "to distinguish between the holy and the profane, and between the unclean and the clean" (Lev 10:10).

The ideology of the authors of the Enoch documents directly opposed that of the Zadokites. The catalyst was a particular concept of the origin of evil that portrayed a group of rebellious angels as ultimately responsible for the spread of evil and impurity on earth.[41]

39. J. Milgrom, *Leviticus 1–16,* AB (New York: Doubleday, 1991); J. E. Hartley, *Leviticus,* WBC (Dallas: Word, 1992); M. S. Jaffee, "Ritual Space and Performance in Early Judaism," in *Early Judaism* (Upper Saddle River, N.J.: Prentice Hall, 1997) 164-212.

40. Jaffee, *Early Judaism,* 171.

41. On the centrality of the problem of the origin of evil in ancient apocalypticism, see J. J. Collins, "Creation and the Origin of Evil," in *Apocalypticism in the Dead Sea Scrolls,* 30-51; P. Sacchi, *Jewish Apocalyptic and Its History,* trans. W. J. Short, JSPSup 20 (Sheffield: Sheffield Academic Press, 1997); M. Barker, "The Origin of Evil," in *The Lost Prophet: The Book of Enoch and Its Influence on Christianity* (Nashville: Abingdon, 1988) 33-48; C. Molenberg, "A Study of the Roles of Shemihaza and Asael in 1 Enoch 6–11," *JJS* 35 (1984) 136-46; P. Sacchi, "Riflessioni sull'essenza dell'apocalittica: Peccato d'origine e liberta' dell'uomo," *Hen* 5 (1983) 31-58; idem, "L'apocalittica e il problema del male," *PdV* 25 (1980) 325-47; P. D. Hanson, "Rebellion in Heaven: Azazel and Euhemeristic Heroes in 1 Enoch 6–11," *JBL* 96 (1977) 195-233; M. Delcor, "Le mythe de la chute des anges et de l'origine des géants comme explication du mal dans le monde dans l'apocalyptique juive: Histoire des traditions," *RHR* 189 (1976) 3-53.

While the Zadokites founded their legitimacy on their responsibility to be the faithful keepers of the cosmic order, the Enochians argued that this world had been corrupted by an original sin of angels, who had contaminated God's creation by crossing the boundary between heaven and earth and by revealing secret knowledge to human beings. Despite God's reaction and the subsequent flood, the original order was not, and could not be, restored. The good angels, led by Michael, defeated the evil angels, led by Semyaz and Azaz'el. The mortal bodies of the giants, the offspring of the evil union of angels and women, were killed, but their immortal souls survived as evil spirits (1 En 15:8-10) and continue to roam about the world in order to corrupt human beings and to destroy cosmic order. While Zadokite Judaism describes creation as a process from past disorder to current divine order, the Enochians claim that God's past order has been replaced by the current disorder. While Zadokite Judaism claims that there were no rebellious angels, the satan also being a member of the heavenly court (Job 1:6-12; 2:1-7; Zech 3:1-2; 1 Chr 21:1), Enochic Judaism would be ultimately responsible for the creation of the concept of the devil.[42] While Zadokite Judaism struggles to separate evil and impurity from the demonic and makes their spread depend on human choice, Enochic Judaism removes control of these disruptive forces from humans. "Rebellion against the order of the Most High unleashes the forces of chaos . . . the defilement of the created order extending from humankind to birds to beasts to reptiles. This, in biblical metaphor, is a description of the collapse of the order of creation, with pugnacious forces unleashed in a vicious process of degeneration and decay."[43]

As a result of angelic sin, human beings cannot control the spread of evil and impurity. Human beings are still held accountable for their actions, but they are victims of an evil that they have not caused and cannot resist. Impurity also spreads out of human control, the boundaries between the clean and the unclean having been disrupted by the angels' crossing over the boundaries between the holy and the profane. Although the concepts of impurity and evil remain conceptually separate in Enochic Judaism, impurity is now more closely connected with evil. The impurity produced by the fallen angels has weakened the human capability of resisting evil.

The myth of the fallen angels was not merely a bizarre or folkloric

42. Sacchi, "The Devil in Jewish Traditions of the Second Temple Period (c. 500 BCE–100 CE)," in *Jewish Apocalyptic,* 211-32.

43. Hanson, "Rebellion in Heaven," 199-200.

expansion of ancient legends; it disrupted the very foundations of Zadokite Judaism. Enochic Judaism directly challenged the legitimacy of the second temple and its priesthood. "We are witnessing a harsh indictment against the temple cult and its expository tradition, an indictment originating within the sectarian perspective of a highly developed apocalyptic eschatology."[44]

For the Enochians, the power that the house of Zadok claims is mere illusion, if not the guilty pretentiousness of evil usurpers. Evil and impurity are uncontrollable, and human beings, including the proud priests of Jerusalem, are powerless. The only hope is in God's intervention. The Enochians completely ignore the Mosaic torah and the Jerusalem temple, that is, the two tenets of the order of the universe. In addition, the attribution to Enoch of priestly characteristics[45] suggests the existence of a pure prediluvian, and pre-fall, priesthood and disrupts the foundations of the Zadokite priesthood, which claimed its origin in Aaron at the time of the exodus, in an age that, for the Enochians, was already corrupted after the angelic sin and the flood.

Finally, the superiority of Enochic Judaism is guaranteed not only by its claimed antiquity but also by the superior status of their revealer, Enoch, who, unlike his rival Moses, lived before the angelic sin and never died but "was taken" by God (Gen 5:24), and being now in heaven has more direct access to God's revelation.

The anti-Zadokite character of Enochic Judaism and its priestly nature are confirmed by the Aramaic Levi, which endorses a pre-Zadokite ideal priesthood. "On one hand, the priests of the author's day . . . are implicitly indicted by the model of Levi that varies from the Pentateuchal norms, and . . . are explicitly accused by Levi's warnings about his apostate descendants. On the other hand there are priests who accept the norms established in Levi, the most ancient priest of all; they are the adherents to the author's views, those who prize purity, wisdom, and learning as traits proper to the priesthood. Aramaic Levi is a rejection of the former kind of priest, and a plea for acceptance of the latter type."[46]

(d) While the terms of the opposition between the Enochians and the

44. Ibid., 226.

45. M. Himmelfarb, "Enoch as Priest and Scribe," in *Ascent to Heaven in Jewish and Christian Apocalypses* (New York: Oxford University Press, 1993) 23-25; G. W. E. Nickelsburg, "Enoch, Levi, and Peter: Recipients of Revelation in Upper Galilee," *JBL* 100 (1981) 575-600.

46. Kugler, *From Patriarch to Priest,* 136-37.

Zadokites are clearly set, it is more difficult to reconstruct the chronology of the schism. The substantial consensus among scholars is that the Enochic literature is rooted in oral and literary traditions that predate the emergence of Enochic Judaism as an established movement. These traditions are as ancient as those preserved by Zadokite literature; they go back to the same Babylonian milieu of the exilic age and to the preexilic mythological heritage of ancient Israel.[47] But when did the schism between Enochians and Zadokites occur?

Ben Zion Wacholder takes Ezekiel as the forerunner of an anti-Zadokite opposition party, emphasizing the importance of the exiled prophet-priest for the development of Enochic Judaism, a role of founding father that scholars in Jewish mysticism and apocalypticism also attribute to Ezekiel.[48] In many ways, the pre-Maccabean Enochic literature, particularly chs. 21–36 of the Book of the Watchers, resembles Ezekiel.

Ezekiel was as important in Zadokite Judaism as in Enochic Judaism, however, and the same father-child relationship has been claimed between

---

47. Recent and less recent scholars have argued for the antiquity of Enochic traditions and their Babylonian roots; see J. C. VanderKam, *Enoch: A Man for All Generations* (Columbia: University of South Carolina Press, 1995); H. S. Kranvig, *Roots of Apocalyptic: The Mesopotamian Background of the Enoch Figure and of the Son of Man*, WMANT 61 (Neukirchen-Vluyn: Neukirchener, 1988); O. Neugebauer, "The Astronomical Chapters of the Ethiopic Book of Enoch (72 to 82)," in M. Black, et al., *The Book of Enoch, or, 1 Enoch*, SVTP 7 (Leiden: Brill, 1985) 387-88; J. C. VanderKam, *Enoch and the Growth of an Apocalyptic Tradition*, CBQMS 16 (Washington, D.C.: Catholic Biblical Association of America, 1984); P. Grelot, "La géographie mytique d'Hénoch et ses sources orientales," *RB* 65 (1958) 33-69; idem, "La légende d'Hénoch dans les apocryphes et dans la Bible: Origine et signification," *RSR* 46 (1958) 5-26, 181-220.

48. B. Z. Wacholder, "Ezekiel and Ezekielianism as Progenitors of Essenianism," in Dimant and Rappaport, eds., *Dead Sea Scrolls*, 186-96. Cf. Himmelfarb, "From Ezekiel to the Book of the Watchers," in *Ascent to Heaven*, 9-28; D. J. Halperin, *The Faces of the Chariot: Early Jewish Responses to Ezekiel's Vision* (Tübingen: Mohr, 1988); J. E. Fossum, *The Name of God and the Angel of the Lord*, WUNT 36 (Tübingen: Mohr, 1985); I. Gruenwald, *Apocalyptic and Merkavah Mysticism*, AGJU 14 (Leiden: Brill, 1980); G. Quispel, "Ezekiel 1:26 in Jewish Mysticism and Gnosis," *VC* 34 (1980) 1-13; C. Rowland, "The Influence of the First Chapter of Ezekiel on Jewish and Early Christian Literature" (diss., Cambridge, 1974); R. G. Hamerton-Kelly, "The Temple and the Origins of Jewish Apocalyptic," *VT* 20 (1970) 1-15; J. Maier, *Vom Kultus zur Gnosis* (Salzburg: O. Müller, 1964); G. G. Scholem, *Major Trends in Jewish Mysticism* (New York: Schocken, 1941).

Ezekiel and Zadokite Judaism. Paul D. Hanson presents Ezekiel's vision of the new temple as "the fountainhead of the hierocratic tradition" and "the promulgation of a program of restoration."[49] More recently, Stephen L. Cook has convincingly demonstrated how "the school of Ezekiel is a starting point for elucidating both the Zadokite priesthood and Zadokite millennialism."[50]

There is no reason to make the "pragmatic" Ezekiel clash with the "visionary" Ezekiel. In the context of the Babylonian exile, Ezekiel's dissociation of God's heavenly abode from the Jerusalem temple offered the common priestly background from which both Enochic and Zadokite traditions arose. The disagreement and therefore the emergence of two distinctive parties would occur only later, after the return from the exile, and would concern the modalities of the restoration. While the Zadokites claimed that God's order had been fully restored with the construction of the second temple,[51] the Enochians still viewed restoration as a future event and gave cosmic dimensions to a crisis that for the Zadokites had momentarily affected only the historical relationships between God and Israel.

Paolo Sacchi argues that the schism between Enochians and Zadokites occurred at the beginning of the fourth century BCE. Studying the Book of the Watchers, he concludes that the complex stratification of the document implies a long redactional process that reaches back to the Persian period.[52] He makes a strong case that the absence of the Enoch character in 1 Enoch 6–11 makes this section the oldest part of the Enochic collection, a section that in turn is based on earlier traditions, inasmuch as it combines two originally independent stories, the one centered on the sexual union of angels and women, the other on the spread of secret knowledge.[53] If Sacchi

49. P. D. Hanson, *The Dawn of Apocalyptic: The Historical and Sociological Roots of Jewish Apocalyptic Eschatology,* rev. ed. (Philadelphia: Fortress, 1983).

50. S. L. Cook, *Prophecy and Apocalypticism: The Postexilic Social Setting* (Minneapolis: Fortress, 1995) 215.

51. P. R. Ackroyd, *Exile and Restoration,* OTL (Philadelphia: Westminster, 1968).

52. P. Sacchi, "Il Libro dei Vigilanti e l'apocalittica," *Hen* 1 (1979) 42-98; idem, "Ordine cosmico e prospettiva ultraterrena nel postesilio," *RivB* 30 (1982) 6-25. These articles are now available in English translation as "The Book of the Watchers and Apocalyptic," and "Cosmic Order and Otherworldly Perspectives in the Post-Exilic Period," in *Jewish Apocalyptic,* 32-71 and 72-87, respectively.

53. G. W. E. Nickelsburg, "Apocalyptic and Myth in 1 Enoch 6–11," *JBL* 96 (1977) 383-405.

is correct, then the myth of the fallen angels would not be an expansion of Gen 6:1-4, but rather a parallel development of the common mythological heritage shared by both the Enochians and the Zadokites.

The historical setting seems to support such a reconstruction of the origins of Enochic Judaism. Zadokite Judaism established itself only gradually through the reforms of Nehemiah and Ezra. The fifth century BCE seems still largely characterized by the conflict with the last representatives of the prophetic movements faithful to the heritage of the Davidic monarchy (Third Isaiah, Ruth, Jonah).[54] It was only in the fourth century BCE that Zadokite Judaism eventually triumphed and its opponents had to adjust themselves to the new situation and to define the terms of their opposition. While the Samaritans were excluded from the Jerusalem temple and founded a schismatic community, a priestly opposition party took shape in Judaea and coalesced around ancient myths with Enoch as their hero.[55]

Michael E. Stone and David W. Suter share the view that the composition of the Book of the Watchers was the catalyst of the schism but point rather to the third century BCE. In their judgment, the process of the hellenization of the Zadokite priesthood gives the most likely setting.[56]

Whether Enochic Judaism emerged in the fourth or third century BCE, one thing is certain: Enochic Judaism arose out of anti-Zadokite priestly circles that opposed the power of the priestly Zadokite establishment. The long debate in scholarship about whether the Enoch books come from priestly or antipriestly circles finds a consistent resolution when considering

54. P. Sacchi, "Il primo sadocitismo (520-400 circa a.C.)," in *Storia del Secondo Tempio,* 89-104; M. Smith, *Palestinian Parties and Politics,* e.g., 161-62.

55. See P. Sacchi, "La corrente enochica, le origini dell'apocalittica e il Libro dei Vigilanti," in *Storia del Secondo Tempio,* 148-55. On the Samaritans see idem, "I Samaritani," in *Storia del Secondo Tempio,* 127-34. Cf. A. D. Crown, ed., *The Samaritans* (Tübingen: Mohr, 1989); R. Pummer, *The Samaritans* (Leiden: Brill, 1987); R. J. Coggins, *Samaritans and Jews: The Origins of Samaritanism Reconsidered* (Atlanta: John Knox, 1975).

56. D. W. Suter, "Fallen Angel, Fallen Priest: The Problem of Family Purity in 1 Enoch 6–16," *HUCA* 50 (1979) 115-35; M. E. Stone, "The Book of Enoch and Judaism in the Third Century BCE," *CBQ* 40 (1978) 479-92 (repr. in M. E. Stone and D. Satran, eds., *Emerging Judaism* [Philadelphia: Fortress, 1989] 61-75); cf. M. E. Stone, *Scriptures, Sects and Visions: A Profile of Judaism from Ezra to the Jewish Revolts* (Philadelphia: Fortress, 1980); G. W. E. Nickelsburg, "Enoch, First Book of," *ABD* 2.508-16.

that the priestly nature of Enochic Judaism does not contradict its anti-priestly attitudes.[57] Enoch's "critique of the Jerusalem priestly establishment . . . takes seriously the priesthood's claim for itself and the importance of priestly duties and categories. This attitude is at once critical of the reality it sees in the temple and deeply devoted to the ideal of the temple understood in a quite concrete way."[58]

At the roots of the Qumran community, therefore, is an ancient schism within the Jewish priesthood between Enochians and Zadokites. We do not know exactly who the Enochians were, whether they were genealogically related to the Zadokites or were members of rival priestly families. Unlike the situation with the Samaritans, we have no evidence that the Enochians formed a schismatic community, in Palestine or elsewhere. The Enochians were an opposition party within the temple elite, not a group of separatists. The words of Robert A. Kugler about Aramaic Levi apply to the entire Enochic literature in pre-Maccabean times: it testifies to "a period of time when there was a dispute regarding the proper character of the priestly office, but when the discussion was still quite tame, and there was yet room for differences of opinion."[59]

In conclusion, the analysis of the ancient literature collected in the Dead Sea Scrolls leads to the striking discovery that the library of Qumran contained records of both pro-Zadokite and anti-Zadokite Judaism. The statements in Sirach supporting the freedom of human will (Sir 15:11-20) and polemically rejecting the idea of the devil (21:27) and the corruption of the universe (39:16-35) show that the conflict between Zadokite Judaism and Enochic Judaism did not belong to a remote past but was still unresolved at the beginning of the second century BCE.[60] Did the people of the Dead Sea Scrolls collect those ancient religious texts regardless of their

57. Hanson argued that the Enochic literature came from nonpriestly circles (*Dawn of Apocalyptic*).

58. Himmelfarb, *Ascent to Heaven*, 27.

59. Kugler, *From Patriarch to Priest*, 135.

60. For a detailed analysis of the confrontation between Sirach and Enochic Judaism, see Boccaccini, "Ben Sira, Qohelet, and Apocalyptic," in *Middle Judaism*, 77-125; idem, "Origine del male, libertà dell'uomo e retribuzione nella sapienza di Ben Sira," *Hen* 8 (1986) 1-37. Comparing Sirach and 1 Enoch, Randall A. Argall has reached the same conclusion: "each tradition views the other among its rivals" (*1 Enoch and Sirach: A Comparative Literary and Conceptual Analysis of the Themes of Revelation, Creation, and Judgment*, SBLEJL 8 [Atlanta: Scholars Press, 1995] 250).

ideological origins? Were they indifferent about the confrontation between Zadokites and Enochians? Or was there a logic in preserving the documents of both parties? The answer may be found in a series of documents that chronologically and ideologically lie between those ancient texts and the sectarian writings of the community of the Dead Sea Scrolls.

CHAPTER 4

The Formative Age

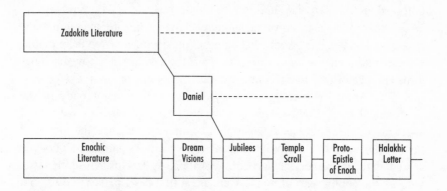

1. Daniel and the Book of Dream Visions

Daniel and Dream Visions provide a convenient starting point for our analysis of the formative age of the community of the Dead Sea Scrolls. Both texts were written during the Maccabean revolt after the death of Onias III, the last legitimate Zadokite high priest. Both texts were present in many copies in the Qumran library and were regarded as authoritative. Both texts are apocalyptic; they share the same literary genre (apocalypse) and the same worldview (apocalypticism).[1] But do they belong ideologically to the same party?[2]

The book of Dream Visions (1 Enoch 83–90) belongs without doubt to Enochic Judaism.[3] The evidence is given by the self-conscious placement of Dream Visions within the Enochic tradition. The protagonist, Enoch, appears on the scene as a character already known, who needs no introduction, and the first-person narration of the preceding Astronomical Book continues without interruption. Foremost, the ideological continuity is guaranteed by the explicit reference to the idea that the spread of evil and impurity is caused by the sin of rebellious angels (1 En 84:4; 86:1-6). As a consequence of angelic sin, the order of creation has been disrupted and the earth has become the victim of chaotic forces. "I saw in a vision the sky being hurled down and snatched and falling upon the earth. . . . I saw the earth being swallowed into the great abyss, the mountains suspended upon mountains, the hills sinking down upon the hills, and tall trees being uprooted and thrown and sinking into the deep abyss" (1 En 83:3-4).

Dream Visions is, however, an innovative text. Greater attention to the historical dimension markedly distinguishes the document from the previous Enochic tradition. The major consequence of the angelic sin is now that it has turned human history into a continuous and inexorable process of degeneration. The Animal Apocalypse, which constitutes the major body of the document (1 En 85:1–90:42), depicts what we could call the strange case of a genetic disease that has changed and continues to change the nature of humankind, subsequently producing inferior species of animals. Nobody is spared: in the metaphorical world of the Animal Apocalypse, even the Jews, who are the noblest part of humankind, are at first described as "cows" but

1. J. J. Collins, "Daniel, Enoch and Related Literature," in *Apocalypticism in the Dead Sea Scrolls* (London and New York: Routledge, 1997) 12-29.

2. In previous studies I have offered a detailed analysis of the reasons, indicating that Daniel and Dream Visions represent two different parties. It is enough here to recall some of the conclusions of my analysis. See G. Boccaccini, "Daniel and the Dream Visions: The Genre of Apocalyptic and the Apocalyptic Tradition," in *Middle Judaism: Jewish Thought, 300 BCE to 200 CE* (Minneapolis: Fortress, 1991) 126-60; idem, "'E' Daniele un testo apocalittico? Una (ri)definizione del pensiero del Libro di Daniele in rapporto al Libro dei Sogni e all'apocalittica," *Hen* 9 (1987) 267-302; cf. P. Sacchi, *Jewish Apocalyptic and Its History,* trans. W. J. Short, JSPSup 20 (Sheffield: Sheffield Academic Press, 1997) 23.

3. The most important monographs on 1 Enoch, including Dream Visions, are listed in the bibliography at the end of this volume.

later become "sheep." Only at the end of time will God purify the universe by fire and restore the original goodness of creation.

In the detailed description of the history of Israel, most striking is the methodical polemic against the tenets of Zadokite Judaism. The exodus from Egypt and the march through the desert are described in detail, including Moses' ascent of Mount Sinai (1 En 89:29-33), but no reference is made to the covenant and the gift of the Mosaic torah. They are simply ignored. As for the temple, its construction under Solomon is emphatically evoked (1 En 89:36, 50), but the entire history of Israel in the postexilic period unfolds under demonic influence ("the seventy shepherds" of 1 En 89:59ff.), until God comes to the earth and the new creation is inaugurated. In an era of corruption and decline, the Zadokite temple is no exception; it is a contaminated sanctuary ("all the bread which was upon it was polluted and impure," 1 En 89:73).

In the eyes of the author of Dream Visions, the Maccabean crisis is only the last chapter of the degenerative process initiated by the angelic sin. The profaning action of Menelaus and Antiochus IV adds nothing to an already compromised situation, and as a result it is not even mentioned. At the time of the judgment, the city of the temple ("the ancient house") will be devoured by the same purifying fire of Gehenna into which the wicked are thrown. In its place God will build a "new house" in which all the elect will be reunited. "I went on seeing until that ancient house caught [fire]. . . . The Lord of the sheep brought about a new house, greater and loftier than the first one. . . . All the sheep were within it. . . . And the Lord of the sheep rejoiced with great joy because they had all become gentle and returned to his house" (1 En 90:28-33).

Daniel shares the idea that history is condemned to inexorable degeneration. Starting with the Babylonians, "four kingdoms" (cf. Dan 7) will rule over Israel, and the Jews will serve "seventy weeks of years" of exile (cf. Dan 9). The common figure of the "iniquitous king," Antiochus IV, allows the two periodizations to be synchronized in a crescendo of evil and corruption. In spite of any similarities, however, a fundamental difference makes Daniel representative of a different party. While sharing the same apocalyptic worldview as Dream Visions, Daniel opposes the Enochic doctrine of evil and strenuously defends the tenets of Zadokite Judaism: the Mosaic torah and the legitimacy of the second temple. The prayer of Daniel in chapter 9, a chapter confirmed by the fragments of Qumran as belonging to the original text rather than being a later addition, makes clear that the degeneration of history is caused not by the sin of the angels but by the Jewish people's transgression of the Mosaic covenant. It is the result not of an uncontrolled spread of evil and impurity but of God's punishment for the unfaithfulness of Israel. The angels never appear as rebellious against God, whose dominion cannot be challenged: "His dominion is an everlasting dominion. . . . He does according to his will with the host of heaven . . . and there is no one who can stay his hand or say to him: What are you doing?" (Dan 4:31-32). The kingdoms and their angelic counterparts (cf. Dan 10) are not stray bullets but instruments of God's punishment. In addition, Daniel stresses that the degeneration of history is limited to a single historical season and is not characteristic of the history in its entirety. It is the consequence of a misused opportunity to observe the covenant on the part of humankind. Despite all challenges from humans, God's order stands firm; human sin cannot destroy it. The evil of this world is not the result of corruption and chaotic disorder.

It is no surprise, therefore, that the covenantal Daniel would be canonized by Rabbinic Judaism, while the Enochic literature, including Dream Visions, would not. Recognition of the contrast between Daniel and Enochic Judaism has led some scholars to argue that, compared with the apocalyptic Dream Visions, Daniel "is not typically apocalyptic (if apocalyptic at all)."[4] Indeed, if we limit the name "apocalyptic" to the Enochic party, as Paolo Sacchi does by using the phrase "Jewish apocalyptic" as a synonym for Enochic Judaism, we have the paradox that both the apocalyptic books par excellence of the Bible, Daniel and Revelation, are nonapocalyptic or even antiapocalyptic, because they do not belong to Enochic Judaism.[5] The difficulty can be overcome by claiming with John J. Collins that apocalypticism denotes not a single party but a worldview that influenced many Jewish parties, including the covenantal party that produced Daniel, the Enochic party that produced Dream Visions, and the Christian party that produced Revelation.[6]

4. P. R. Davies, "Eschatology in the Book of Daniel," *JSOT* 17 (1980) 33-53 (repr. in P. R. Davies, *Sects and Scrolls: Essays on Qumran and Related Topics* [Atlanta: Scholars Press, 1996] 23-44); cf. A. C. Welch, *Visions of the End* (London and Boston: Pilgrim, 1922).

5. See Sacchi, *Jewish Apocalyptic,* 26; cf. Boccaccini, *Middle Judaism,* 160.

6. J. J. Collins, *The Apocalyptic Imagination: An Introduction to the Jewish Matrix of Christianity* (New York: Crossroad, 1984). On the distinction between Enochic Judaism and apocalypticism, see also the discussion in Ch. 1 above.

Even within the coalition of forces (the Hasidim) that supported the Maccabees,[7] Daniel and Dream Visions occupied different positions. Daniel endorsed passive resistance, while Dream Visions promoted a more militant activism.[8] In its anti-Enochic stance, the apocalyptic Daniel also took much more seriously than the apocalyptic Dream Visions the profanation of the Zadokite temple, which was a sacrilegious action against God and God's legitimate temple (Dan 8:10-12; 11:36-39). This situation would last "two thousand and three hundred evenings and mornings; then the sanctuary shall be restored to its rightful state" (Dan 8:13-14). The figure of "two thousand and three hundred evenings and mornings" (1,150 days) approximates the "three and a half years" (1,260 days) of Antiochus's persecution (Dan 9:27; cf. 7:25; 12:7). The discrepancy is intentional; Daniel argues that God would restore the temple *before* the end of times as an act of justice owed to its legitimate cult.[9]

Although sympathetic to the principles of Zadokite Judaism, Daniel was not a supporter of the Zadokite priesthood. The glorious period of the return from exile and of the second temple is not such for Daniel. On the contrary, it is a time of punishment; the exile has not ended yet. "Seventy weeks of years are decreed . . . to finish the transgression, to put an end to sin, and to atone for iniquity" (Dan 9:24). As in Dream Visions, the exile will end only by the intervention of God and the inauguration of the eschatological era, which it was hoped would follow the events of the Maccabean period. After the divine punishment there is no more history; God's forgiveness marks the end of history.[10]

Exactly this anti-Zadokite element, which Daniel shares with Dream Visions, made Daniel popular at Qumran, as attested by the presence among the Dead Sea Scrolls of an abundant pseudo-Danielic literature. The extant fragments (4Q243 [4QpsDan[a] ar], 4Q244 [4QpsDan[b] ar], 4Q245 [4QpsDan[c] ar]) indicate clearly that the tendency was to read

---

7. J. Sievers, *The Hasmoneans and Their Supporters: From Mattathias to the Death of John Hyrcanus I* (Atlanta: Scholars Press, 1990); P. R. Davies, "Hasidim in the Maccabean Period," *JJS* 28 (1977) 127-40.

8. G. Boccaccini, "Faced with the Events of History," in *Middle Judaism,* 156-59.

9. Ibid., 148, 158-59.

10. In a seminal article in 1976, Michael A. Knibb was the first to notice, almost with surprise, that most of the apocalyptic literature shares the idea that Israel is still in exile ("The Exile in the Literature of the Intertestamental Period," *HeyJ* 17 [1976] 253-72).

Daniel in light of Dream Visions, not vice versa.[11] In order to make Daniel compatible with Enochic Judaism, it was enough to add a few elements so that the "seventy weeks" and the "four kingdoms" were turned from a special period of punishment for human sins into the final era in the comprehensive degeneration of history. Where Daniel limits historical determinism to the exilic and postexilic time of punishment, Pseudo-Daniel contains a prophecy about the entire course of history, from the flood to the end of days, that seems similar to Dream Visions. Where Daniel puts the angelic world under God's control, Pseudo-Daniel claims that Israel is led astray by the power of evil spirits. Those who collected the Dead Sea Scrolls were ideologically closer to the apocalyptic circles that wrote Dream Visions than to the apocalyptic circles that wrote Daniel.

2. The Book of Jubilees

Jubilees is demonstrably later than the early Enochic books: Jub 4:17-19 alludes to the Book of the Watchers, the Astronomical Book, and Dream Visions.[12] Particularly important for the date of Jubilees is the reference to Enoch having a dream revelation about the history of humankind. "[Enoch] saw what was and what will be in a vision of his sleep as it will happen among the children of men in their generations until the day of judgment" (4:19). Since the form and content of the vision correspond exactly to Dream Visions and have no parallel in the previous Enochic literature, Jubilees was undoubtedly written after the Maccabean crisis. Jubilees played an important role at Qumran, as demonstrated by the quantity of manuscripts found there. Nonetheless, Jubilees is clearly a presectarian text. Its quotation as an authoritative work by the Damascus Document

---

11. On the Pseudo-Danielic writings, see Collins, *Apocalypticism in the Dead Sea Scrolls,* 15-18; idem, "Pseudo-Daniel Revisited," *RevQ* 17/65-68 (1996) 111-35; P. W. Flint, "4Pseudo-Daniel arc (4Q245) and the Restoration of the Priesthood," *RevQ* 17 (1996) 137-50; F. García Martínez, *Qumran and Apocalyptic: Studies on the Aramaic Texts from Qumran,* STDJ 9 (Leiden: Brill, 1992) 137-61; J. T. Milik, "Prière de Nabonide et autres écrits d'un cycle de Daniel," *RB* 63 (1956) 407-15.

12. The most important monographs on the book of Jubilees are listed in the bibliography at the end of this volume.

(CD 16:2-4) shows that its composition precedes the flourishing of the sectarian literature of Qumran.[13]

The book of Jubilees stems from the same priestly party that produced the books of Enoch. Jubilees gives great importance to Enoch as a writer and a revealer (4:17ff.), and Enochic traditions play an important role in Jubilees.[14] Most importantly, Jubilees shares the generative idea of Enochic Judaism, the idea that evil is superhuman and is caused by the sin of the Watchers (7:21ff.). The universe and human history are under the influence of rebellious demonic forces.[15]

Like the author of Dream Visions, the author of Jubilees holds the idea that history is a process of decline and degeneration (Jub 23:8-23). He also agrees that his time is the end, even though he envisages the end as a more gradual series of events. "In those days," immediately after a climax of persecution in which "there will be none who will be saved from the hands of the Gentiles" (23:24-25), a new faithful generation shall arise ("children will begin to search the law and to search the commandments and to return to the way of righteousness," 23:26). The author of Jubilees expects "those days," his days, to be the beginning of the final era of everlasting peace and righteousness (23:27-31).

Ideologically related to Enochic Judaism, Jubilees also reflects the same sociological background. The author voices a priestly tradition different from, yet claims a dignity equal to, the Zadokite tradition. Levi and his sons were entrusted with a library of books (45:16) containing heavenly lore revealed to Jacob (32:21-26) and sacred traditions passed down from earlier patriarchs. It is the duty of Levi and his sons to preserve and renew the books "until this day." "And [Jacob] gave all his books and his fathers' books to Levi, his son, so that he might preserve them and renew them for his sons until this day" (45:15). This written tradition ultimately goes back to Enoch. He was "the first who learned writing and knowledge and wisdom. . . . He saw and knew everything and wrote his testimony and

13. On the dating of Jubilees, see J. C. VanderKam, "Jubilees, Book of," *ABD* 3.1039-32.

14. J. C. VanderKam, "Enoch Traditions in Jubilees and Other Second Century Sources," in *SBL Seminar Papers, 1978,* 1.229-51.

15. For Jubilees as an Enochic document, see P. Sacchi, "Libro dei Giubilei," in idem, ed., *Apocrifi dell'Antico Testamento,* 2 vols. (Turin: Unione Tipografica-Editrice Torinese, 1981-89) 1.179-411. The ideological continuity between 1 Enoch and Jubilees is also emphasized by O. S. Wintermute, "Jubilees," in *OTP* 2.35-142.

deposited the testimony upon the earth against all the children of men and their generation" (4:17-19). Through Methuselah and Lamech, the teachings of Enoch reached his great-grandson Noah (7:38-39). Noah also "wrote everything" he was taught by the angels of God, and "gave everything which he wrote to Shem, his oldest son" (10:13-14). This literature was then inherited by Abraham, who "took his father's books . . . and he copied them. And he began studying them thereafter" (12:27). In short, the party behind Jubilees claims to be the recipient of a Levitical tradition other than Zadokite, a family tradition that recognizes Enoch as its progenitor and has all the distinctive marks of Enochic Judaism.

Unlike the previous texts of Enochic Judaism, however, Jubilees has an amazing feature: it presents itself as a book given to Moses, the chief revealer of the Zadokite tradition. The book of Jubilees gives us evidence that after the Maccabean crisis, the Enochians, or at least some Enochians, now considered the Mosaic revelation as no longer a competitive revelation to pass over in silence, as Dream Visions did, but as a common heritage that could neither be ignored nor dismissed.

The way in which Zadokite and Enochic traditions were mingled is ingenious. From the Astronomical Book (1 En 81:1-10) the author of Jubilees takes up the idea that in heaven are some tablets on which "all the deeds of humanity and all the children of the flesh upon the earth for all the generations of the world" are written down (81:2). Enoch "looked at the tablets of heaven, read all the writing (on them), and came to understand everything" (81:2). In the Astronomical Book the tablets of heaven are only one among the many things that Enoch sees in his heavenly journeys, and it is not clear if human events are written there before or, most probably, after they occur. At any rate, in the earlier Enochic literature the heavenly tablets are not central; Dream Visions does not even mention them as a source of revelation.

In the Astronomical Book, however, the vision of the heavenly tablets has a significant position: it immediately precedes God's order that sends Enoch back to earth "on the ground in front of the gate of [his] house." There Enoch is commanded to "make everything known to [his] son Methuselah" and to "write down" what he saw (81:5-6). One could interpret this command, which concerns the entire revelation Enoch received from the angel Uriel, as a command to write down what Enoch had read on the heavenly tablets. This is exactly what Jubilees did, turning an incidental detail of the Astronomical Book into the main source of God's revelation. Jubilees claims that, after Enoch, other revealers had the opportunity to see and write down some parts of the heavenly tablets. The experience of Jacob in Jub 32:21-26 repeats, stage by stage, that of his ancestor and shows how the revealer is now seen as somebody who read, memorized, and copied from a heavenly archetype. "[Jacob] saw in a vision of the night, and behold an angel was descending from heaven, and there were seven tablets in his hands. And he gave (them) to Jacob, and he read them, and he knew everything which was written in them, which would happen to him and to his sons during all the ages. And he showed him everything which was written in the tablets. . . . And [Jacob] woke up from his sleep and he recalled everything that he had read and seen and he wrote down all of the matters which he had read and seen" (Jub 32:21-26). From a passage like this, we learn that the continuity and consistency of the priestly tradition that Jubilees advocates are guaranteed by the common reference to the tablets of heaven.

The genius of Jubilees is to make Moses part of the same tradition. The introduction of the document makes Moses a revealer like Enoch and Jacob. The angel also showed Moses "the tablets of the division of years from the time of the creation of the law and testimony according to their weeks (of years), according to the jubilees . . . from [the day of creation until] the day of the new creation" (Jub 1:29). Like Enoch and Jacob, Moses also received from God the command: "write down . . . all the matters which I shall make known to you on this mountain" (1:26). In this way, the heavenly tablets became the center of a complex history of revelation involving several revealers (Enoch, Noah, Abraham, Jacob, Moses). The heavenly tablets were shown to them; the revealers saw, recalled, and wrote; and their work generated a written tradition eventually handed down by Levi and his sons "until this day," a tradition that encompasses the Enochic literature and the Zadokite torah, as well as the book of Jubilees itself.

The acceptance of the Mosaic revelation must not obfuscate the real intentions of the author. By acknowledging the connection between the Mosaic revelation and the heavenly tablets, Jubilees also emphasizes the incompleteness of the Zadokite torah. No writing, Enochic or Mosaic, is the exact transcript of the heavenly tablets; the most that even Jubilees can do is to quote them occasionally (4:5, 32; 23:32; 30:9).

From the literary point of view, one can describe Jubilees as an example of rewritten Bible,[16] but its composition was not motivated by an

---

16. G. W. E. Nickelsburg, "The Bible Rewritten and Expanded," in M. E. Stone,

outburst of exegetical curiosity and trust in the inexhaustible comprehen-
siveness of the Mosaic revelation. Even less is Jubilees a eulogy on the
centrality of the Zadokite torah. On the contrary, Jubilees claims that the
Zadokite torah does not contain God's entire will; it is only one of several
incomplete versions of the heavenly tablets, a version to be completed and
corrected in its true meaning by comparing it with the writings of other
revealers, who had a better glimpse at the heavenly tablets. The Zadokite
torah does not even contain the entire revelation given to Moses; it is only
"the book of the first torah" (6:22), with Jubilees also claiming a Mosaic
origin. If in Jubilees the ancient patriarchs are said to keep some of the
laws later revealed to Moses, it is not because the Mosaic torah was
preexistent, as it would be in later Rabbinic Judaism,[17] but because the
patriarchs had direct access to the heavenly archetype. The centrality and
uniqueness of the Zadokite torah are lost in its being only one document
in a larger written tradition, including Enochic documents and Jubilees, a
tradition in which human beings can find traces of God's will. The heavenly
tablets are the only and all-inclusive repository of God's revelation.

After congratulating the author of Jubilees on the brilliant solution he
found in harmonizing Mosaic revelation and Enochic revelation, and in
subordinating the former to the latter, the modern historian has also the
responsibility to explain the phenomenon. In the aftermath of the Maccabean
revolt the Zadokite torah was apparently no longer understood as a document
of the house of Zadok only. Dream Visions and Jewish-Hellenistic authors,
like Artapanus,[18] show that before the Maccabean war, in non-Zadokite
circles the Mosaic torah could still be ignored or was susceptible to syncretis-
tic developments. When the non-Zadokite high priest Menelaus took power,
as representative of a different priestly family, that of "Bilgah,"[19] with the

---

ed., *Jewish Writings of the Second Temple Period,* CRINT 2/2 (Assen: Van Gorcum;
Philadelphia: Fortress, 1984) 89-156.

17. G. Boccaccini, "The Pre-existence of the Torah: A Commonplace in Second
Temple Judaism or a Later Rabbinic Development?" *Hen* 17 (1995) 329-50.

18. On Artapanus see J. J. Collins, "Artapanus," in *OTP* 2.889-903.

19. The report that Simon (and consequently his brother Menelaus; cf. 2 Macc 4:23)
was from the priestly family of "Bilgah" (cf. 1 Chr 24:14), is according to the Vetus Latina
and the Armenian readings of 2 Macc 3:4. The tradition of the Greek text that they were
from the tribe of "Benjamin," that is, from a nonpriestly family, is to be rejected as a later,
biased report after the death of the "evil" high priest Menelaus. See P. Sacchi, *Storia del
Secondo Tempio* (Turin: Società Editrice Internazionale, 1994) 196-97.

support of the Greek king Antiochus IV he also tried to change the Zadokite torah. Many did not object.[20] As the Zadokites had imposed the Mosaic torah as the "law of [their] God and the law of the [Persian] king" (Ezra 7:26), so a new non-Zadokite house of high priests supported by a new Greek king might have now the legitimacy of changing the law. Menelaus had deceitfully succeeded in becoming the high priest of a well-established temple. He had neither any intention nor any interest in destroying Judaism, and so the roots of his power and wealth; his reforms, no matter how radical, were aimed at destroying only a certain kind of Judaism, and so strengthening the roots of his power and wealth.

The greatness of the Maccabees was to present themselves not as the leaders of a rival priestly family, as they were, but as the champions of the national tradition against the Greeks. From the beginning of the revolt, Mattathias and Judas Maccabee proclaimed their faithfulness ("zeal") to the Mosaic torah, which they identified as the foundation of Jewish identity (see 1 Macc 3 and 2 Macc 8). The Maccabees' capture of the flag of Zadokite Judaism proved to be the most effective way to replace the power of the house of Zadok and to prevent its restoration. The Maccabees convinced most of the Jewish people that the Mosaic torah could be restored even without restoring the Zadokite priesthood.

It was through the experience of the Maccabean revolt that the Zadokite torah became the Jewish torah *tout court* as the essential element of Jewish national identity. The Letter of Aristeas, composed at the end of the second century BCE, shows that even in most "dialogical" circles of the Western diaspora the Mosaic torah and its Greek version, the Septuagint, gained a centrality that they did not have before.[21] The Maccabean revolt was the catalyst for the emergence of Jewish nationalism. The change is apparent also in non-Jewish sources that use the term *Ioudaismos* for the first time to define the way of life of ethnic Jews, based on obedience to the Mosaic torah.[22]

---

20. Contemporary historians stress that the Maccabean revolt was primarily a civil strife, not the national war for independence celebrated in the Hasmonean sources and in the later rabbinic tradition. See K. Bringmann, *Hellenistische Reform und Religionsverfolgung in Judäa* (Göttingen: Vandenhoeck & Ruprecht, 1983).

21. G. Boccaccini, "The *Letter of Aristeas:* A Dialogical Judaism Facing Greek *Paideia*," in *Middle Judaism,* 161-85; cf. J. M. G. Barclay, *Jews in the Mediterranean Diaspora: From Alexander to Trajan (323 BCE-117 CE)* (Edinburgh: T. & T. Clark, 1996) 138-50.

22. P. R. Davies, "Scenes from the Early History of Judaism," in D. V. Edelman, ed.,

Jubilees reflects this new climate, after the last of the Oniads fled to Egypt[23] and the house of Zadok was definitely out of the picture. While the Maccabees had created the political framework, Daniel had, quite unwillingly, ideologically opened the path for a harmonization between Enochic and Mosaic traditions. Daniel testifies to an apocalyptic circle that aimed to subordinate the principles of Enochic Judaism into a revised form of covenantal Judaism; the terms of its compromise, however, could be easily reversed. Daniel turned the postexilic period into a time of punishment in order to show that the degeneration of history depends on the transgression of the Mosaic torah. But in so doing, Daniel also made it possible to understand the transgression of the Mosaic torah as part of the process of degeneration of history that began with angelic sin.

The way in which Enochic Judaism already had interpreted the history of the temple offered a suitable parallel: as the temple, so the Mosaic torah. Their bestowal was an act of grace from God; but the temple was destroyed and never properly rebuilt, and the covenant was broken and never properly restored. The disobedience to the torah became just another clear indication that Israel was still living in exile, as Enochic Judaism had always claimed. In the prologue of Jubilees (1:9-18), God reveals to Moses that the people of Israel will forget the covenant. This would lead Israel to a time of punishment and exile, a time that for the author of Jubilees would last until the end of days. The second temple period is dismissed as an age in which the Jews "will forget all my laws and all my commandments and all my judgments, and will go astray concerning new moons, sabbaths, festivals, jubilees, and ordinances" (1:14). The period foretold for that restoration belongs to the *eschaton,* when God would come and dwell with God's people; it does not belong to the history of Israel. The time of Israel's repentance also will be the time when the temple is rebuilt. "After this,

---

The Triumph of Elohim: From Yahwisms to Judaisms (Grand Rapids: Eerdmans, 1996) 145-82; D. Mendels, *The Rise and Fall of Jewish Nationalism* (New York: Doubleday, 1992); S. J. D. Cohen, "Religion, Ethnicity and Hellenism in the Emergence of Jewish Identity in Maccabean Palestine," in P. Bilde, et al., eds., *Religion and Religious Practice in the Seleucid Kingdom* (Aarhus: Aarhus University Press, 1990) 204-23; D. Mendels, *The Land of Israel as a Political Concept in Hasmonean Literature* (Tübingen: Mohr, 1987).

23. Josephus, *J.W.* 7.423-36; *Ant.* 12.237-38, 387; 13.62-73. On the temple built there by the Zadokites, see R. Howard, "The Jewish Temple at Leontopolis: A Reconsideration," *JJS* 33 (1982) 429-43; M. Delcor, "Le temple d'Onias en Egypte," *RB* 75 (1968) 188-205.

they will turn to me from among the nations . . . and I shall transplant them as a plant of righteousness. . . . And I shall build my sanctuary in their midst, and I shall dwell with them. And I shall be their God and they will be my people in truth and righteousness" (1:15-18). With Jubilees, Enochic Judaism has incorporated and digested the tenets of Zadokite Judaism, without losing its own identity. The temple that is praised is the first temple that was destroyed. The Mosaic torah that is praised is the law that was broken. The restoration belongs to the *eschaton,* while evil and corruption dominate the present.

The second important element that distinguishes Jubilees from the previous Enochic tradition is a special doctrine of election, based on God's predeterminism, which results in an identification between evil and impurity, and in a strict, almost dualistic theology of separation. Commentators agree that such a sophisticated doctrine of election is the closest link to the sectarian texts of Qumran.[24]

In line with the early Enochic concept of evil, Dream Visions does not set clear boundaries to separate the chosen from the wicked. The Jews are described as the noblest form of humankind. Evil and impurity affect all human beings, however, including the Jews. Salvation also is not foreign to non-Jewish individuals. The chosen are vaguely defined. In a tradition that describes the spread of evil and impurity as a plague, the chosen are those people, Jews and Gentiles, who, for whatever mysterious reasons, are not affected by this mortal disease and thus survive the day of the final purification of the world.

Jubilees reacts strongly against the dissolution of the Jewish people's prerogatives. They, and only they, are the chosen. Harmonizing the Enochic doctrine of evil and the idea of the election of the Jewish people was by no means an easy task. In this case also, Jubilees was able to find a coherent innovative solution that corrects yet does not challenge, and ultimately even strengthens, the principles of Enochic Judaism. The first step was a much stronger emphasis on God's predeterminism and God's control over the universe. Despite the angelic sin, history unfolds, stage by stage, according to the times (the jubilees) that God has dictated from the beginning. The election of the Jewish people also belongs to the predestined order, which no disorder can change. Since creation, God selected the Jews as a special

---

24. M. Testuz, *Les idées religieuses du Livre des Jubilés* (Geneva: Druz; Paris: Minard, 1960).

people above all nations, and separated them from the other nations as a holy people (2:21). Those marked by circumcision (15:11) are called to participate with the angels in the worship of God. Those who do not belong to the children of Israel belong to the children of destruction (15:26).

This incipient dualism was unknown in the previous Enochic tradition and was equally far from the principles of Zadokite Judaism. In Jubilees the separation between Jews and Gentiles belongs not to the history of humankind but to the order of creation. More significantly, purity is not, as with Zadokite Judaism, an autonomous rule of the universe to which the chosen people also have to adjust, but the prerequisite of their salvation. Being elected means being separate from the impure world. The boundary between purity and impurity becomes the boundary between good and evil.

Now, from the Enochic tradition, Jubilees knows that the fallen angels contaminated the order of creation by crossing the boundary between heaven and earth. Their taking wives for themselves was an act of "fornication" and "made a beginning of impurity" on earth (7:21). Their bloodthirsty children, the giants, polluted the earth as "they poured out much blood upon the earth" (7:24). The spread of impurity they caused was a threat not only to the purity of the cosmos but also to the future election of Israel. In order to make Israel the chosen people, the effects of the contamination caused by the angelic sin must be limited, and the boundaries between the holy and the profane, the clean and the unclean, must be restored.

Jubilees eliminates a major difficulty by arguing that the purity of the cosmos was reestablished with the flood. "And [God] made for all his works a new and righteous nature so that they might not sin in all their nature forever, and so that they might all be righteous, each in his kind, always" (5:12). The cosmos is not in itself contaminated, as it was for the earlier Enochic tradition.

A problem remains: the presence of the "polluted demons" (10:1), the "evil spirits" whose "fathers were the Watchers" (10:4-5), the "cruel spirits . . . [who] lead [people] astray so that they [may] commit sin and impurity" (11:4). If the Jews have no power to control the demonic forces, their election is meaningless. Noah realizes this and begs God: "Do not let them have power over the children of the righteous henceforth and forever" (10:1-6). God will not, or cannot, fulfill Noah's prayer completely. "The chief of the spirits, Mastema," obtains his wish that "a tenth of them remain so that they might be subject to Satan upon the earth" (10:7-9, 11).

94

But Noah is taught by the angels of God about "the healing of all the illnesses [caused by the evil spirits] together with their seductions, so that he might heal by means of herbs of the earth. And Noah wrote everything in a book just as we taught him according to every kind of healing. And the evil spirits were restrained from following the sons of Noah. And he gave everything which he wrote to Shem, his oldest son, because he loved him much more than all his sons" (10:10-14). Alone among the nations, Israel has a remedy against the evil spirits and is not defenseless in the hands of "Prince Mastema."

This does not mean that the chosen people are completely safe. The evil knowledge that the fallen angels have brought to earth (cf. 1 En 8:1-4) is still present. The grandson of Shem, Cainan, "found a writing which the ancestors engraved on stone. And he read what was in it. And he transcribed it. And he sinned because of what was in it, since there was in it the teaching of the Watchers" (Jub 8:1-4). One-tenth of the evil spirits are still present. "Prince Mastema" seeks any opportunity to cause harm to the chosen and arouses the nations against them. Moses would have been killed and the Jews annihilated by the Egyptians had God not delivered them (48:1-4, 9-19).

Foremost, Israel has to be on its guard against itself. The message is clear, consoling and frightening at the same time. The dike that defends the purity, and therefore the salvation, of Israel holds but is subjected to great pressure and is always on the verge of collapsing. Most dangerous are the moral sins that produce impurity: murder (7:33; 21:19), idolatry (1:9; 11:4, 16-17; 20:7; 21:5; 30:10), and, in particular, sexual immorality (4:22; 7:20-21; 9:15; 16:5-6; 20:3-6; 23:14; 25:1, 7; 30:2-17; 33:7-20; 41:16-17, 25-26; 50:5): "There is no sin greater than the fornication which they commit upon the earth because Israel is a holy nation to the Lord his God, and a nation of inheritance, and a nation of priests, and a royal nation, and a (special) possession. And there is nothing which appears which is as defiled as this among the holy people" (33:20).

Jubilees is obsessed with maintaining boundaries between the clean and the unclean, the holy and the profane. Any violation of God's order that produces impurity is a mortal danger for the salvation of the chosen people. Hence Jubilees insists on following the ritual laws with the utmost accuracy and respecting the liturgical times that God has established since the beginning of creation. The Jewish feasts are written in the heavenly tablets and are celebrated in heaven before being performed on earth (cf.

6:18). The 364-day solar calendar is the heavenly calendar that regulates the heavenly liturgy by establishing a series of holy and profane days. No one is allowed to change the appointed times (6:32-35). Jubilees' *post-eventum* prophecy envisages the present, when some "evil" people, "examining the moon diligently, will corrupt the appointed times . . . and will make a day of testimony a reproach and a profane day a festival, and will mix up everything, a holy day (as) profaned and a profane (one) for a holy day" (6:36-37).

For the first time in Jewish thought we have an explicit polemic against the lunar calendar. Although the solar calendar in Jubilees is the same as in the earlier Enochic tradition, the Astronomical Book does not bear traces of a rival lunar calendar but only of a slightly different solar calendar.[25] Jubilees attributes the calendrical change to the influence of the Gentiles and presents it as a new phenomenon to be corrected with the greatest urgency. The best way to assess the evidence is to assume, with James C. VanderKam, that the solar calendar was the traditional priestly calendar of the second temple, shared by both the Zadokites and the Enochians, while the lunar calendar was introduced by Menelaus and Antiochus IV during the Maccabean crisis, as the book of Daniel attests, blaming the "iniquitous king" for "changing the feast days" (Dan 7:25). The lunar calendar was the Hellenistic calendar, as Jubilees records: "they [will] forget the feasts of the covenant and walk in the feasts of the Gentiles" (Jub 6:35).[26]

While the Maccabees took the Zadokite torah as the foundation of Jewish identity, there is no indication that they did the same with the Zadokite calendar. The doctrine of predestination, a fundamental principle in Jubilees, was apparently not as relevant for the Maccabees or, in general, for many Jews who accepted the change with ease. Jubilees made its plea for the restoration of the solar calendar soon after the calendrical change, when it was still possible to consider it as an unfortunate yet temporary side effect of the Maccabean crisis.

25. Sacchi, "The Two Calendars of the Book of Astronomy," in *Jewish Apocalyptic*, 128-39.

26. J. C. VanderKam, "The Origin, Character, and Early History of the 364-Day Calendar: A Reassessment of Jaubert's Hypotheses," *CBQ* 41 (1979) 390-411; idem, "2 Maccabees 6:7a and Calendrical Change in Jerusalem," *JSJ* 12 (1981) 52-74; Sacchi, "I due calendari," in *Storia del Secondo Tempio,* 454-61.

In Jubilees the restoration of the solar calendar was an irreplaceable element in a comprehensive platform aimed at strengthening the purity of the chosen people and the boundaries that separate them from the wicked nations (cf. 9:14-15). "Separate yourself from the Gentiles, and do not eat with them, and do not perform deeds like theirs. And do not become associates of theirs. Because their deeds are defiled, and their ways are contaminated, and despicable, and abominable" (22:16). Even on the individual level, relations with Gentiles are a mortal danger for the entire chosen people. Bringing with it the contamination of evil and impurity, a relationship with a Gentile signifies the weakening and eventually the end of the requirements for salvation. It is therefore a possibility that must be attacked with every means available, with the conscious and unpitying energy of a doctor trying to avoid the spread of a contagious disease. The ruthless revenge of Jacob's sons, led by Levi, against the Shechemites (cf. Gen 34) is raised to the level of a paradigm: "And if there be any man in Israel who wishes to give his daughter or his sister to any man who is from the seed of the Gentiles, let him surely die, and let him be stoned. . . . And also the woman will be burned with fire. . . . And there is no limit of days for this law. And there is no remission or forgiveness . . . because it is a defilement and is contemptible to Israel. And Israel will not be cleansed from this defilement" (Jub 30:7-17).

The identification between evil and impurity makes separation the new password for salvation in a way that was previously unknown in Judaism, in both the Enochic and the Zadokite traditions. Although the harshest words are reserved for those Jews who risk the purity of Israel, the separation that Jubilees promotes is essentially between Jews and Gentiles, not properly within the Jewish people themselves. Jubilees does not use the language of the remnant. No special group appears on the scene as the recipient of divine instruction. Jubilees claims to represent the majority of the Jews against a minority of traitors in a time that in its view was the beginning of the *eschaton*. The theology of separation in Jubilees is not the last recourse of people devoured by a minority complex, who feel persecuted and isolated and struggle to defend themselves. On the contrary, it betrays a majority complex of people who were confident that their time was the time of the conversion of Israel and that their hopes would soon be fulfilled. They expected to see the deviants persecuted and rejected. The audience of Jubilees is evidently to be found among the nation as a whole, not among an embattled sectarian community. "The most significant difference between Jubilees and the [sectarian] writings from Qumran . . . is the fact that Jubilees does not reflect any significant break with the larger national body. . . . The priestly author of Jubilees presents his theological work with the authority of one who understands himself to be representing 'the normative, orthodox' position. . . . He is writing at a time when he expects a general return to the 'normative' position which he represents. . . . Undoubtedly, his hope was frustrated. It would not be too long before his views would be ignored or contested."[27]

In the aftermath of the Maccabean revolt, the Enochians gained momentum, confidence, perhaps even popularity, to such an extent that they attempted to speak as the most authentic voice of the entire people of Israel. The decline of the house of Zadok not only proved the truth of their opposition but also made them look at themselves as the most obvious candidates to become the spiritual guides of Israel during the final days. For a long time they had been dreaming of, and preparing themselves for, this moment. In the euphoria of their victory over their Zadokite adversaries, they could not imagine that new adversaries and competitors soon would make their great illusion turn into disappointment.

3. The Temple Scroll (11QT)

The book of Jubilees opened the path not only to a harmonization between Zadokite and Enochic literature but also to the production of "pseudo-Zadokite" or "pseudo-Mosaic" texts. The best example of this literature is the Temple Scroll (11Q19-20 [11QT[a,b]]).[28]

When Yigael Yadin first published the Temple Scroll,[29] he presented it as a sectarian document, a product of the Qumran community. This view, perpetuated and popularized in subsequent influential introductions to the

27. O. S. Wintermute, "Jubilees," in *OTP* 2.44, 48; cf. P. R. Davies, *Behind the Essenes: History and Ideology in the Dead Sea Scrolls,* BJS 94 (Atlanta: Scholars Press, 1987) 117.

28. The most important monographs on the Temple Scroll are listed in the bibliography at the end of this volume.

29. Y. Yadin, *Megillat ha-miqdaš,* 3 vols. (Jerusalem: Sifriyat maariv, 1977). In English: *The Temple Scroll,* 3 vols. (Jerusalem: Israel Exploration Society, 1983).

Dead Sea Scrolls, is now questioned by most specialists, who (albeit from different perspectives) see the Temple Scroll as a presectarian document.[30]

Many elements closely relate the Temple Scroll and Jubilees.[31] Some have even attempted to show that the two documents were separate halves of a single work or were written by the same author.[32] Although the presence of disagreements makes common authorship "quite unlikely," scholars agree with James C. VanderKam that Jubilees and the Temple Scroll "are very closely related works, despite their sharply divergent character. . . . They express the same line of thought. . . . The authors of the two books belonged to the same legal and exegetical tradition."[33]

Gershon Brin has recently shown how the phrase "which I tell you on this mountain" (11QT 51:6-7), unparalleled in the biblical text, depends on Jubilees. The phrase presupposes that "the author refers to a text that included such a description of God calling Moses to come up to Mount Sinai in order to write the law and the stone tablets according to his dictation."[34] A comparison between the Temple Scroll and the Hebrew fragments of Jubilees demonstrates that that text was Jubilees ("[pay at-

30. For the older view see G. Vermes, *The Dead Sea Scrolls in English,* 3rd ed. (Sheffield: Sheffield Academic Press, 1988) 128-58; E. Schürer, *The History of the Jewish People in the Age of Jesus Christ,* rev. G. Vermes, et al., 3/1 (Edinburgh: T. & T. Clark, 1986) 406-20. Among the first to criticize Yadin's position were B. A. Levine, "The Temple Scroll: Aspects of Its Historical Provenance and Literary Character," *BASOR* 232 (1978) 5-23; L. H. Schiffman, "The Temple Scroll in Literary and Philological Perspective," in W. S. Green, ed., *Approaches to Ancient Judaism: Theory and Practice,* vol. 2, BJS 9 (Chico, Calif.: Scholars Press, 1983) 143-58; H. Stegemann, "Das Land in der Tempelrolle und in anderen Texten aus den Qumranfunden," in G. Strecker, ed., *Das Land Israel in biblischer Zeit* (Göttingen: Vandenhoeck & Ruprecht, 1983) 154-71.

31. On the relationship between Jubilees and the Temple Scroll, see G. Brin, "Regarding the Connection between the Temple Scroll and the Book of Jubilees," *JBL* 112 (1993) 108-9; J. C. VanderKam, "The Temple Scroll and the Book of Jubilees," in G. J. Brooke, ed., *Temple Scroll Studies,* JSPSup 7 (Sheffield: JSOT Press, 1989) 211-36; C. M. H. Lignée, "La place du livre des Jubilés et des Rouleau du Temple dans l'histoire du mouvement Essénien: Ces deux ouvrages ont-ils été écrits par le Maître de Justice?" *RevQ* 13 (1988) 331-45.

32. For the former see B. Z. Wacholder, *The Dawn of Qumran: The Sectarian Torah and the Teacher of Righteousness* (Cincinnati: Hebrew Union College Press, 1983). For the latter see Lignée, "La place du livre des Jubilés."

33. VanderKam, "The Temple Scroll and the Book of Jubilees," 231-32.

34. Brin, "Regarding the Connection," 108.

tention to all the wo]rds which I tell you [on this mountain]," 4Q216 [4QJub[a]] 1:12-13 = Jub 1:5).[35]

Brin's contribution is particularly important because it illuminates the nature of the Temple Scroll and its special relationship with Jubilees. Like Jubilees, the Temple Scroll presents itself as a Mosaic revelation parallel to the Zadokite torah. From a literary point of view, one can say that the document is a harmonized torah, or better, the work of a "creative legalist, who exploited divine revelation in recognizable, logical ways in order to allow its hidden meanings to surface."[36] The self-identification of the Temple Scroll, however, is otherwise. It does not recognize the Mosaic torah as its source. It claims to be an independent revelation from God that drew its authority from the same archetype, the heavenly tablets.

Like Jubilees, the Temple Scroll expresses the view of a priestly circle that opposes the Jerusalem establishment and has serious reservations about the legitimacy of the second temple. The preeminence of Levi over Judah ("the high priest will offer the [holocaust of the Levites] first, and, after it, he will burn the holocaust of the tribe of Judah," 11QT 23:10-11; cf. 24:10-11) parallels the blessing of Isaac in Jub 31:8-32, where Levi and Judah are similarly singled out among Jacob's sons and Levi obtains the primacy. Studies on the sources of the Temple Scroll have also concurrently shown that the document is rooted in pre-Maccabean traditions reflecting a dissident Levitical interpretation of the Zadokite torah.[37] Jubilees provided the setting that made it possible to

35. On the Jubilees fragments from Qumran, see J. C. VanderKam and J. T. Milik, "The First Jubilees Manuscript from Qumran Cave 4: A Preliminary Publication," *JBL* 110 (1991) 243-70; J. C. VanderKam, "The Jubilees Fragments from Qumran Cave 4," in J. Trebolle Barrera and L. Vegas Montaner, eds., *The Madrid Qumran Congress: Proceedings of the International Congress on the Dead Sea Scrolls, Madrid, 18-21 March, 1991,* STDJ 11/1-2 (Leiden: Brill, 1992) 2.635-48.

36. P. R. Callaway, "Extending Divine Revelation: Micro-Compositional Strategies in the Temple Scroll," in Brooke, ed., *Temple Scroll Studies,* 148-62 (quotation on p. 161). For the view that it is a harmonized torah, see Y. Yadin, *The Temple Scroll: The Hidden Law of the Dead Sea Sect* (New York: Random House, 1985).

37. D. D. Swanson, *The Temple Scroll and the Bible: The Methodology of 11QT,* STDJ 14 (Leiden: Brill, 1995); F. García Martínez, "Sources et rédaction du Rouleau du Temple," *Hen* 13 (1991) 219-52; M. O. Wise, *A Critical Study of the Temple Scroll from Qumran Cave 11,* SAOC 49 (Chicago: Oriental Institute, 1990); A. M. Wilson and L. Wills, "Literary Sources for the Temple Scroll," *HTR* 75 (1982) 275-88.

mingle this anti-Zadokite tradition with the Mosaic revelation, as a better, additional, and more reliable copy of the heavenly tablets.

Like Jubilees, the Temple Scroll endorses a solar calendar that is identical to the 364-day cultic calendar of the Astronomical Book and Jubilees. The correspondence of rituals and festivals between Jubilees and the Temple Scroll is virtually total.[38]

The sum of the evidence leads to the conclusion that those who composed the Temple Scroll belong to the same group within Enochic Judaism that shortly before had produced the book of Jubilees.

However, the Temple Scroll goes beyond Jubilees in transposing Jubilees' theology of separation into a detailed and consistent constitution for the present, the final days of Israel in this world before the end of days and the world to come. This constitution provides the plan for an interim temple, not envisaged in Jubilees, as well as a new, stricter code of purity laws, which, with greater accuracy, meets the requirements set by Jubilees.

Dream Visions and Jubilees had foretold the restoration of the temple as a divinely created sanctuary in the world to come (cf. 1 En 90:29; Jub 1:15-17, 26-29). 11QT 29:2-10 indicates clearly that the purpose of the Temple Scroll was not to describe that eschatological temple and its rituals, the temple as it will be in the world to come but is not yet. Instead, the Temple Scroll provides a construction plan and a system of laws for an interim temple, "until the day of [the new] creation, when I [[= God]] shall create my temple, establishing it for myself forever." The Temple Scroll describes a temple for the present world, a temple as it is not but should be and will be as soon as the author's party obtains the authority to build and operate it.

The "gigantic dimensions of the visionary temple," with its additional third courtyard that would have encompassed most of the city of Jerusalem,[39] betray the other major concern of the document, that of protecting

---

38. VanderKam, "The Temple Scroll and the Book of Jubilees"; cf. Y. Yadin, "The Temple Scroll," *BA* 30 (1967) 135-39; J. M. Baumgarten, "The Calendars of the Book of Jubilees and the Temple Scroll," *VT* 37 (1987) 71-78.

39. M. Broshi, "The Gigantic Dimensions of the Visionary Temple in the Temple Scroll," *BARev* 13 (1987) 36-37. Cf. L. H. Schiffman, "Architecture and Law: The Temple and Its Courtyards in the Temple Scroll," in J. Neusner, et al., eds., *From Ancient Israel to Modern Judaism: Intellect in Quest of Understanding: Essays in Honor of Marvin Fox*, vol. 1, BJS 159 (Atlanta: Scholars Press, 1989) 267-84.

the purity of Israel as the chosen people. A comparison between the Temple Scroll and the decree of Antiochus III (223-187 BCE) recorded by Josephus (*Ant.* 12.145-46) gives us the measure of how and why the author of the Temple Scroll wanted to change the purity code. Published at the beginning of the second century BCE, when the Seleucids took control of Jerusalem, the decree of Antiochus III marked the new king's acceptance of the principles of Zadokite Judaism.[40] According to Josephus the text was written "in honor of the temple," that is, confirming the status quo. The decree recognizes the authority and the rights of the Zadokite priests by making them the payees of the penalty of "three thousand drachmae of silver" against "whomever would transgress any of [the king's] orders."

The text contains two sets of laws about purity, one concerning the temple and the other concerning the city of Jerusalem. Access to the temple is barred to all Gentiles and to Jews who do not follow proper purity laws. "It shall be lawful for no foreigners to come within the limits of the temple; which thing is forbidden also to the Jews, except to those who, according to their own customs, have purified themselves" (*Ant.* 12.145). The second part of the royal decree regulates access to Jerusalem. The city is off limits for "any animal which is forbidden for the Jews to eat"; the law extends also to their "flesh" and their "skin" (*Ant.* 12.146). In line with the traditional principles of Zadokite Judaism, the temple and the city are subjected to different degrees of purity.

The Temple Scroll promotes a stricter code of purity that does not make any distinction between the degree of purity of the temple and the city. Jacob Milgrom calls it "one of the far-reaching innovations of the Temple Scroll,"[41] and it was indeed. The requirements of purity for the temple are extended to the whole city of Jerusalem. While in Lev 15:18 sexual impurity is a bar to participation in the temple cult, according to the Temple Scroll it makes people unworthy of dwelling in Jerusalem: "Anyone who lies with his wife and has an ejaculation, for three days shall not enter anywhere in the city of the temple in which I shall install my name" (11QT 45:11-12). Correspondingly, the requirements of purity for the

---

40. On the decree of Antiochus III, see L. L. Grabbe, *Judaism from Cyrus to Hadrian,* 2 vols. (Minneapolis: Fortress, 1992) 1.246-47.

41. J. Milgrom, "The Qumran Cult: Its Exegetical Principles," in Brooke, ed., *Temple Scroll Studies,* 165-80 (quotation on p. 174); cf. L. H. Schiffman, "Exclusion from the Sanctuary and the City of the Sanctuary," *HAR* 9 (1985) 315-17.

priests are extended to the entire people of Israel. The blind, who in Lev 21:17-20 are excluded from the priesthood, are now barred from entering the city of Jerusalem. "No blind person shall enter it throughout his whole life; he shall not defile the city in the center of which I dwell" (45:12-13).

The basic principle is that the temple-city is equivalent to the camp of Israel in the wilderness, and correspondingly the biblical laws concerning the purity of the Sinai encampment (Heb. *mhnh;* Deut 23; Num 5; Lev 13) are strictly applied to Jerusalem. "The city which I will sanctify, installing my name and my temple [within it] shall be holy and shall be clean from all types of impurity which could defile it. Everything that there is in it shall be pure and everything that goes into it shall be pure" (11QT 47:3-6). The prohibition on introducing skins of unclean animals is extended to include even the skins of pure animals. The higher degree of purity that distinguishes Jerusalem from any other Jewish city is now the same degree of purity as that of the temple. "All the hides of pure animals which they sacrifice in their cities they shall not bring into it. . . . You shall not defile the city within which I shall install my name and my temple. . . . You shall not purify any city among your cities like my city. What you sacrifice in my temple is pure for my temple; what you sacrifice in your cities is pure (only) for your cities" (11QT 47:7-17).

Compared with the rules of the decree of Antiochus III, the Temple Scroll signals a dramatic change from the principles of Zadokite Judaism. Lawrence H. Schiffman is correct in saying that "the text is a polemic against the existing order, calling for radical change in the order of the day, putting forward reforms in the areas of cultic, religious and political life."[42] As with Jubilees, however, the Temple Scroll promotes a concrete agenda of political and religious reform. It "is a program for the state during the period of the eschaton. It is not concerned with a sectarian separation from broader society — rather, it mandates what the 'establishment' is to be."[43] The spirit of the Temple Scroll is not isolationist but includes the whole of Israel as a homogeneous entity. Its protest is neither a hopeless cry nor a sad lamentation by an isolated minority group over the irreparable corruption of Israel. The experience of the Maccabean crisis has turned

42. L. Schiffman, "The Temple Scroll and the Nature of Its Law: The Status of the Question," in E. C. Ulrich and J. C. VanderKam, eds., *The Community of the Renewed Covenant: The Notre Dame Symposium on the Dead Sea Scrolls* (Notre Dame: University of Notre Dame Press, 1994) 37-55 (quotation on p. 51).

43. Wise, *Critical Study of the Temple Scroll,* 203.

Enochic Judaism from an opposition party to a party that is ready and eager to rule. With Jubilees and the Temple Scroll, the oppositional ideology of the earlier Enochic literature has been transformed into a platform for a new government of Israel.

4. The Proto-Epistle of Enoch, Including the Apocalypse of Weeks

Like the other Enochic books, the Epistle of Enoch (1 En 91–105) was already known before the discovery of the Dead Sea Scrolls through the Ethiopic version and a large Greek fragment containing 97:6–104:13.[44] But the Aramaic fragments found at Qumran have made an extraordinary contribution to the study of the document. On the one hand, quite unexpectedly, they have shown that ch. 105, missing in the Greek text (which jumps directly from 104:13 to 106:1) and generally considered a later addition, was part of the original composition. On the other hand, they have confirmed what scholars had been saying for some time, that the order of the opening chapters (91–93) was corrupt. Daniel C. Olson offers the simplest and most convincing reconstruction of the original sequence. He shows that the transmission of the Ethiopic text was disarranged, at a certain point, by the dislocation of one page in an ancient codex. With some confidence, we can say that the reconstructed sequence of chapters (91:1-10; 92:3–93:10; 91:11–92:2; 93:11–105:3) gives the original text of the Epistle.[45] The Qumran fragments have also shown that the document, which may have once circulated as an autonomous work (see 4QEn^g ar), was already associated with the previous Enochic texts by the end of the second or the beginning of the first century BCE, forming a single composition that had chs. 106–7 as its closing section (see 4QEn^c ar).

But the discovery of the Qumran fragments has not solved all the

---

44. The most important monographs on 1 Enoch, including the Epistle of Enoch, are listed in the bibliography at the end of this volume. On the Greek version, see M. Black, *Apocalypsis Henochi Graece,* PVTG 3 (Leiden: Brill, 1970); C. Bonner, *The Last Chapters of Enoch in Greek* (London: Christophers, 1937).

45. D. S. Olson, "Recovering the Original Sequence of 1 Enoch 91–93," *JSP* 11 (1993) 69-104.

mysteries of the Epistle. Scholars are divided about the composite or unitary nature of the document. Some isolate the Apocalypse of Weeks (93:1-10; 91:11–92:1) as a previous (pre-Maccabean) and independent piece of literature that the (post-Maccabean) author of the Epistle of Enoch incorporated into his work, a hypothesis that was traditional among former interpreters.[46] Others see no compelling reason to reject the view that the (pre-Maccabean) author of the Apocalypse of Weeks is also the author of the rest of the Epistle.[47]

Each party seems to have a string in its bow, a strong argument to support its view. On the one hand, the Epistle of Enoch, in its present form, displays several internal inconsistencies, both literary and ideological, a fact that would better fit in a composite document. On the other hand, the Qumran fragments show that the Apocalypse of Weeks can hardly be isolated from its immediate literary context, a fact that would suggest a unitary composition.

A reassessment of the Qumran fragments and of the internal structure of the Ethiopic text may let us overcome the conflicting evidence and develop a new hypothesis about the origin and the date of the Epistle of Enoch. It is widely recognized that the document has a nonsectarian authorship. Because of the fragments found among the Dead Sea Scrolls, however, scholars take for granted that the Epistle of Enoch, as we know it from the Greek and Ethiopic versions, was read and preserved by the Qumran community. The pre-Maccabean date of the Apocalypse of Weeks, or of the entire Epistle, depends largely on this assumption. But the evidence that the Epistle of Enoch was known at Qumran is far from being conclusive.

I argue here that the sectarian community preserved only a much shorter mid-second-century-BCE text, a presectarian document that I would call the Proto-Epistle of Enoch. This hypothesis restores the original literary context of the Apocalypse of Weeks, that larger context from which the Qumran fragments have shown it cannot be isolated. The Apocalypse of Weeks was part of the Proto-Epistle and was written by the same author.

46. M. Black, "The Apocalypse of Weeks in the Light of 4QEn," *VT* 28 (1978) 464-69; G. W. E. Nickelsburg, "The Epistle of Enoch and the Qumran Literature," *JJS* 33 (1982) 333-48. Cf. R. H. Charles, *The Book of Enoch* (Oxford: Clarendon, 1893); F. Martin, *Le livre d'Hénoch* (Paris: Letouzey et Ané, 1906).

47. Milik, *Books of Enoch;* García Martínez, *Qumran and Apocalyptic;* J. C. VanderKam, "The Epistle of Enoch," in *Enoch: A Man for All Generations* (Columbia: University of South Carolina Press, 1995) 89-101.

Furthermore, this hypothesis ascribes to the Proto-Epistle and to the Apocalypse of Weeks a more likely post-Maccabean setting and provides a coherent explanation for the internal inconsistencies of the Epistle by stating that the text we know from the Greek and the Ethiopic was a later, first-century-BCE composition unattested at Qumran.

The Epistle of Enoch consists of three speeches that Enoch delivered to his sons: (a) 91:1-10; 92:3-5; (b) 93:1-10; 91:11-17; and (c) 91:18–92:2; 93:11–105:3. Each speech is preceded by an introduction, which consists of a short opening statement by Enoch. The introductions sing the praises of Enoch as the supreme revealer and summarize the content of each speech.

In the introduction to the first section (91:1-2), Enoch asks his son Methuselah to gather the family, "for a voice calls me and the spirit is poured over me so that I may show you everything that shall happen to you forever." The speech is a consistent apocalyptic description of the history of humankind until the day of the great judgment (91:3-10; 92:3-5). Enoch exhorts his sons "to walk in righteousness" and not to associate "with those who walk with two hearts" (91:4). The reference is primarily to the Book of the Watchers (chs. 10–11), and to "those days" (91:8; cf. 10:13ff.) when evil and iniquity will be destroyed and the righteous will live forever. But the insistence on the concept of the degeneration of history ("I know that the state of violence will intensify upon the earth," 91:5), a concept unknown in the earliest Enochic literature, points to a post-Maccabean setting. The connection of the speech with Dream Visions is so obvious that in the tradition of the Ethiopic text, and in the view of some modern commentators, ch. 91 was often read as an appendix to Dream Visions rather than as an introduction to a new book of Enoch.[48]

The first section of the Epistle is consistent and bears no traces of later interpolations. That it was part of the Proto-Epistle is proved by 4Q212 (4QEn^g ar), where the end of the first speech is attached to the beginning of the second section that includes the Apocalypse of Weeks.

In the introduction to the second section (93:1-2), Enoch announces that this time the subject of his speech is the chosen ("the children of righteousness, the elect ones of the world, and the plant of righteousness"),

---

48. According to Ms. Kebran 9/II (Hammerschmidt-Tanasee 9/II), 1 En 92:1 is the beginning of the "fifth" Book of Enoch. Cf. S. Uhlig, *Das äthiopische Henochbuch* (Gütersloh: Mohr, 1984).

which is exactly what Jubilees had found missing in Dream Visions and what the Apocalypse of Weeks is about. The relationship with Jubilees is emphasized also by another significant detail. To the established authority that the earlier Enochic tradition had given to Enoch as a heavenly seer, now the text adds the specific authoritive claim that Jubilees made the essential foundation of any revelation: "I have learned from the words of the angels and understood from the heavenly tablets."

The second speech of Enoch is the one known as the Apocalypse of Weeks, a sketch of human history divided into ten periods ("weeks") and ending with the final everlasting age of righteousness ("many weeks without number forever"). While the division of history into ten periods is a common pattern in apocalyptic literature (e.g., the "seventy weeks" of years of Daniel could be also seen as ten jubilees),[49] a reading of the Apocalypse of Weeks against its own context suggests, once again, a post-Maccabean setting. As in Jubilees and in contrast to Daniel, history is not preordained only in its final development or in one of its segments, but since the beginning, in all its stages. As in Jubilees and in contrast to Dream Visions, comprehensive historical determinism is the necessary foundation for the existence in the corrupted world of a group of chosen people ("the plant of righteousness"; cf. Jub 1:15). History is marked not only by degeneration but also by the uninterrupted presence of the chosen.

The first week shows the starting point; it was the time in which Enoch was born and "righteousness was sti[ll enduring]" (4QEn^g ar 3:23-24 = 1 En 93:3). The second week is the time of the flood, when "deceit and violence will increase," but also the time when "a man [[= Noah]] will be saved." The text does not, however, leave room for any optimism: "iniquity will grow" even after the flood (4QEn^g ar 3:24-25 = 1 En 93:4). The third week is the time of the election of Abraham and Jacob-Israel, "the plant of righteousness forever" (1 En 93:5). Although the first three weeks follow the traditional path of the earlier Enochic literature, the fourth week signals a dramatic change by mentioning the gift of the Mosaic torah (1 En 93:6), showing that Enochic Judaism had learned the lesson of Jubilees and the Temple Scroll in now also embracing this tenet of Zadokite Judaism as a constitutive element of Jewish identity.

By putting the temple at the center of its discourse, the author of the

---

49. A. Yarbro Collins, "Numerical Symbolism in Apocalyptic Literature," *ANRW* 2.21.2 (1984) 1222-87.

Apocalypse reveals his priestly roots. In the chiastic structure of the Apocalypse, the core is the construction of the first temple in the fifth week ("a house of glory and sovereignty will be built forever," 1 En 93:7) and its destruction at the end of the sixth week ("the house of sovereignty will be burnt with fire; and therein the whole race of the chosen root will be dispersed," 93:8). The sixth week also makes clear that both the law and the temple will be betrayed during the time of the monarchy; it is a time when "all [people] will be blindfolded, and the hearts of them all will forget wisdom."

Consistent with the principles of Enochic Judaism, the Apocalypse describes the postexilic period, "the seventh week," not as the time of restoration but as a time of increasing sin: "an apostate generation will arise; all their deeds will be at fault." No reference is made to the construction of the second temple. The restoration has not occurred yet; Israel is still in exile. Here, however, a significant change occurs, even from the tradition of Jubilees and the Temple Scroll. In the Apocalypse we have the emergence of the idea of a chosen group (a minority) destined in the seventh week to receive the "wisdom" that the majority has forgotten. This minority group is not completely separate from Israel, which, as in Jubilees, remains the "plant of righteousness"; but its appearance is a necessary step that defines an interim time. The group is the nucleus of the future true and restored Israel. They are the chosen among the chosen, a minority group, which testifies to the righteousness of the plant, the majority of the Jewish people. "At the close [of the seventh week], the chosen ones will be selected as witnesses of the righteousness of the plant; they will be given wisdom and knowledge sevenfold. They will uproot the foundations of violence and the work of deceit in it in order to carry out righteousness" (4QEn^g ar 4:11-14 = 1 En 93:9-10).

Unlike the author of Dream Visions and in line with the tendency of Jubilees, the author of the Apocalypse of Weeks does not believe that the world to come is at hand. The emergence of the chosen among the chosen does belong to the end of times, but it is only the beginning of the long process. "The end is not exactly a fixed point. Rather we have an eschatological scenario in which there is a series of 'ends' as the old order passes away and is replaced by the new."[50] The three-stage scenario following the election of the chosen among the chosen parallels in reverse

50. J. J. Collins, *Apocalypticism in the Dead Sea Scrolls,* 54.

the first three weeks. The first stage is the restoration of Israel and the rebuilding of a new temple, a concept that is very similar to the interim temple described by the Temple Scroll. As in the Temple Scroll, a new temple on earth belongs to the next future of the author (the end of the eighth week) but is not yet the eschatological temple in the world to come. "After this, the eighth week will come, the one of righteousness, in which [a sword] will be given to all the righteous, for them to carry out righteous judgment against the wicked who will be delivered into their hands. At its close, they will gain riches in righteousness and there will be built the house of sovereignty of the Great One, in his magnificence, for all eternal generations" (4QEn§ ar 4:15-18 = 1 En 91:12-13).

The second stage is the restoration of humankind. "And after that, the ninth week. [In it] will be revealed jus[tice and just judgment] to all the sons of the whole earth. All those who ac[t wickedly will vanish] from all the whole earth and they shall be hurled into the [eternal] well. All [will see] the just eternal path" (4QEn§ ar 4:19-22 = 1 En 91:14).

Finally, we have the return to the primordial stage with the final judgment and the new creation, which opens the path to the eternal glory of the world to come. "And after [that, the tenth week. In its seventh part] there will be an eternal judgment and the time of the great judgment [. . .]. The first heaven will pass away [and there will appear a new heaven and all the powers] of heaven will rise throughout all eternity, shining [seven times more]" (4QEn§ ar 4:22-25 = 1 En 91:15-16).

The glorious description of the world to come fulfills the vision of the ten weeks and closes Enoch's second speech. "[After that, there will be] many weeks [the number of which will not] have an end [ever, in which goodness and justice] will be achieved [and there shall be no more sin forever]" (4QEn§ ar 4:25-26 = 1 En 91:17).

The second section of the Epistle, including the Apocalypse of Weeks, is the best-preserved section from Qumran. The unity of the literary structure and the common reference to the "plant of righteousness" offer no reason, ideological or literary, for isolating the Apocalypse of Weeks from the context that the Aramaic fragments give to it, the context of three connected speeches by Enoch.

Given the consistency of the first two sections, one would expect the third part of the Epistle to follow the same pattern. The introduction (91:18–92:1) is consistent; it contains all one would expect to find. The brief eulogy of Enoch ("he is the writer of all the signs of wisdom among all the people, he is blessed and noble in all the earth," 92:1) certifies the authority of the revealer, while connecting him to the gift of wisdom promised to the chosen. The opening statement, an admonition "to walk in the ways of righteousness . . . for all those who walk in the ways of injustice shall perish" (91:18-19 = 4QEn^g ar 2:17-21), repeats the invitation to "his sons" made in the first speech. Now, after the Apocalypse of Weeks, it is clear that for the author "the sons of Enoch" are the forerunners of a group that belongs to the present, "the chosen of the seventh week." The third speech is thus announced as a discourse about the two ways, the way of the righteous and the way of the sinners. It begins with an encouragement by Enoch to his sons (and to later followers) not to worry about what they have learned from the Apocalypse of Weeks. "Let not your spirit be troubled by the times, for the Holy and Great One has appointed times for all things" (92:2).

A series of rhetorical questions follows, introduced by the clause, "Who among all men can know . . . ?" (93:11-14). This part, which many modern commentators call the Nature Poem, has always been something of an enigma. In the present context, it is rather obscure and sounds a generic warning that, after all, nobody can fully understand the mysteries of God, an odd statement in a tradition that is claiming exactly the contrary, thanks to its connection with a revealer, Enoch, who lives in heaven.

Then the text makes some sense again. Consistent with the Apocalypse of Weeks and the introductory statement, in a first admonition (94:1-2) Enoch invites "his sons" to "walk in righteousness" and announces to them that a group of chosen people will finally arise. They will be the ones to whom "the ways of injustice and death shall be revealed," and "they shall keep themselves at a distance from (those ways) and would not follow them" (94:2). To "those righteous ones" a second admonition is reserved ("now to you, those righteous ones, I say," 94:3-5). They are commanded "not to walk in the evil way, or in the way of death" and "not to draw near to them lest you be destroyed." The time of their election is not yet the final end; they have to face the opposition of the "sinners."

After 94:5 the tone changes; the discourse is suddenly interrupted. The Ethiopic text contains a long series of woes (94:6-10; 95:4-7; 96:4-8; 97:7-10; 98:8–99:2; 99:11-15; 100:7-9; 103:5) against the sinners and blessings for the righteous, now identified with the well-to-do and the poor, respectively. No further mention is made of the existence of a group of chosen among the chosen, while any reference to the "wisdom" that God has to provide them suddenly disappears. The focus shifts from the present relationship between the righteous and the sinners in this world to the *eschaton* of their respective destinies on judgment day ("in those days," 96:8; 97:5; 99:3, 10; 100:1, 4, 13; 102:1). The text is direct and apodictic in threatening the sinners and encouraging the righteous ("I swear to you," 98:1, 4, 6; 99:6; 103:1; 104:3). By taking up the same language of God against the fallen angels as used in the Book of the Watchers (cf. chs. 12–16), Enoch reminds his readers of God's inescapable judgment against sinners: "they shall have no peace" (94:6; 98:11, 15; 99:13; 101:3; 102:3; 103:8). This complex literary development makes the third speech of Enoch disproportionate and confused.

The change in content and vocabulary, which extends to the beginning of ch. 104, makes it highly probable that an interpolation was made in the original text at 94:5. Indeed, the consolatory discourse of Enoch continues at 104:7. According to the classical procedure of interpolation, a redactional verse (104:6) resumes the thread of the speech that the interpolated material has interrupted. "Now fear not, righteous ones, when you see the sinners waxing strong and their ways become benefiting; do not be partners with them, but keep far away from those who lean onto their own injustice, for you are to be partners with the good-hearted people of heaven" (104:6). The verse repeats the admonition of Enoch to the "righteous ones" (94:3-5), adding only a reference to the angels that smooths the transition by making the verse also the conclusion of the preceding section: "I swear unto you that in heaven the angels will remember you for good" (104:1-5). The change of tone is once again apparent. The focus shifts back from the *eschaton* to the present. Not accidentally, the text resumes with a new admonition, the third one of the original series, reserved for the sinners ("Now, you sinners," 104:7-9), who were the last group mentioned at the end of the second admonition, exactly as the second admonition had addressed the "righteous," who were mentioned at the end of the first admonition. The sinners are reproached and reminded that their "sins are being written down every day." Interestingly, the passage, similar to the first two admonitions but unlike the interpolated material, does not refer to the final judgment. This detail is striking when one considers that the interpolator duplicates the same text almost verbatim in 98:6-8 with the significant double addition of the phrase "until the day of your judgment."

If we eliminate the section 94:6–104:6, the third section of the Proto-Epistle of Enoch regains its consistency. After the series of three admonitions (to the "sons of Enoch," to the "righteous ones," and to the "sinners"), which were the core of the speech, Enoch describes himself as the one who knows the "mysteries" of heaven and once again announces that "wisdom" will be given to the chosen in this world, "to the righteous and the wise." He also knows "Scriptures of joy, and all the righteous ones who learn from them the ways of truth shall rejoice" (104:10-13).

Now the Nature Poem at the beginning of Enoch's speech finally makes sense. "Once the reader moves beyond the first two questions, the transparent answer to each of them should be 'Enoch' . . . [he is] the one who knew and understood all these deep matters. Nevertheless, if that is the point, we have to infer it for ourselves; the author does not help us with it."[51] This is true for the Epistle of Enoch but was not true for the original text of the Proto-Epistle. The chiastic structure of Enoch's speech makes clear that the Nature Poem was not an invitation to humility. On the contrary, it was an overt exaltation of Enoch, who is "the one who among all men" knows the "mysteries" of heaven. We cannot blame the author for what the interpolator did.

Finally, the close of Enoch's speech (105:1-2) matches the beginning (92:2), with the common reference to the historical framework given by the Apocalypse of Weeks. The chosen have no reason to be "troubled by the times." God would assist them through history, and at the end they will become the guides of the children of the earth.

The third speech of Enoch was originally a shorter and consistent literary unit (92:2; 93:11–94:5; 104:7–105:2), similar in length and content to the previous two speeches. In the following chapter we explore why and when a later interpolator added to the text the long section 94:6–104:6 and created the new composition called the Epistle of Enoch. It is enough here to state that we have no evidence that the Epistle of Enoch, in the form we have from the Ethiopic and the Greek, was known at Qumran. The fact that the extant Aramaic fragments contain only the beginning of ch. 93 and a few remnants of the end of ch. 104 and ch. 105, with no traces of the interpolated section, may not be accidental.

The message of the Proto-Epistle is simple, direct, and entirely focused on the concept of election. As in Dream Visions, history is subjected to inexorable degeneration until the end, but, as Jubilees had claimed, in this world there is a distinctive group of chosen people, the plant of

---

51. VanderKam, *Enoch: A Man for All Generations,* 91.

righteousness, Israel. The Proto-Epistle adds that, at the beginning of the final times (the present of the author), God will choose a group from among the chosen. This group will receive special "wisdom" and will keep themselves separate from the rest of the people while acting on their behalf and thus preparing the way for the redemption of Israel and of the entire creation.

With its doctrine of double election, the Proto-Epistle of Enoch testifies to a further stage in the development of Enochic Judaism. By reestablishing clear boundaries and privileges for the chosen people based on an ambitious agenda of reforms to be shared by the entire community of Israel, Jubilees and the Temple Scroll signaled the emergence within Enochic Judaism of an attempt to distinguish clearly the chosen from the wicked, the faithful Jews from the non-Jews (to whom the minority of Jewish "traitors" was assimilated). This approach was apparently unsuccessful. While the Hasmoneans consolidated their power in Jerusalem, Enochic Judaism gradually came to realize that, within the Jewish people, they were the minority. With the Proto-Epistle of Enoch, the emphasis shifted from the entire people of Israel to a minority group that was the recipient of a special revelation and was called to a special mission on behalf of the entire people of Israel, as the first stage in the long series of final events.

It was a controversial move. The reference in the Proto-Epistle to "sinners," altering the Enochic scripture's "on the basis of their own speech" (104:10-11), seems to indicate that there were conflicts and disagreements, perhaps even within Enochic Judaism. It was the beginning of a period of controversy marked by growing sectarian attitudes. Without betraying their loyalty to the people of Israel, the Enochians now believed they did not have to wait for the conversion of Israel in order to carry out what they thought was the true interpretation of God's will. As the chosen among the chosen, they began developing a separate identity, and perhaps building a separate society, within Judaism.

5. The Halakhic Letter (4QMMT)

To the same stage in the development of the Enochic movement also belongs the Halakhic Letter (4QMMT; also known as Some of the Works of the Law), a document whose initial announcement in 1984 and subse-

quent publication in 1994 have produced the most recent outburst of ex-
citement in Qumran studies.[52]

The Halakhic Letter describes the birth of a schismatic group (the
"we" party) that addresses someone having authority (the "you" party)
about the reasons for their separation from a majority group (the "they"
party). The text is marked by a repetition of the refrains: "we maintain,"
"you know," "they do."

The "we" party, that is, the author's group, exhibits the distinctive
marks of Enochic Judaism. It promotes a calendar that is the same as the
solar calendar of the Astronomical Book, Jubilees, and the Temple Scroll
("the year is complete, three hundred and si[xty-four] days," 4QMMT 2).
The halakhah, centered on a code of purity laws, agrees with and depends
on the Temple Scroll.[53] Following the same trend of thought, the regulations
of the Sinai encampment are extended to the temple-city. "We think that
the temple [is the place of the tent of meeting, and Je]rusalem is the camp;
and outside the camp is [outside Jerusalem;] it is the camp of their cities. . . .
Jerusalem is the holy camp, the place which [God] has chosen from among
all the tribes of Is[rael, since Jer]usalem is the head of the camps of Israel"
(4QMMT 32-34, 63-65).

As in the other documents of Enochic Judaism, the exile belongs not
to the past but to the present of the Jewish people. Their sins have not yet
been forgiven. Consistent with the development of Enochic Judaism in the
post-Maccabean period, both the destruction of the first temple and the
transgression of the Mosaic torah are signs of sin and decline. "[And it is
written in the book of] Moses and in [the words of the prop]hets that
[blessings and curses] will come . . . [the bl]essings which c[ame upon]
him in the days of Solomon the son of David and also the curses which
came upon him from the [days of Je]roboam son of Nebat right up to the
capture of Jerusalem and of Zedekiah, king of Judah" (4QMMT 103-5).

As in the Proto-Epistle of Enoch, however, the process of degeneration has already begun to reverse. The present is the beginning of the final
events that would ultimately lead to the new creation. The present is the
time at the end of the seventh week, which was foretold in the Proto-Epistle

52. The most important monographs on the Halakhic Letter are listed in the
bibliography at the end of this volume.

53. L. H. Schiffman, "The Temple Scroll and the Systems of Jewish Law of the
Second Temple Period," in Brooke, ed., *Temple Scroll Studies,* 239-55.

as the first step toward the final conversion of Israel. "We are aware that part of the blessings and curses which are written in the b[ook of Mo]ses have come to pass, and that this is the end of days, when they will convert in Isra[el] for[ever . . .] and they will not backsli[de]" (4QMMT 20-22). This is the time in which God has selected the chosen from among the chosen. While the rest of Israel is under the influence of "the evil scheming and the counsel of Belial" (4QMMT 115), the chosen have to walk in the path of righteousness and keep separate from the sinners. "[You know that] we have separated from the rest of the peop[le and that we avoid] mingling in these affairs and associating with them in these matters. And you k[now that there is not] to be found in our hands deceit or betrayal or evil" (4QMMT 92-94).

Florentino García Martínez also points to "a pre-Qumranic context," and understands the Halakhic Letter "as coming from the parent group of the Qumran community. This pre-Qumranic group had already adopted the calendar, followed the halakhah we know from other Qumran compositions and started to develop some of the characteristic theological ideas we know in a much more developed form from the same Qumranic compositions."[54] But his conclusion that "the Halakhic Letter [4QMMT] seems to be directed not at the political power of Jerusalem or at the Hasmonean kings but at the religious group from which the [Qumran] sect detached itself" has many difficulties.[55] On the one hand, the "you" party is someone who has both religious and political authority over the entire people of Israel, someone who has "intellect and knowledge of the torah" and is asked to remember the example of the ancient "kings of Israel," in particular David. "Whoever of them who respected the torah was freed from his many afflictions; those who sought the torah [were forgiven] their sins" (4QMMT 109-14). The data better fit the Hasmonean dynasty, as most commentators recognize.

On the other hand, the "we" party does not seem to have the features of an extreme group that separates from an already sectarian community.

54. F. García Martínez, "4QMMT in a Qumran Context," in J. Kampen and M. J. Bernstein, eds., *Reading 4QMMT: New Perspectives on Qumran Law and History* (Atlanta: Scholars Press, 1996) 15-27 (quotation on p. 27).

55. F. García Martínez, "The Origins of the Essene Movement and of the Qumran Sect," in F. García Martínez and J. Trebolle Barrera, *The People of the Dead Sea Scrolls*, trans. W. G. E. Watson (Leiden: Brill, 1995) 77-96 (quotation on p. 93).

Lawrence H. Schiffman has made a strong case that the Letter is "a document from the earliest stage of the sect's development, when its members still hoped to return to participation in temple worship."[56] Schiffman also has convincingly demonstrated the similarities between the halakhah of the Letter and what rabbinic sources attribute to the Sadducees. Claiming, however, that "its origins and the roots of its halakhic tradition lie in the Sadducean Zadokite priesthood" goes beyond the evidence.[57] Whoever considered the postexilic period as a period of sin and degeneration could not be a nostalgic Zadokite. Not even the most dissident Zadokite could have denied the legitimacy of the second temple without denying his or her own identity. The presence of Sadducean elements in the Halakhic Letter is better explained by the fact that Enochic Judaism was a rival priestly tradition that challenged Zadokite Judaism from within, sharing, to a large extent, the same worldview and the same ideological categories. The common priestly roots of Zadokite and Enochic Judaism are enough to explain the Sadducean traits of the Halakhic Letter. The title of "dissident Zadokites" better applies to the Enochians than to any group of post-Maccabean Sadducees.

There is clear indication that the "we" party has only recently separated from the majority, the "they" party, and considers the estrangement only temporary. The "we" party still sees in the new situation, with the end of the power of the house of Zadok, the opportunity to restore an order that they considered absent since the destruction of the first temple. There is a self-imposed separation, but not isolationism. The "we" party still views itself as part of the community of Israel. The tone of the Letter is respectful and conciliatory; the goal is to explain to the leaders of Israel, the "you" party, the reasons that forced them to separate. The "we" party speaks to the entirety of Israel and seeks reconciliation. There is even hope that the Hasmoneans would eventually side with them. "We have written to you some of the precepts of the torah which we think are good for you and for your people, for in you we see intellect and knowledge of the torah. Reflect on all these matters and seek from him so that he may support your counsel and keep far from you the evil scheming and the counsel of Belial,

56. L. H. Schiffman, "Origin and Early History of the Qumran Sect," *BA* 58/1 (1995) 37-48 (quotation on p. 41); cf. idem, "Evidence of the Halakhic Letter," in *Reclaiming the Dead Sea Scrolls* (Philadelphia and Jerusalem: Jewish Publication Society, 1994) 83-89.

57. Schiffman, "Origin and Early History," 41.

so that at the end of time, you may rejoice in finding that some of our words are true. And it shall be reckoned to you as in justice when you do what is upright and good before him, for your good and that of Israel" (4QMMT 112-18).

Even the traditional polemics of Enochic Judaism against the Jerusalem priesthood are softened. Now that the Zadokites have lost their power, the author of the Halakhic Letter clarifies that his party does not contest the legitimacy of the Aaronite priesthood. His anger is directed only against "a part" of the sons of Aaron, which leaves the door open to the possibility of an agreement with the other part. "And the sons of Aaron are the [holiest of the holy,] but you know that a part of the priests and of the peo[ple mingle] and they squeeze each other and defile the [holy] seed [and also] their (own) [seed] with fornications" (4QMMT 81-85).

The attitude of the "we" group is similar to that of the Proto-Epistle of Enoch. The group is determined to keep its separate identity; but, at the same time, they are convinced about having a mission for the entirety of Israel, and confident that at the end the people and the Jewish authorities would recognize the truth of their position. Rather than testifying to the birth of the Qumran community, the Halakhic Letter seems to testify to the time in which the parent Enochic group, or part of it, decided that, as the chosen of the seventh week and the witnesses of the truth, they had to walk in the path of righteousness without mingling with the sinners, who were then the majority of the people. Still awaiting the conversion of the rest of Israel, the members of the group were asked to be content with, and proud of, their otherness and their separate way of life. It was a dangerous mixture of pride and expectation that could easily turn into frustration and hatred with the negative reaction of those they wished to convert. The history of the Qumran community would be the history of a lost illusion.

CHAPTER 5

The Schism between Qumran
and Enochic Judaism

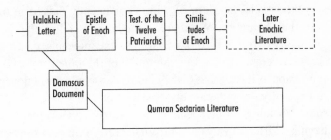

1. The Damascus Document (CD)

Scholars widely recognize that the Damascus Document is a key text for
understanding the origins of the Qumran community.[1] For example,
Philip R. Davies states, "in CD we find a meeting of pre-Qumran . . . and
Qumran ideology and materials, giving us a link between such works as
Jubilees, [1] Enoch, and 11QT on the one hand, and 1QS in particular on

---

1. The most important monographs on the Damascus Document are listed in the
bibliography at the end of this volume.

the other."[2] The document presents a unique combination of presectarian and sectarian elements. To a large extent its theology and its sociological background are presectarian.

The theology of the Damascus Document gives a certain role to human free will. "And now, my son, listen to me and I shall open your eyes so that you can see and understand the deeds of God, so that you can choose [Heb. *bḥr*] what he is pleased with and repudiate what he hates, so that you can walk perfectly on all his paths and not follow after the thoughts of a guilty inclination [*yṣr*] and lascivious eyes" (CD 2:14-16). Although one can find similar phrases in the later Qumran literature, the Damascus Document lacks the deterministic emphasis of the sectarian scrolls. Dualism is not yet preeminent. Belial is God's opponent, and in CD 5:18 he is already paired with an angelic counterpart, the "prince of lights." Yet Belial was not created evil. In line with the previous Enochic tradition, which describes a conscious plot of rebellious angels, the Damascus Document believes in the angels' freedom of will. "For having walked in the stubbornness of their hearts the Watchers of the heavens fell; on account of it they were caught, for they did not follow the precepts of God" (CD 2:17-18). The reference to the Enochic myth of the fallen angels is particularly significant, as it would be conspicuously absent in the major sectarian texts that explicitly deny the angels' freedom of will.[3]

From a sociological perspective, the Damascus Document reflects a people having a different way of life from the rest of the Jewish population, yet not completely isolated from the common social and religious institutions of Israel. Echoing the language of the Temple Scroll and the Halakhic Letter, the Damascus Document speaks of people living in the "city of the temple" (CD 12:1-2) or in "the camp" (10:23), as well as living in the "cities of Israel" (12:19) or in the "camps" (7:6; 19:2); people "who take women and beget children" (7:6-7; cf. 12:12:1-2; 15:5-6), are "owners" of property (9:10-16), have a job and earn a salary (14:12-17), and attend the temple in Jerusalem and offer sacrifices (12:17-21; 16:13-14). According to Julio Trebolle Barrera, "from [the Damascus Document] it seems to follow that the members of the community lived in cities and villages,

2. P. R. Davies, *Behind the Essenes: History and Ideology in the Dead Sea Scrolls,* BJS 94 (Atlanta: Scholars Press, 1987) 30.

3. Cf. J. J. Collins, *Apocalypticism in the Dead Sea Scrolls* (London and New York: Routledge, 1997) 48-50.

surrounded by their relatives and servants, devoted to business, farming and herding, although separate from the rest of the Jews and Gentiles."[4]

The authorship of the Damascus Document belongs to the same Enochic party I have described in the previous two chapters. Commentators agree in locating the document within the same trajectory of thought. The halakhah of the Damascus Document is so closely related to the Temple Scroll and the Halakhic Letter that Michael O. Wise claims that "the author [of the Temple Scroll] was a member of the CD community."[5] The *Heilsgeschichte* of the Damascus Document also resembles that of Jubilees, the Temple Scroll, and the Apocalypse of Weeks, as Philip R. Davies has demonstrated in a series of articles.[6] In this case also, Davies's conclusion is that a direct link unites the Damascus Document to the previous Enochic literature: "Both [Jubilees and CD] come from the same circles, which probably produced parts of [1] Enoch as well."[7]

At the same time, however, the Damascus Document has an unmistakably sectarian trait that is missing from the previous Enochic literature and that makes it the forerunner of the sectarian literature of Qumran. The Damascus Document already presupposes the existence of a special group, that of the followers of the "teacher of righteousness," a group having its own separate identity within the Enochic movement. The Damascus Document is the bridge text between the earlier Enochic literature and the sectarian literature of Qumran.

The prologue of the Damascus Document (CD 1:1–2:1) offers a general summary of the history of the group to which the author belonged. The

4. J. Trebolle Barrera, "The Essenes of Qumran: Between Submission to the Law and Apocalyptic Flight," in F. García Martínez and J. Trebolle Barrera, *The People of the Dead Sea Scrolls,* trans. W. G. E. Watson (Leiden: Brill, 1995) 49-76 (quotation on p. 58).

5. M. O. Wise, *A Critical Study of the Temple Scroll from Qumran Cave 11,* SAOC 49 (Chicago: Oriental Institute, 1990) 202.

6. Davies, "A Comparison of Three Essene Texts," in *Behind the Essenes,* 107-34; idem, "The Temple Scroll and the Damascus Document," in G. J. Brooke, ed., *Temple Scroll Studies: Papers Presented at the International Symposium on the Temple Scroll, Manchester, December 1987* (Sheffield: JSOT Press, 1989) 201-10.

7. P. R. Davies, *The Damascus Covenant: An Interpretation of the "Damascus Document,"* JSOTSup 25 (Sheffield: JSOT Press, 1983) 203. Cf. idem, "The Temple Scroll and the Damascus Document," in Brooke, ed., *Temple Scroll Studies,* 209: "There is simply too much evidence to permit us the option of denying a relationship between 11QT, CD, Qumran, and Jubilees."

opening verses immediately establish a connection with Enochic Judaism. "[God] has a dispute with all flesh and will carry out judgment on all those who spurn him" (1:2). The passage may allude specifically to Dream Visions: "The angels of your heavens are now committing sin (upon the earth), and your wrath shall rest upon the flesh of the people until the great day of judgment" (1 En 84:4). After recalling the general Enochic framework of decline and degeneration, the Damascus Document jumps to the time of the Babylonian exile: "When they were unfaithful in forsaking him, [God] hid his face from Israel and from his sanctuary and delivered them up to the sword" (CD 1:3-4). In line with the post-Maccabean development of Enochic Judaism, the Damascus Document is determined to trace the continuous presence of the chosen in this world as a well-defined group. At the end of his first dream vision, Enoch had begged God to spare "a plant of eternal seed": "Do not destroy, O my Lord, the flesh that has angered you from upon the earth, but sustain the flesh of righteousness and uprightness as a plant of eternal seed; and hide not your face from the prayer of your servant, O Lord" (1 En 84:6). Now, the Damascus Document intends to show how the prayer of Enoch has been fulfilled, depicting a three-stage history that leads to the birth of its own community.

After the Babylonian exile, God first "saved a remnant for Israel and did not deliver them up to destruction" (CD 1:4-5). The reference to Babylon and the "remnant" of Israel is no surprise. Drawing from the same environment of exiled priests, Enochic Judaism shares with Zadokite Judaism the view that Israel is "the community of the exile" (cf. Ezra 9:7-8), but rejects the idea that the second temple period was a time of blessing and restoration (cf. Ezra 9:9). Israel is living in the "time of wrath" that precedes the judgment (CD 1:5). The lay author of Daniel goes back to Jeremiah and his prophecy of the "seventy years" in order to extend the time of God's punishment to the entire postexilic period. The priestly author of the Damascus Document, instead, summons the testimony of Ezekiel, the founding father of both Enochic and Zadokite Judaism. Did Ezekiel not foretell that the exile of "Israel" would last "390 years" (Ezek 4:5)? Coherent with the message of the Proto-Epistle of Enoch and the Halakhic Letter, the Damascus Document interprets the present as the time in which a special group of chosen has emerged within Israel. "And in the period of wrath, three hundred and ninety years from delivering them into the hand of Nebuchadnezzar, king of Babylon, [God] visited them and caused to sprout from Israel and from Aaron a root for planting in order to possess his land and to become fat with the good things of his soil" (CD 1:5-8). Here we have a first significant change from the previous Enochic tradition. Now the group of the chosen is not simply a community of witnesses of the righteousness of the plant, Israel, as the Proto-Epistle had defined them. Instead, they are "a root of planting" that replaces Israel as the chosen people. A second change is even more striking. The emergence of this community is still only a preparatory step toward the final stage. "They realized their sin and knew that they were guilty men; but they were like blind persons and like those who grope for the path over twenty years. And God appraised their deeds, because they sought him with a perfect heart and raised up for them a teacher of righteousness in order to direct them in the path of his heart" (CD 1:8-11). "Twenty years" after the separation of the Enochians from the rest of the Jewish people (the separation evidenced by the Halakhic Letter), a "teacher" has come to disclose the ultimate truth to the members of the splinter group. His followers are the true chosen.

In the following section (CD 2:1-14a), the Damascus Document stresses that God's election is based on historical determinism. "[God] knows the years of their existence, and the number and detail of their ages, of all those who exist over the centuries, and of those who will exist, until it occurs in their ages throughout all the everlasting years" (CD 2:9-10). The link between election and historical determinism is common in the post-Maccabean documents of Enochic Judaism. However, the Damascus Document goes much further. In an astonishing statement that contradicts everything Enochic Judaism had said since Jubilees, the Damascus Document claims that at the beginning of the world God did not choose the entirety of Israel but only a remnant of it. "Those persons who turn aside from the path and abominate the precept. . . . God did not choose at the beginning of the world" (CD 2:6-7). With words that anticipate the sectarian dualism, the text continues by arguing that God "in all [ages] has established for himself men called by name, . . . and their names were established with precision, but those he hates he allows to go astray" (CD 2:11-13). God chose as a remnant not the people of Israel, not a tribe, not some families, not even a minority group, but individuals "by name."

The third section of the Damascus Document (CD 2:14b–4:12a) repeats, and adds more details to, the three-stage reconstruction of the origins of the community of the teacher of righteousness. Once again, Enochic Judaism provides the ideological and literary starting point. A detailed description of the fallen angels and of the subsequent degeneration of history ("all flesh . . . decayed," 2:20) is matched by the continuous presence of a faithful remnant, from the sons of Noah to Abraham, Isaac, Jacob, and Moses. Nevertheless, the Jewish people went astray and "were delivered up to the sword, for having deserted God's covenant . . . and having followed the stubbornness of their heart" (3:10-12). After the Babylonian exile, God "established his covenant with Israel forever," first "with those who remained steadfast in God's precept" (i.e., the early Enochians) and then "with those who were left among them . . . revealing to them hidden matters in which all Israel had gone astray" (3:12-13). Even this community of chosen among the chosen is not the ultimate goal of God's election. They also "defiled themselves with human sin and unclean paths. . . . But God, in his wonderful mysteries, atoned for their failings and pardoned their sins. And he built for them a safe home in Israel, such as there has not been since ancient times, not even till now" (3:17-20). The proof text is once again drawn from Ezekiel: "As God established for them by means of Ezekiel the prophet, saying: 'The priests and the levites and the sons of Zadok who maintained the service of my temple when the children of Israel strayed far away from me, shall offer the fat and the blood'" (3:20–4:2; cf. Ezek 44:15). While in Ezekiel the opposition was between the Levitical priests and the sons of Zadok, in this quotation the Damascus Document slightly corrects the Ezekiel text in order to make it fit into the threefold historical scheme. "The priests are the converts of Israel who left the land of Judah [[= at the time of the Babylonian exile]]; and (the levites) are those who joined them [[= the parent group after the 390 years of exile]]; and the sons of Zadok are the chosen of Israel, 'those called by name' who stood up at the end of days [[= the followers of the teacher of righteousness]]" (CD 4:2-4).

This passage, more than any other, has led scholars to the idea that the founders of the Qumran community were a group of Zadokite priests who separated themselves from the rest of Judaism when it became clear that they would never regain their power in Jerusalem. The Enochic roots of the community of the teacher of righteousness and of its parent movement are the strongest argument against such a hypothesis. The reference to the same Ezekiel text on which the Zadokites had built their power simply confirms that the roots of Enochic Judaism are in the same priestly environment in which Zadokite Judaism originated. Significantly, the expression "sons of Zadok" denotes here only the last stage in the development of the movement, not the entire movement since its origins. Moreover, the members of this final community are not chosen because of their belonging to a particular family group, but are called individually "by name," as the Damascus Document has already clarified in its second section. Davies correctly pointed out that the Damascus Document "treats the term [sons of Zadok] typologically and applies it to all the present members of the community, who we have no reason to assume were all Zadokite. . . . Scholars of Qumran simply must stop talking Zadokite. . . . Accordingly, we might be better advised to speak of the non-Zadokite nature of the community at Qumran."[8]

In the aftermath of the Maccabean revolt, the Enochians celebrated a complete victory over the Zadokites; the enemies are not simply defeated and humiliated — they are even deprived of their name. For centuries the Zadokites claimed to have fulfilled the words of Ezekiel, but, the sectarians now say, they were dead wrong. The only authentic "sons of Zadok" are the sectarians, who are the true recipients of Ezekiel's prophecy. The long confrontation between Enochians and Zadokites has reached its ultimate stage: the community of the teacher of righteousness has superseded the house of Zadok.

The Damascus Document aimed to promote a stricter separation from the rest of Israel than the previous Enochic tradition had claimed. Jubilees warned Israel against the possibility of some occasional raids by Mastema, but also reassured the chosen people of God's protection. With even greater emphasis the Halakhic Letter warned the Jewish authorities against "the evil scheming and the counsel of Belial," but with optimism that the situation could still be reversed. Now, the Damascus Document, while maintaining the strictest separation from the Gentiles (CD 12:6-11), claims that Israel at large is living in sin and error and is caught in the "three nets of Belial: . . . fornication, . . . wealth, . . . defilement of the temple" (4:15-17). The door for conversion will remain open for some time, until "the period corresponding to the number of these years is complete" (4:10).

Now, "the wall is built" (4:11) and the members of the group have "to separate themselves from the sons of the pit . . . to separate unclean from clean and differentiate between the holy and the common; to keep the sabbath day according to the exact interpretation, and the festivals and

8. P. R. Davies, "Sons of Zadok," in *Behind the Essenes,* 51-72 (quotation on pp. 54, 71, 72).

the day of fasting, according to what they had discovered, those who entered the new covenant in the land of Damascus" (6:15-19).

Many scholars take "the new covenant in the land of Damascus" (6:5, 19; 7:14-15, 18-19; 8:21; 20:12) as a reference to the exile of the Qumran community in the Judaean desert. For Lawrence H. Schiffman, "Damascus" is "a code word for Qumran."[9] As Davies has correctly pointed out, however, every time "Damascus" is mentioned in the Damascus Document, "only one historical context is provided, and it is the Babylonian exile. . . . There are cogent reasons for preferring Damascus as a symbol for Babylonia. . . . It is the claim made by the community of CD . . . that the true Israel (or Judah) arose in Babylon . . . [and] that its covenant and its legal tradition and its organization originated in Babylon in the wake of the exile. . . . Damascus lies not at the end of the process, but the beginning."[10]

This does not mean that the parent community actually developed in the eastern Diaspora and returned to Palestine only during the Maccabean period, as Jerome Murphy-O'Connor suggested.[11] The point of the Damascus Document is not that the parent sect lived in Babylon, but that its roots were there. As Davies concludes, "the ideology of CD has powerful roots in priestly exilic literature, especially the Holiness Code and Ezekiel."[12] The Damascus Document "celebrates a group which claims authentic descent from the Babylonian exile, has its own covenant, exegetical tradition, based on the same scripture, its genealogy (now missing), and an only slightly different version of the 'official' history of 'Israel.' "[13] In his description of this unnamed group, Davies has unawares released a quite accurate composite picture of Enochic Judaism: a Palestinian movement whose exegetical, halakhic, and liturgical traditions are rooted in the exiled priesthood, as it was for their Zadokite siblings and opponents.

The three-stage reconstruction of the origins of the community of the

9. L. H. Schiffman, "Origin and Early History of the Qumran Sect," *BA* 58/1 (1995) 37-48 (quotation on p. 45).

10. P. R. Davies, "The Birthplace of the Essenes: Where Is 'Damascus'?" in *Sects and Scrolls: Essays on Qumran and Related Topics* (Atlanta: Scholars Press, 1996) 95-111 (quotation on pp. 102-4, 109) (repr. from *RevQ* 14 [1990] 503-19).

11. J. Murphy-O'Connor, "The Essenes and Their History," *RB* 81 (1974) 215-44.

12. Davies, *Damascus Covenant,* 202.

13. Idem, *Sects and Scrolls,* 108.

teacher of righteousness, which emerges from the opening sections of the Damascus Document, corresponds to what systemic analysis confirms was the actual prehistory of the community that collected the Dead Sea Scrolls. The Babylonian exile was the starting point of an opposition priestly tradition that, in the postexilic period, did not recognize the legitimacy of the Zadokite restoration; after the Maccabean crisis, it gradually developed the self-consciousness of being a distinct and separate group of the chosen, having a special mission to accomplish on behalf of the entire people of Israel. Eventually, a single community emerged, led by the teacher of righteousness, and claimed to be the ultimate fulfillment of God's promises, the true "sons of Zadok" and the true "house of Judah" (CD 4:11).

Although the Damascus Document "betrays an organized, well-developed community with a clearly-expressed ideology and historical traditions,"[14] it bears no evidence that the followers of the teacher of righteousness lived all together in the same place and formed a community that was also geographically isolated. On the contrary, as we have seen, the document addresses people living either in Jerusalem or in other Judaean cities and villages. In this sense, the Damascus Document is a pre-Qumranic document that "achieved its outline and substantially its present form before the foundation of the Qumran community,"[15] inasmuch as there is no reference to the Qumran settlement or any other sectarian settlement. Nonetheless, the Damascus Document is a sectarian document, inasmuch as it gives people no other choice but "entering" the new community "in order to atone for their sins" (CD 4:4-10).

The best way to reconcile the evidence seems to me that of interpreting the document as the initial attempt of the community of the teacher of righteousness to define itself in relation to its parent movement. The Damascus Document was a pre-Qumranic document written by a sectarian elite within Enochic Judaism, addressing the larger Enochic communities in an attempt to gain the leadership of the movement.

The parent movement was reproached and flattered at the same time, lectured with severity but never totally condemned. "They realized their sin and knew that they were guilty men, but they were like blind persons and like those who grope for the path over twenty years. And God appraised their deeds, because they sought him with a perfect heart and raised up for

---

14. Idem, *Damascus Covenant,* 202.
15. Ibid.

them a teacher of righteousness" (CD 1:8-11). The same carrot-and-stick treatment is repeated soon afterward. "They had defiled themselves with human sin and unclean paths . . . but God atoned for their failings and pardoned their sins" (3:17-18). The parent movement is presented not as a contemporary phenomenon but as a group that belongs to the past. They are righteous precursors who have prepared the way for the preaching of the teacher of righteousness and now have to stand aside in favor of the new leadership that is the fulfillment of the Enochic ideals.

In writing the Damascus Document the sectarians may have had simply to modify and adapt an already existing text produced by Enochic Judaism after the Halakhic Letter ratified the split from the rest of Israel. Textual analysis actually supports such a possibility; Florentino García Martínez speaks of a presectarian "nucleus of CD, completed with a series of halakhic prescriptions from the formative period."[16]

It is therefore likely that most of the regulations contained in the Damascus Document originated outside the group of the teacher of righteousness and reflect the way of life of the Enochic communities. In its comprehensive approach, however, the Damascus Document is not detached and disinterested. It betrays the determination to regulate the lives of the members of the parent movement, living either in Jerusalem or in camps. No right to self-determination is assigned to them; on the contrary, they are required to accept the leadership of an elite that claims special authority from God.

The Damascus Document, therefore, does not testify to the beginning of the communal life in Qumran, but to the stage immediately preceding the foundation of the Qumran settlement, the time in which the community of the teacher of righteousness tried to gain leadership over the Enochic movement, claiming that they had been chosen by God to guide it into a path of stricter separation from the rest of Israel. Did the community of the teacher of righteousness succeed? The continuity, both literary and ideological, between the Damascus Document and the Community Rule proves undoubtedly that the foundation of the Qumran settlement was the subsequent step in the life of the same group. Did their retreat to Qumran mark the defeat or the triumph of their ideals? The answer to these questions is to be sought outside the Qumran library, in a series of documents related

---

16. F. García Martínez, "The Origins of the Essene Movement and of the Qumran Sect," in García Martínez and Trebolle Barrera, *People of the Dead Sea Scrolls,* 77-96 (quotation on p. 86).

to the Dead Sea Scrolls but not attested there. After examining what is at Qumran, we have to turn toward what is missing there and examine the case of some conspicuous absences.

2. Missing Texts (I): Sectarian Censorship

The character of a library is given not only by what it contains but also by what it does not contain. What is missing, therefore, is not less important than what is there, and we can learn from what is absent as much as from what is present. It cannot be accidental that among the Dead Sea Scrolls "no writing has been found which contradicts the basic ideas of this community or represents the ideas of a group opposed to it."[17] The documents in the Qumran library have told us about the origins of the group; the missing texts will now reveal to us its location within the pluralistic world of middle Judaism.

The scrolls have some possible allusions to the sect of the Pharisees, but "no literature representative of the Pharisaic stream."[18] The document that most often has been associated with the Pharisees among the pre-70 Old Testament Pseudepigrapha is the Psalms of Solomon,[19] and no copy of it was found at Qumran.

Similarly, no Qumran writings reflect the views of the Hasmoneans. The absence of 1 Maccabees and the book of Judith (and Esther) does not come as a surprise, when one considers the many anti-Hasmonean statements in the sectarian literature, especially the *pesharim,* and the rejection of feasts such as Hanukkah and Purim. What is surprising is to find a text like 4Q448, which the editors describe as a prayer for King Alexander Jannaeus.[20] At any rate, 4Q448 cannot be counted as a Hasmonean document. Rather, it bears

17. García Martínez, "Dead Sea Scrolls," in ibid., 9.

18. Y. Shavit, "The 'Qumran Library' in the Light of the Attitude towards Books and Libraries in the Second Temple Period," in M. O. Wise, et al., eds., *Methods of Investigation of the Dead Sea Scrolls and the Khirbet Qumran Site: Present Realities and Future Prospects* (New York: New York Academy of Sciences, 1994) 299-317 (quotation on p. 300).

19. Cf. J. Schüpphaus, *Die Psalmen Salomos* (Leiden: Brill, 1977).

20. E. Eshel, H. Eshel, and A. Yardeni, "A Scroll from Qumran which Includes Part of Psalm 154 and a Prayer for King Jonathan and His Kingdom," *IEJ* 42 (1992) 199-229.

witness to a pro-Hasmonean stance by the sectarians, intended not to endorse the Jerusalem authorities but simply to state their "temporary support" concerning a particular political circumstance.[21]

In cave 7 some fragments of Greek texts have been found. The only ones that have been identified belong to the Septuagint, namely, 7QSeptuagint Exodus (7Q1) and 7QEpistle of Jeremiah (7Q2). No trace has appeared of any of the texts of Hellenistic Judaism, such as the Letter of Aristeas, 3 Maccabees, the Wisdom of Solomon, the works of Philo, and the like.

Finally, the scrolls do not refer to John the Baptist, Jesus, Paul, or James; one finds no reference whatsoever to the beginnings of the Christian movement, nor has any Christian text been found in the Qumran library. The possible identification in cave 7 of tiny fragments from the New Testament, which the Spanish papyrologist José O'Callaghan announced in 1972, has not overcome the burden of proof and is falling into oblivion despite the many efforts to keep the hypothesis alive.[22] The contribution of the Dead Sea Scrolls to knowledge about Christian origins is exceptional, yet "it does not include having provided us with the oldest copy of Mark's Gospel or of any other writing from the New Testament."[23]

The most remarkable absence of all, however, is also the least noticed: the later Enochic literature. This phenomenon, first highlighted by Jósef T. Milik, could not escape the notice of a specialist in the Old Testament Pseudepigrapha, James H. Charlesworth.[24] "The Aramaic portions of

21. Collins, *Apocalypticism in the Dead Sea Scrolls,* 79-80.

22. J. O'Callaghan, "Papiros neotestamentarios en la cueva 7 de Qumrân?" *Bib* 53 (1972) 91-100 (English trans. by W. L. Holladay, "New Testament Papyri in Qumrân Cave 7?" JBLSup 91/2 [1972] 1-14); idem, *Los papiros griegos de la cueva 7 de Qumrân* (Madrid, 1974); idem, "Sobre el papiro de Marcos en Qumrân," *Filología Neotestamentaria* 5 (1992) 191-98. Cf. C. P. Thiede, *Die älteste Evangelium-Handschrift? Das Markus-Fragment von Qumran und die Anfänge der schriftlichen Überlieferung des Neuen Testaments* (Wuppertal: Brockhaus, 1986; 2nd ed. 1990; English ed.: *The Earliest Gospel Manuscript? The Qumran Papyrus 7Q5 and Its Significance for New Testament Studies* [Exeter: Paternoster, 1992]). A bibliography of the controversy surrounding O'Callaghan's announcement is in J. A. Fitzmyer, "The New Testament at Qumran?" in *The Dead Sea Scrolls: Major Publications and Tools for Study,* rev. ed., SBLRBS 20 (Atlanta: Scholars Press, 1990) 168-72.

23. García Martínez, "Dead Sea Scrolls," 14.

24. See J. T. Milik with M. Black, *The Books of Enoch: Aramaic Fragments of Qumrân Cave 4* (Oxford: Clarendon, 1976) 7; J. H. Charlesworth, "The Origins and

1 Enoch reveal that by the end of the first century BCE, the Qumran [sectarians] had lost interest in this document."[25] Charlesworth, however, did not know how to explain the phenomenon: "Does the apparent disinterest in the Books of Enoch suggest that the community [of Qumran] had become less apocalyptic?"[26]

We have seen that the earliest Enochic literature is preserved at Qumran (the Book of the Watchers, the Astronomical Book, Dream Visions, and the Proto-Epistle) and played a central role in the origins of the community of the Dead Sea Scrolls. But no evidence has been found in the Qumran library of the three most important documents of Enochic Judaism written in the first century BCE (the Epistle of Enoch, the Testaments of the Twelve Patriarchs, and the Similitudes of Enoch). The absence "suggests that the [Enochic] corpus was transmitted and developed in at least one context other than Qumran."[27]

The sectarian documents of Qumran also show a decreasing interest in traditions associated with the patriarch Enoch. "In view of the strong manuscript evidence for interest in the books of Enoch at Qumran, there is remarkably little appeal to the Enoch tradition in the major sectarian documents of Qumran."[28]

This is much more than "a loss of interest" in Enochic Judaism — this is a dramatic departure from the parent movement. The mystery of the missing Enochic texts is the key to understanding the parting of the ways between Enochic Judaism and the community of the Dead Sea Scrolls.

3. Enochic Documents Unknown at Qumran; or, Enoch vs. Qumran

(a) *The Epistle of Enoch.* As we have seen in the previous chapter, the Epistle of Enoch is the result of a long interpolation in an autonomous

---

Subsequent History of the Authors of the Dead Sea Scrolls: Four Transitional Phases among the Qumran Essenes," *RevQ* 10 (1980) 213-34.

25. Charlesworth, "Origins," 227.

26. Ibid., 228.

27. G. W. E. Nickelsburg, "Enoch, First Book of," *ABD* 2.508-16 (quotation on p. 515).

28. Collins, *Apocalypticism in the Dead Sea Scrolls,* 35-36.

document, the Proto-Epistle of Enoch.[29] There are compelling reasons to believe that, while the Proto-Epistle was presectarian, the Epistle was postsectarian, written by a group other than the Qumran sect. As a result, the Epistle remained unknown in the Qumran library, or, if it was known, it was not accepted there.

The first and most obvious reason is the absence of Qumran fragments. This is hardly to be dismissed as accidental, considering the numbers of Aramaic fragments that extensively cover the entirety of 1 Enoch, the only exceptions being the Similitudes (or Parables) of Enoch, the section 94:6–104:6, and the final chapter (108). According to Milik, "for the first book of Enoch, the Book of the Watchers, we can calculate that exactly 50 percent of the text is covered by the Aramaic fragments; for the third, the Astronomical Book, 30 percent; for the fourth, the Book of Dreams, 26 percent; for the fifth, the Epistle of Enoch, 18 percent."[30] Statistics makes it difficult to assume that this 18 percent of the recovered text of the Epistle was concentrated only by chance in the shorter sections that I have reconstructed as belonging to the Proto-Epistle, while no fragment has been recovered of the much longer section 94:6–104:6 that I have identified as a later addition. As no one questions, on the basis of the calculus of probability, that the Similitudes of Enoch and ch. 108 were unknown at Qumran, the same criterion should apply to the section 94:6–104:6, or at least one should concede the benefit of the doubt.

A second clue is given by the structure of the Enoch collection known at Qumran. The Aramaic fragments show that the sectarians knew an ensemble of Enoch books that had chs. 106–7 as its ending. It is likely that this section, which a two-line *vacat* in 4QEnoch[c] separates from ch. 105, was added by the compiler as an appendix to the entire Enoch collection. García Martínez has demonstrated that the compiler took these two chapters from the lost Book of Noah and supplemented them with an interpolation, 106:19–107:1.[31] In so doing, the compiler turned chs. 106–7 into a sort of general summary of the entire Enoch collection.

When Noah was born, his father Lamech and his grandfather Me-

---

29. The most important monographs on 1 Enoch, including the Epistle of Enoch, are listed in the bibliography at the end of this volume.

30. Milik, *Books of Enoch*, 5.

31. F. García-Martínez, *Qumran and Apocalyptic: Studies on the Aramaic Texts from Qumran*, STDJ 9 (Leiden: Brill, 1992) 27-28.

thuselah were shocked: "He is not like an (ordinary) human being, but he looks like the children of the angels of heaven" (1 En 106:5). Unlike his descendants, the great-grandfather Enoch is not so easily impressed; he knows the secrets of heaven. He reminds his son Methuselah of the earliest revelation he gave him ("I have already seen this matter in a vision and made it known to you," 106:13). From the words of Enoch (here the reader's thought immediately turns back to the Book of the Watchers and Dream Visions), Methuselah already should have understood that Noah is the "remnant" in a world that, because of the sin of the fallen angels, is full of evil and impurity and would remain such even after the flood, until the time of the final catharsis (106:1-18).

At this point, the compiler felt compelled to integrate the text from the Book of Noah by adding a few sentences to Enoch's speech. "After that there shall occur still greater oppression than that which was fulfilled upon the earth the first time; for I do know the mysteries of the holy ones, for he, the Lord, has revealed them to me and made me know — and I have read (them) in the tablets of heaven" (106:19). The reference to the tablets of heaven reminds the reader of the Astronomical Book and prepares the path for a synopsis of the central message of the Proto-Epistle. As Noah and his sons were spared from the flood, so a new remnant will be selected at the end of the final tribulation. "Then I beheld the writing upon them that one generation shall be more wicked than the other, until a generation of righteous ones shall arise" (107:1). The theology of the interpolation is very close to the doctrine of election in the Proto-Epistle. The compiler aims to say that the words which Enoch addressed to his sons are equally addressed to the righteous of the final days, and to show how the message of the Proto-Epistle fits into the context of the entire Enochic revelation. That the interpolation does not refer to the contents of section 94:6–104:6 suggests that the latter was unknown to the compiler. The last part of Enoch that the compiler knew and summarized was the Proto-Epistle.

Finally, more light on the relationship between the Proto-Epistle and the Epistle comes from a comparison of their different ideologies. In a seminal study on the Epistle of Enoch and the Qumran literature, George W. E. Nickelsburg argued for the presence in the document of two contradictory ideologies.[32] While he sees "strong evidence for a historical con-

---

32. G. W. E. Nickelsburg, "The Epistle of Enoch and the Qumran Literature," *JJS* 33 (1982) 333-48.

nection between the author of [the Apocalypse of Weeks] and the authors of the relevant Qumran writings," he rejects the hypothesis of a Qumranic origin of the final composition. "I have found in the Epistle neither the specific exegetical traditions nor the specific polemics against temple, cult, and priesthood characteristic of Qumran, nor the heightened dualism which would confirm [sectarian] authorship."[33] García Martínez shares Nickelsburg's opinion: "All specific polemic against the temple, the cult or priesthood, is lacking in the Epistle, as are the specific exegetic traditions of the Qumranic community and its characteristic ideas, such as dualism."[34] Since Nickelsburg and García Martínez believe that the Epistle was known at Qumran, the only possibility for them is that the Epistle is also a presectarian document, that is, a document from the parent movement from which the Qumran community arose.

The Epistle does not simply lack specific Qumranic elements, however — it has specific anti-Qumranic elements. The most obvious is 1 En 98:4. The passage explicitly condemns those who state that since human beings are victims of a corrupted universe, they are not responsible for the sins they commit, and they blame others (God or the evil angels) for having exported "sin" into the world. "I have sworn unto you, sinners: In the same manner that a mountain has never turned into a servant, nor shall a hill (ever) become a maidservant of a woman; likewise, neither has sin been exported into the world. It is the people who have themselves invented it. And those who commit it shall come under a great curse" (98:4).

Paolo Sacchi and John J. Collins understand the passage as a reaction against the early Enochic doctrine of the fallen angels,[35] and, to a certain extent, it is. The central point, however, seems to be otherwise. The author does not deny that evil has a superhuman origin, but holds human beings responsible for the sinful actions they commit. What the author aims to introduce is a clearer distinction between evil, which is from the angels, and sin, which is from humans, in order to show that the Enochic doctrine of evil does not contradict the principle of human responsibility. Evil is a contamination that prepares a fertile ground for sin (we might now use the

---

33. Ibid., 347.

34. García Martínez, *Qumran and Apocalyptic,* 89.

35. P. Sacchi, *Jewish Apocalyptic and Its History,* trans. W. J. Short, JSPSup 20 (Sheffield: Sheffield Academic Press, 1997) 146; Collins, *Apocalypticism in the Dead Sea Scrolls,* 23.

term "temptation"), but it is the individuals themselves who have "invented" sin and therefore are responsible for their own deeds.

This strong and uncompromising appeal to human freedom and responsibility may seem surprising in a tradition, such as the Enochic, that from its inception had consistently repeated the view that human beings are victims of evil. It is much less revolutionary, however, than it might seem at first sight. Since its origin, the major concern of Enochic Judaism was never to absolve human beings and angels from their sins. On the contrary, the purpose of the myth of the fallen angels was to absolve the merciful God from being responsible for a world that the Enochians deemed evil and corrupted. "The idea that angels have the capacity for moral choice is fundamental to the myth of the fallen angels."[36] Less clear, at the origin of the myth, was the degree of human freedom and accountability, which, however, could not be totally denied without denying the justice of God and the sense of God's wrath and judgment. The Epistle made explicit what was implicit in the myth of the fallen angels. As Nickelsburg has pointed out, over the centuries the Enochic authors were persistent and consistent in making "human beings . . . responsible for their actions. . . . Nonetheless, the Enochic authors attributed a significant part of the evils in this world to a hidden demonic world."[37] In the Enochic system of thought, the two contradictory concepts of human responsibility and human victimization had to coexist between the Scylla of an absolute determinism and the Charybdis of an equally absolute antideterminism. Accept either of these extremes and the entire Enochic system would collapse into the condemnation of God as the unmerciful source of evil or as the unjust scourge of innocent creatures.

By clarifying that evil is a temptation more than an uncontrollable contamination, the Epistle corrects rather than disowns the position of the earlier Enochic texts. The real opposition is against those who claim that human beings are not responsible because "sin has been exported into the world." The only Jewish group that made such a radical claim was the Qumran community, who must be recognized as the target of the Epistle. García Martínez also recognizes that 1 En 98:4 "is incompatible with the characteristic determinism of Qumran, according to which the portion of

36. M. J. Davidson, *Angels at Qumran: A Comparative Study of 1 Enoch 1–36, 72–108 and Sectarian Writings from Qumran*, JSPSup 11 (Sheffield: JSOT Press, 1992) 289.
37. Nickelsburg, *ABD* 2.514.

light or darkness inherent to each man determines his fate."[38] An overall analysis of the section 94:6–104:6 confirms this interpretation.

The study of the Epistle of Enoch is basically the study of how the interpolated material modifies the Proto-Epistle. The goal of the interpolator is to correct the message of the Proto-Epistle by developing it according to a different theological trajectory from that followed by the sectarians of Qumran. In Jubilees and the Temple Scroll the opposition is between Jews and Gentiles. The Proto-Epistle and the Halakhic Letter signal the emergence of a group of chosen among the chosen as the first step toward the *eschaton*. The followers of the teacher of righteousness identify themselves as the only chosen of the last days. The Epistle's doctrine of election is a systematic demolition of the principles of inaugurated eschatology that the Qumran community had brought to its ultimate conclusion.

The author of the Epistle abandons the complex historical determinism on which Jubilees, the Proto-Epistle, and the Damascus Document built their doctrines of election. The Epistle knows only the distinction between "now" and "those days," this world and the world to come, the present and the future of the final judgment. At the end of days, "the angels shall descend into the secret places. They shall gather together into one place all those who gave aid to sin. And the Most High will arise on that day of judgment in order to execute a great judgment upon all the sinners. He will set a guard of holy angels over all the righteous and holy ones, and they shall keep them as the apple of the eye until all evil and all sin are brought to an end" (1 En 100:4). The reference to "secret places" where "those who gave aid to sin" are gathered is reminiscent of the Book of the Watchers and Dream Visions. It is an allusion to the imprisonment of the fallen angels "underneath the rocks of the ground until the day of their judgment and of their consummation" (10:12). The last judgment is first of all the day of the punishment of the rebellious angels, who are the first enemies of God (cf. 90:20-27). Angels as well as humans are free and accountable to God for their misbehavior.

The author of the Epistle does not deny that already in this world there is a clear distinction between the chosen and the wicked. This dualism, however, is transferred to the sociological level. The chosen (the righteous

---

38. García Martínez, *Qumran and Apocalyptic,* 89; cf. G. W. E. Nickelsburg, "Enoch 97–104: A Study of the Greek and Ethiopic Texts," in M. E. Stone, ed., *Armenian and Biblical Studies* (Jerusalem: St. James, 1976) 90-156.

and the wise) and the wicked (the sinners and the foolish) are identified respectively with the poor (and powerless) and the rich (and powerful). Such a taxonomy was not unknown at Qumran (1QpHab 12:3, 6, 10; 1QH 5:22; 4QpPs37 2:10).[39] While the sectarians viewed themselves as the poor, however, in the Epistle of Enoch (as well as later in the nascent Christian movement) the category of the poor does not lose its primary significance as a sociological and inclusive category. Before being the label of a specific group, the poor are all the oppressed of this world. This leads the Epistle to reject the sectarian claim, made by the community of the teacher of righteousness since the Damascus Document, that the chosen are called individually, "by name." God's election concerns a broad category of people rather than named individuals, a fact that leaves more room for human freedom. God did not choose individuals to form an isolated community but elected a social category, the poor, as the recipient of God's promises. Individuals remain free to choose to which group they want to belong.

As the Epistle passes over in silence the special "wisdom" that the Proto-Epistle had promised to the righteous before the final end, so it also rejects the idea that the chosen, either Israel or a remnant of it, have in this world the sure "medicine" against evil. Of course, "(salutary) medicine is far from you [sinners] on account of your sins" (1 En 95:4), but even to the righteous this is a promise that will be fulfilled only at the end of days. "But you, who have experienced pain, fear not, for there shall be a healing medicine for you" (96:3). Therefore, the chosen are such only to a limited extent: they are not the "saved," but candidates for salvation. No individual, no community of people, can claim to possess salvation as a present and permanent gift and profess not to be in need of salvation.

The author of the Epistle strenuously opposes the theology of separation as developed by the community of the Dead Sea Scrolls. In this world, the poor and the rich live side by side. The separation between the chosen and the wicked will occur only at the end of time. The emphasis on human responsibility allows the possibility of conversion. The author opposes any kind of predestination; in this world, the boundaries between the chosen and the wicked remain permeable. The door to salvation, which the Damascus Document kept open only for a limited period of time and the sectarian documents barred from the beginning for those who have not

39. L. E. Keck, "The Poor Among the Saints in Jewish Christianity and Qumran," *ZNW* 57 (1966) 54-78.

been chosen by God, will be open until the very last moment. "In those days, blessed are they all who accept the words of wisdom and understand them, to follow the path of the Most High; they shall walk in the path of his righteousness and not become wicked with the wicked; and they shall be saved" (99:10). Moreover, the reference in the previous verses to "those who carve images of gold and of silver and of wood and of clay, and those who worship evil spirits and demons, and all kinds of idols" (99:7), indicates that the possibility of conversion even for the Gentiles was not excluded, according to the universalistic approach that had been traditional in Enochic Judaism up to and including Dream Visions.

While the Epistle signals a return to some of the traditional themes of earlier Enochic Judaism, it also marks a fresh start away from those old foundations. No text of Enochic Judaism had ever before stated with such clarity that the superhuman origin of evil does not eliminate or deny human responsibility. The Epistle had a lasting impact in shifting the emphasis from the ancient myth of the angelic sin to the mechanisms through which evil surfaces within each individual and, therefore, to the possibility of controlling the emergence of evil and resisting its temptation. It was the Epistle's greatest success: the answer of Qumran was not the only possible answer to the questions raised by the earlier Enochic tradition.

(b) *The Testaments of the Twelve Patriarchs.* That something went wrong in the relationship between the community of the Dead Sea Scrolls and Enochic Judaism is confirmed by the absence of another fundamental document of the first century BCE related to Enochic Judaism: the Testaments of the Twelve Patriarchs.[40]

In their present form, the Testaments are Christian and must have received that form sometime in the second half of the second century CE. This fact has led some specialists, in particular Marinus de Jonge, to advocate the absence of a Jewish original. Although these scholars recognize the presence of Jewish materials, they claim that the authorship of the Testaments is Christian, because "the Christian interpolations cannot be removed without damaging the fabric of large sections of the work."[41]

40. The most important monographs on the Testaments of the Twelve Patriarchs are listed in the bibliography at the end of this volume.

41. M. de Jonge, "Testaments of the Twelve Patriarchs," *ABD* 5.180-86. For the numerous works M. de Jonge has devoted to the Testaments of the Twelve Patriarchs, see the bibliography at the end of this volume.

When we realize that Rabbinic Judaism became normative only after the destruction of the second temple, however, we understand that it is incorrect to label some ideas as non-Jewish (either Christian or Hellenistic) only because they were nonrabbinic. The nonrabbinic flavor of the Testaments comes primarily from the multifaceted world of middle Judaism, not from later Christian authorship or Hellenistic influence. A detailed and well-informed study by Jarl Henning Ulrichsen seems now to vindicate the opinion of many specialists in middle Judaism: underneath the Christian layer is a coherent Jewish original.[42] When the relatively few Christian additions are removed, the Testaments are recognizably a pre-Christian Jewish document. More specifically, as David Flusser has been felicitously saying for some time, the Testaments are a "Jewish work composed in circles close to the [Qumran sectarians], but differing from them in some of its views," the work of an "author . . . [who] was a member of a movement in Judaism of which the Dead Sea sect was a part."[43]

The link between the Testaments of the Twelve Patriarchs and Enochic Judaism is visible through the former's sharing of the basic principles of the movement. The author maintains that evil has a superhuman origin, and blames the devil, Belial (Gk. *Beliar*), and the evil spirits for instigating human acts of sin (TReu; TDan 1:7; 3:6; TBenj 6:1; 7:1; et passim). The author voices a pre-Mosaic priestly written tradition that proclaims the superiority of Levi over Judah (TReu 6:5-12; TSim 7:1; TLevi; TIss 5:7; TNaph 5:1-5; TJos 19:11) and that, through Jacob, Isaac, Abraham, and Seth (TBenj 10:6), goes back to Enoch (TSim 5:4; TLevi 10:5; 14:1; TDan 5:6; TNaph 4:1; TBenj 9:1). Finally, the author considers Israel as still living in exile, "scattered as captives among the nations" after the destruction of the first temple (TLevi

---

42. See J. H. Ulrichsen, *Die Grundschrift der Testamente der Zwölf Patriarchen: Eine Untersuchung zu Umfang, Inhalt und Eigenart der ursprünglichen Schrift*, AUUHR 10 (Uppsala: Almqvist & Wiksell, 1991). Among those scholars who have argued for the Jewish Palestinian origin of the Testaments, see in particular P. Sacchi, "I Testamenti dei Dodici Patriarchi," in idem, ed., *Apocrifi dell'Antico Testamento*, 2 vols. (Turin: Unione Tipografica-Editrice Torinese, 1981-89) 1.725-948; A. Hultgård, *L'Eschatologie des Testaments des Douze Patriarches*, AUUHR 6-7 (Uppsala: Almqvist & Wiksell, 1977-82); D. Flusser, "The Testaments of the Twelve Patriarchs," *EncJud* 13.184-86; M. Philonenko, *Les interpolations chrétiennes des Testaments des Douze Patriarches et les manuscrits de Qoumran* (Paris: Presses Universitaires, 1960).

43. The quotations are, respectively, from D. Flusser, *The Spiritual History of the Dead Sea Sect* (Tel Aviv: MOD Books, 1989) 95; idem, *EncJud* 13.185.

10:1-5; cf. 15:1-4; 16:1-5; et passim), and announces that the restoration would occur only at the end of time: "the latter temple will exceed the former in glory" (TBenj 9:2). As Michael A. Knibb has demonstrated, the study of the "sin-exile-return" passages (TLevi 10, 14-15, 16; TJud 18:1, 23; TIss 6; TZeb 9:5-9; TDan 5:4-13; TNaph 4:1-3; 4:4-5; TAsh 7:2-4; 7:5-7) shows that "the understanding of the exile to be found in the Testaments represents in reality only a more extreme form of the kind of interpretation found already in Daniel, [1] Enoch and the Damascus Document."[44]

Interestingly, as in the case of the Epistle of Enoch, the Testaments seem to be familiar with, or to have used, some material preserved at Qumran. In particular, the Testament of Levi is based on Aramaic Levi (4Q213-14 [4QTLevi[a,b] ar]),[45] while the Testament of Naphtali might share the same source as the Hebrew Testament of Naphtali (4Q215 [4QTNaph]). Three other fragmentary texts (3Q7 [3QTJud[a]], 4Q538 [4QAJu ar], 4Q539 [4QAJo ar]) manifest occasional verbal links with parts of the Testaments of the Twelve Patriarchs. The evidence suggests the existence at Qumran of a testamental literature associated with the sons of Jacob. The author(s) of the Testaments of the Twelve Patriarchs shared the same literary background that fostered the sectarian literature of Qumran.

On the ideological level, the Testaments of the Twelve Patriarchs also present some striking similarities to the sectarian documents of Qumran. The dualistic vocabulary is virtually identical, with the same emphasis on the opposition between God and Belial, "light and darkness" (TLevi 19:1), "the spirit of truth and the spirit of error" (TJud 20:1). Besides, the Testaments of the Twelve Patriarchs are the Enochic documents that in their eschatology are closest to the messianic expectations seen in the sectarian scrolls: the "unique prophet" (TBenj 9:2; cf. 1QS 9:11; 4Q175), and the "messiah(s) from Levi and Judah" (TSim 7:2; TDan 5:10; TGad 8:1; cf. CD 12:23–13:1; 14:19; 19:10-11; 20:1; 1QS 9:11; 1QSa 2:11-21; 4Q175).[46]

---

44. M. A. Knibb, "The Exile in Intertestamental Literature," *HeyJ* 17 (1976) 253-72 (quotation on p. 266). These passages were first identified by M. de Jonge, *The Testaments of the Twelve Patriarchs* (Assen: Van Gorcum, 1953) 83-86.

45. R. A. Kugler, *From Patriarch to Priest: The Levi-Priestly Tradition from Aramaic Levi to Testament of Levi,* SBLEJL 9 (Atlanta: Scholars Press, 1996).

46. J. J. Collins, *The Scepter and the Star: The Messiahs of the Dead Sea Scrolls and Other Ancient Literature* (New York: Doubleday, 1995); Hultgård, *L'Eschatologie;* J. Liver, "The Doctrine of the Two Messiahs in Sectarian Literature in the Time of the Second Commonwealth," *HTR* 52 (1959) 149-85.

The most typically sectarian elements are, however, conspicuously missing from the Testaments of the Twelve Patriarchs, which seem rather to follow the trajectory of the Epistle of Enoch in emphasizing the freedom and responsibility of angels and humans. The duel between God and Belial is a real conflict, not a prestaged drama. There is no doubt that Belial will be defeated at the end (TLevi 18:12-13), but until that moment the devil is a rebellious and aggressive challenger of God's power and authority.

The human soul is the battlefield. Belial has a key for direct access to human selfhood. That is, Belial placed "seven spirits of deceit" in every human being "against humankind" (cf. TReu 2:1-2). These seven spirits of deceit interact against the seven spirits that God placed in the human being, but more significantly, they interact with the last of these spirits, "the spirit of procreation and intercourse, with which comes sin [Gk. *hamartia*] through fondness for pleasure" (TReu 2:8).

The distance of the anthropology of the Testaments from the Qumran doctrine of the spirits could not be greater. In the Testaments God is not the source of both the good and evil spirits; the presence of evil spirits is against both God and humankind. Not only is the internal struggle a deviation from the original plan of creation, but also God has not preordained the outcome. The number of good and evil spirits is the same in each individual, which guarantees humans fairness in the struggle and gives the last word over to human responsibility. It is the "conscience of the mind" that ultimately makes the difference. "So understand, my children, that two spirits await an opportunity with humanity: the spirit of truth and the spirit of error. In between is the conscience of the mind which inclines as it will" (TJud 20:1-2). If Jürgen Becker and Paolo Sacchi are correct in viewing the Testament of Reuben as the development of a sectarian nucleus in which God was originally said to be the source of both the evil and the good spirits,[47] the redactional history of the text would tell us of the parting of the ways between Qumran and Enochic Judaism.

In the Testaments the emphasis on human responsibility reaches a degree of intensity that was unknown in the previous Enochic tradition. The document signals an epochal change in the interpretation of the sin of the Watchers. Human beings are not mere victims of the angelic sin but

---

47. J. Becker, *Untersuchungen zur Entstehungsgeschichte der Testamente der zwölf Patriarchen*, AGJU 8 (Leiden: Brill, 1970); Sacchi, "I Testamenti dei Dodici Patriarchi."

jointly responsible. The blame shifts from angels to women. "They [women] charmed the Watchers, who were before the flood. As they continued looking at the women, they were filled with desire [Gk. *epithymia*] for them. . . . Then they were transformed into human males. . . . Since the women's minds were filled with desire for these apparitions, they gave birth to giants" (TReu 5:6-7).

The psychologization of the myth of the fallen angels denies the equation of impurity and evil that Jubilees had established and the Qumran sectarians turned into one of the foundations of their doctrine of evil. The Testaments passes over in silence the ontological contamination caused by the angelic sin. The only kind of impurity that produces evil is the ethical impurity that springs forth from the hearts of human beings filled with "desire" (Gk. *epithymia*).

Having turned evil into an inner temptation fostered by the devil, Enochic Judaism for the first time could develop an ethic capable of opposing the power of evil. The goal is to attain an integrity (Gk. *haplotēs*) of soul that can defeat the duplicity of Belial, who, as TBenj 6:7 effectively states, "knows no integrity."

An ethic that does not address the ambivalence of human nature is condemned to fail. Without integrity of heart, the practice of any moral code, including the Mosaic torah, is ineffective. "The commandments of God are double" (TNaph 8:7), their goodness depending on the goodness of the human soul. "If the soul is disposed toward evil, all of man's deeds are wicked; driving out the good, he accepts the devil and is overmastered by Beliar. Even when man does good, it is turned into evil" (TAsh 1:8).

Although no longer ignoring the Mosaic torah as the pre-Maccabean Enochic literature did, the Testaments of the Twelve Patriarchs follow the traditional Enochic teaching that the power of evil makes obedience to the law insufficient for salvation. With the Qumran literature the Testaments share the paradox of a human being who does good but is evil. What one is, is more important than what one does. What one is depends on the cosmic conflict between God and Belial. Yet, unlike the Qumran literature, the Testaments mention a way out: to fill the heart with an undivided love for God and the neighbor, thus leaving no more room for desire and duplicity. "The Lord I loved with all my strength; and I love every human being. You do these as well, my children, and every spirit of Beliar will flee from you, . . . so long as you have the God of heaven with you, and walk with all humankind in integrity of heart" (TIss 7:6-7; cf. 3:6–5:3; TReu 4:1; TBenj 3:4).

142

The alternative is between "desire" (Gk. *epithymia*) and "love" (Gk. *agapē*). One who "is subjected to the passion of desire and is enslaved by it" (TJos 7:8) loses integrity, is "overmastered by Belial," and is led to the "deadly sin" (Gk. *hamartia eis thanaton,* TIss 7:1). But if one "lives in integrity of heart . . . then the spirits of error have no power over him" (TIss 4:1-6; cf. TReu 3:5; TDan 5:1-4; et passim). In particular, in contrast to the Qumran texts, the Testaments insist on the possibility of repentance and even banish any feeling of hatred toward the sinners. The twelve patriarchs provide formidable examples (cf. TReu 1:9-10; TSim 2:13; TJud 15:4) and plenty of good advice. "Love one another from the heart, and if anyone sins against you, speak to him in peace. Expel the venom of hatred. . . . If anyone confesses and repents, forgive him. . . . Even if he is devoid of shame and persists in his wickedness, forgive him from the heart and leave vengeance to God" (TGad 6:3-7).

Since the struggle between good and evil is common to all human beings and only ethical impurity stands in the way of salvation, the Testaments of the Twelve Patriarchs give more strength to the universalistic approach of the earlier Enochic tradition. God does not show partiality; God loves all those who fear God and love their neighbor, regardless of any boundary between groups of people. "If you continue to do good, even the unclean spirits will flee from you and wild animals will fear you. For where someone has within himself respect for good works and has light in the understanding, darkness will slink away from that person" (TBenj 5:2-3; cf. 3:4; 6:1). As the anthropology and ethics of the Testaments state about the common solidarity of all humankind in sin and goodness, so the eschatology of the document does not make any distinction between Jews and Gentiles. Echoing Dream Visions' prophecy of God's new house in which "the [faithful] sheep [[= the elect from among the Jews]] . . . are gathered together with all the beasts of the field and the birds of the sky [[= the elect from among the Gentiles]]" (1 En 90:33), the Testaments describe the world to come as a time of salvation for all humankind. "God will appear . . . to save the race of Israel, and to assemble the righteous from among the nations" (TNaph 8:3; cf. TSim 7:2; TAsh 7:3; TBenj 9:2).[48]

48. G. Boccaccini, "Boundless Salvation: Jews and Gentiles in Middle Judaism," in *Middle Judaism: Jewish Thought, 300 B.C.E. to 200 C.E.* (Minneapolis: Fortress, 1991) 251-65; idem, "Dallo straniero come categoria sociale allo straniero come problema religioso: Alle radici dell'universalismo cristiano e rabbinico," *RSB* 8/1-2 (1996)

David Flusser is the scholar who has emphasized most strongly the anti-Qumranic nature of the Testaments of the Twelve Patriarchs. "These people rebelled against the [Qumranic] doctrine of hatred, and abandoned its sharp dualism and its characteristically strict doctrine of predestination, and in their place developed a very humane and humanistic doctrine of love."[49] While remaining faithful to the same foundations, the Testaments of the Twelve Patriarchs gave to Enochic Judaism a completely different trajectory from that imparted by the Qumran community.

(c) *The Book of the Similitudes (or Parables) of Enoch.* My analysis of the post-Qumranic Enochic text ends with the Book of the Similitudes of Enoch (1 En 37–71).[50] Similitudes is not the last document of Enochic Judaism (2 Enoch, the Apocalypse of Abraham, 4 Ezra, and many others would follow in the same trajectory of thought), but it is the first one that does not bear literary traces of a common origin with the sectarian documents of Qumran. Its absence from the Dead Sea Scrolls led many scholars to believe that it was a later Christian document. The editor of the Qumran fragments of 1 Enoch, Jósef T. Milik, suggested a very late date "around the year 270 CE."[51] At present, the overwhelming majority of scholars would disagree and point to the turn of the era as the time in which this pre-Christian, Enochic document was composed.[52] But no scholar has been able to solve the mystery of its absence from the Qumran library. Now, at the end of our journey through the ancient Enochic literature, we have a perfectly reasonable explanation for why the document was not preserved among the Dead Sea Scrolls: it was composed after the schism between Qumran and Enochic Judaism.

Similitudes confirms the Enochic choice for a view of historical determinism that assumes God's control over historical events without going into the details of too rigid periodization. "Even before the world was created, he knows what is forever and what will be from generation

---

163-72; idem, "Prospettive universalistiche nel tardo-giudaismo," *PSV* 16 (1987) 81-98; cf. M. Pérez-Fernández, "La apertura a los gentiles en el judaísmo intertestamentario," *EstBib* 41 (1983) 83-106.

49. Flusser, *Spiritual History,* 79.

50. The most important monographs on 1 Enoch, including the Book of the Similitudes, are listed in the bibliography at the end of this volume.

51. Milik, *Books of Enoch,* 96.

52. Nickelsburg, *ABD* 2.508-16; J. H. Charlesworth, *The Old Testament Pseudepigrapha and the New Testament,* SNTSMS 54 (Cambridge: Cambridge University Press, 1985); S. Chialà, *Libro delle parabole di Enoc* (Brescia: Paideia, 1997).

to generation" (1 En 39:11). Like the Epistle of Enoch and the Testaments of the Twelve Patriarchs, Similitudes knows only a fundamental periodization that opposes this world to the world to come.

This world is characterized by a certain dualism between good and evil, light and darkness. "The Lord of the Spirits . . . created the distinction between light and darkness and separated the spirits of the people, and strengthened the spirits of the righteous in the name of his righteousness" (1 En 41:8). The doctrine of individual predestination is rejected, however, thus preventing human responsibility and God's justice from collapsing. "Surely, neither an angel nor Satan has the power to hinder; for there is a judge to all of them, he will glance, and all of them are before him, he is the judge" (41:9). Following the path opened by the Epistle of Enoch, the two groups of the righteous and the sinners are identified respectively with the well-to-do and the poor; salvation is not predetermined by an individual call from God but depends on different moral behavior. With words that echo the Testaments of the Twelve Patriarchs, Similitudes confirms that the distinction between rich and poor is not simply economic but ethical as well. Because it divides the human heart, the love of money leads to idolatry. Sinners "manifest all their deeds in oppression; all their deeds are oppression. Their power (depends) upon their wealth. And their devotion is to the gods which they have fashioned with their own hands" (46:7; cf. TJud 19:1).

Another important step is carried out in the psychologization of the ancient myth of the fallen angels. The emphasis is not on the universe's contamination, of which human beings are passive victims, but overwhelmingly on the spread of secret knowledge passed on to human beings by the angels (1 En 64:1-2; 69:1-26). This revelation, aimed to mislead human beings, is described as a process of temptation that started at the beginning of humankind. The angel who taught human beings the art of making instruments of war is the same who first "misled Eve" (69:6). As we have already noticed in the analysis of the Testaments of the Twelve Patriarchs, Enochic Judaism, while rejecting the Qumran equation of evil and impurity, is seeking for a balance between the superhuman origin of evil and human responsibility. The time is ripe for the original sin of the Watchers to be replaced by the original sin of Adam as the new Enochic myth about the origin of evil. This change will be apparent in the Enochic or Christian documents of the first century CE, such as the Life of Adam and Eve, the Letter of Paul to the Romans, 2 Enoch, and 4 Ezra. The three-character drama, staging Satan, Eve, and Adam, gives a more active role to human beings without denying the superhuman origin of evil, and makes the human heart the source through which evil entered and continues to enter the world.[53]

Central to Similitudes is what James C. VanderKam calls the "notion of reversal."[54] While this world is under the dominion of rebellious angels, in the world to come "the elect one . . . would sit in the throne of glory and judge Azaz'el and all his company, and his army, in the name of the Lord of the Spirits" (1 En 55:4). While in this world the well-to-do rule over and oppress the poor, "in those days, the kings of the earth and the mighty landowners shall be humiliated on account on the deeds of their hands" (48:8; cf. 46:4-6). While light and darkness coexist in this world, in the world to come "there shall be light that has no end . . . for already darkness has been destroyed" (58:6). The "reversal" that Similitudes announces excludes any form of inaugurated eschatology that would annul human responsibility.

Chapter 42 is a short poem telling how wisdom once visited the earth but was frustrated in her search: "Wisdom went out to dwell with the children of the people, but she found no dwelling place" (42:1-2). So she returned to heaven, while iniquity took her place: "Wisdom returned to her place and she settled permanently among the angels. Then iniquity went out of their rooms" (42:2-3). Coherent with the Enochic doctrine of evil, Similitudes knows that this world is a place of iniquity; wisdom is exclusively an eschatological gift (cf. 48:1; 49:1).

The poem of ch. 42 is a direct attack against the sapiential myth of the torah as the earthly embodiment of heavenly wisdom.[55] However, the tradition of Sirach and 1 Baruch may not be the only target. The Enochic poem also denies the suggestion of the Proto-Epistle of Enoch and of the sectarian literature of Qumran that on earth a special group of people have received "wisdom" as a permanent possession.

Similitudes does not deny that such a group would ultimately emerge but stresses that this time is yet to come. While the Qumran community claimed to be the "house" established by God in this world, Similitudes

53. I. Levi, *Le péché original dans les anciennes sources juives* (Paris: Imprimerie Nationale, 1907); L. Ligier, *Péché d'Adam et péché du monde* (Paris: Aubier, 1960).

54. J. C. VanderKam, *Enoch: A Man for All Generations* (Columbia: University of South Carolina Press, 1995) 134.

55. G. Boccaccini, "The Preexistence of the Torah: A Commonplace in Second Temple Judaism, or a Later Rabbinic Development?" *Hen* 17 (1995) 329-50.

reminds its readers that the "house of [God's] congregation" would be established only by God's messiah. "And after this the righteous and the chosen one will cause the house of his congregation to appear . . . and the righteous will have rest from the ill-treatment of the sinners" (1 En 53:6-7; cf. 38:1). While the sectarian community called itself the "righteous plant," Similitudes reserves this imagery for the messianic congregation that "shall be planted" when God will "reveal the Son of Man to the holy and the elect ones" (62:7-8). While the Apocalypse of Weeks had granted the gift of wisdom to the chosen among the chosen at the end of the seventh week, Similitudes claims that "all the secrets of wisdom shall come out from the conscience of [the messiah's] mouth" (51:3; cf. 49:3-4).

The explicit link of all eschatological gifts with the coming of the messiah guarantees that no confusion is possible. The gift of wisdom and the establishment of the community of the saints belong not to a preliminary stage but only to the future of the world to come, when God and God's messiah will overthrow the evil forces, angelic and human.

Until that time, unpleasant as it may be, the righteous and the sinners have to live together. The sinners "deny the name of the Lord of the Spirits, yet they like to congregate in his houses and with the faithful ones who cling to the Lord of the Spirits" (1 En 46:7-8). The later Enochic literature is clearly not isolationist. The tendency is even to soften the elements of disagreement with Jewish society at large. For example, the author of Similitudes knows that, depending on the sun or on the moon, "one festival is celebrated more than the other" (41:5). Nevertheless, this does not seem to bother him. Both the sun and the moon execute their courses in accordance with God's command (41:1-7). Calendrical divergence is only one of many obvious consequences of the presence in this world of the righteous and sinners. "The course of the moon's path is light to the righteous and darkness to the sinners" (41:8).

Similitudes does not deny that the distinction between the oppressed and the oppressors is clearly set, and that the righteous have the right, and the duty before God, to walk in their way. The attitude is similar, however, to that of the Testaments of the Twelve Patriarchs: "even if one is devoid of shame and persists in his wickedness, forgive him from the heart and leave vengeance to God" (TGad 6:7). The major interest of these later Enochic texts is to keep contact with fellow Jews and to show that the boundary between the righteous and the sinners is not impassable. Repentance belongs to this world. Contrary to what the Qumran community proclaimed, the door would be closed only at the time of the final judgment. "At that moment, kings and rulers shall perish . . . and from thenceforth no one shall induce the Lord of the Spirits to show them mercy" (1 En 38:5-6). The importance of the statement is emphasized by repetition. Similitudes alludes to a typical phrase in the Epistle ("they shall have no peace," 94:6; 98:11, 15; 99:13; 101:3; 102:3; 103:8) and clarifies that it must be interpreted as referring only to the time after the last judgment. "The Lord of the Spirits has said that from thenceforth he will not have mercy on them" (50:5). Facing God's judgment, "the governors, kings, high officials, and landlords" would regret that they missed the opportunity of enjoying God's salvation and now "have no (more) chance to become believers" (63:8), and "their face shall be filled with shame before that Son of Man" (63:11).

In Similitudes the figure of the messiah assumes an emphasis that was unknown in the previous Enochic tradition and would remain foreign to the Qumran community. Because of the emphasis on predestination, at Qumran the messiahs are not, and could not possibly be, "the ultimate focus of the hopes of the sect";[56] messianic expectation never reaches the center of the stage. Instead, Similitudes makes the Danielic Son of Man a key character in the Enochic doctrine of evil.[57] As the one to whom all the eschatological gifts are related, the Son of Man strengthens the Enochic stance against any form of inaugurated eschatology, while his preexistence confirms God's foresight and control over this world without denying the freedom of angels and humans. The superhuman nature of the Son of Man enables him to defeat the angelic forces responsible for the origin and the spread of evil, a task that no human messiah (either priestly or kingly) could ever accomplish. The superhuman nature of the Son of Man also enables him to carry out the judgment, a task that makes fully consistent the Enochic concern that the merciful God cannot be directly involved in any manifestation of evil, from its origin and spread to its final destruction.

56. Collins, *Apocalypticism in the Dead Sea Scrolls,* 90.

57. On the figure of the Son of Man in the context of middle Jewish messianic expectations, see Collins, *Scepter and the Star;* J. H. Charlesworth, ed., *The Messiah: Developments in Earliest Judaism and Christianity* (Minneapolis: Fortress, 1992); J. Neusner, W. S. Green, and E. S. Frerichs, eds., *Judaisms and Their Messiahs at the Turn of the Christian Era* (Cambridge: Cambridge University Press, 1987); S. Mowinckel, *He That Cometh: The Messiah Concept in the Old Testament and Later Judaism,* trans. G. W. Anderson (New York and Nashville: Abingdon, 1956).

Similitudes is the mature product of an anti-Qumranic Enochic stream that, drawing on the same ideological and literary background as the Dead Sea Scrolls, has now reached ideological and literary autonomy. While the redactional history of the Epistle of Enoch and the Testaments of the Twelve Patriarchs is closely interwoven with the sectarian literature of Qumran, Similitudes is non-Qumranic more than anti-Qumranic. A gulf now separates the two movements.

From this point on, interaction and exchange of documents between the two groups ceases. While the community of the Dead Sea Scrolls engages in enforcing its doctrine of cosmic dualism and individual predestination, Enochic Judaism engages in other matters, such as conversion and deliverance from evil, which do not make sense if good and evil are preordained by God. Why should God warn people to convert and offer them divine help, if God's choice makes individuals what they are? Why should God be removed from any relationship with evil, if God is the creator of it?

None of these concerns makes sense in light of Qumran sectarian theology. At Qumran the freedom of God's decision annuls any other freedom, including God's own freedom to be merciful toward God's creatures. Enochic Judaism explores a different path that, while confirming the superhuman origin of evil, preserves the freedom of Satan to rebel, the freedom of human beings to choose, and the freedom of God to bring deliverance. Evil is against God's will and is the unfortunate result of an act of rebellion, which only the joint efforts of God, humans, and the heavenly messiah can successfully defeat.

We can now answer Charlesworth's question, "Does [the lack of interest in Enochic literature] mean that the Qumran community had become less apocalyptic?" The Qumran community did not become less apocalyptic, if we consider its roots and its worldview;[58] but it certainly became less Enochic the further it parted from the parallel development of mainstream Enochic Judaism since the first century BCE. Therefore, the decreasing influence of Enochic literature on the sectarian texts is by no means surprising; it is the logical consequence of the schism between Qumran and Enochic Judaism.

---

58. Collins, *Apocalypticism in the Dead Sea Scrolls*.

4. Sectarian Documents in Context; or, Qumran vs. Enoch

It is now possible to locate the sectarian literature and its theology, which I have described systematically in Chapter 3, within a dynamic historical trajectory. Among the sectarian documents are no writings that one could properly call historical. Nevertheless, some scrolls offer a glance at the inner history of the sect and its relationship to the pluralistic environment of middle Judaism. Credit goes to the Groningen hypothesis for showing that the sectarian literature, especially the *pesharim,* contains some intriguing allusions to the parting of the ways between Qumran and its parent movement. A reconstruction of the schism, as seen from the Qumran side, can now be offered.

The sectarian literature consistently presents the teacher of righteousness as a former member, not the founder, of the parent movement from which the Qumran community split. The teacher of righteousness was a "priest" (1QpHab 2:8; 4Q171 [4QpPsᵃ] 3:15), who claimed to have received a special revelation to be the leader of the chosen. The *pesharim* remember him as the one "to whom God has disclosed all the mysteries of the words of his servants, the prophets" (1QpHab 7:4-5; cf. 2:8-9), and whom "God chose to stand [in front of him, for] he installed him to found the congregation [of his chosen ones] for him, [and stra]ightened out his path, in truth" (4Q171 [4QpPsᵃ] 3:15-17). The Damascus Document speaks of him as a reformer who began preaching "twenty years" after the constitution of an organized movement within Israel (CD 1:9-11). The Damascus Document also reveals that the catalyst of the schism between the parent movement and the teacher of righteousness was his decision to call for a stricter segregation from the rest of Israel, whom he considered under the dominion of Belial.

As expected, the strongest reaction came from the authorities of the Jerusalem temple, who saw their legitimacy threatened. The literature of Qumran bears the memory of the persecution of the teacher of righteousness by the Hasmonean high priests, who were labeled "wicked priest(s)" (1QpHab 8:8-13; 8:16–9:2; 9:9-12; 11:4-8, 12-15; 12:2-6, 7-10).[59]

---

59. A. S. van der Woude, "Wicked Priest or Wicked Priests? Reflections on the Identification of the Wicked Priest in the Habakkuk Commentary," *JJS* 32 (1982) 349-59; idem, "Once Again: The Wicked Priests in the Habakkuk Pesher from Cave 1 of Qumran," *RevQ* 17 (1996) 375-84; W. H. Brownlee, "The Wicked Priest, the Man of Lies, and the Righteous Teacher: The Problem of Identity," *JQR* 73 (1982) 1-37.

The sectarian documents also contain a series of obscure allusions to rival groups who were enemies of the community, such as "the arrogant men who are in Jerusalem" in the Isaiah *pesher* (4Q162 [4QpIs^b] 2:6-7, 10). In some cases, commentators recognize more specific references to middle Jewish sectarianism. In particular, "those who seek smooth things" (CD 1:18; 4Q163 [4QpIs^c] frag. 23:10-11; 1QH 10:23) would be the Pharisees, or the "house of Ephraim," which the Nahum *pesher* (4Q169 [4QpNah]) reproaches and contrasts with the "house of Manasseh," or the Sadducees, while identifying the sectarians with the glorious "house of Judah."

For my analysis of the parting of the ways between Qumran and Enochic Judaism, it is more important to notice the existence of internal opposition. In addition to the authorities of Jerusalem and rival sects, the sectarian texts also count among their enemies some "traitors," people who "entered the new covenant in the land of Damascus and turned and betrayed and departed from the well of living waters" (CD 19:33-34).

The Damascus Document refers to an opponent of the teacher of righteousness as the "scoffer," "the liar," or "the preacher of lies" (CD 8:13; 19:26; 20:15; cf. 1QpHab 2:1-2; 5:9-12; 10:9; 4Q171 [4QpPs^a] 1:26; 4:14). This individual appears to be the leader of a group that broke away at an early stage from the movement led by the teacher of righteousness. This group of traitors is labeled "the house of Peleg." The reference is to a descendant of Noah and Seth who was called Peleg, from the Hebrew root *plg* ("to divide"), "because in the days when he was born the sons of Noah began dividing up the earth for themselves" (Jub 8:8; cf. Gen 10:25; 1 Chr 1:19). That Peleg is a direct ancestor of the Israelites underlines that the division is within the same family.

The Damascus Document says that "the house of Peleg . . . went out of the holy city and relied on God at the time when Israel was unfaithful and made the sanctuary unclean,[60] but returned again [to the wa]y of the people in a few respec[ts]" (CD 20:22-24). In other words, the house of Peleg is a group of people who share the Enochic view of the contamination of postexilic Judaism, but are now accused by the

---

60. With P. R. Davies and M. A. Knibb, I take "Israel," not the house of Peleg, as the subject of the temple's defilement. Cf. Davies, *Damascus Covenant,* 190-94; M. A. Knibb, *The Qumran Community* (Cambridge: Cambridge University Press, 1987) 74-76.

teacher of righteousness of being inconsistent with their own positions and too ready to compromise.

The reference to Peleg in the Nahum *pesher* supports this interpretation: "they are the wick[ed people of Judah], the house of Peleg, which consorted with Manasseh" (4Q169 4:1). Because the Nahum *pesher* denotes the sectarians as the house of Judah, it confirms that "Peleg" was a code word for the internal opposition (cf. in the Psalms *pesher* the reference to "the ruthless ones of the covenant who are in the house of Judah, who plot to destroy those who observe the law, who are in the Community Council," 4Q171 [4QpPsᵃ] 2:14-15). Even more interestingly, the association of Peleg with Manasseh, or the Sadducees, confirms that at stake was the separation from the Jerusalem temple and priesthood.

In light of the history of the Enochic movement, it is not difficult to understand the reasons why many Enochians resisted the pressure for a more radical opposition. The teacher of righteousness called for a separation from Israel and the temple in a way that many were not prepared to do. The conciliatory tone of the Halakhic Letter shows that the Enochic movement, although critical of the religious and political institutions of Israel, had no intention of breaking off completely from Jewish society and the Jerusalem authorities, including the Sadducean priesthood.

The confrontation within the parent movement between the followers of the teacher of righteousness and the others apparently grew in intensity. The attitude of the Damascus Document, which is polemical against the entirety of the Jewish people, is still conciliatory toward the house of Peleg. The door is still open for its members and "each one according to his spirit, shall be judged in the holy council" (CD 20:24-25). "As a group they are to be neither recognized as members nor rejected, but each one of them shall be considered on his merits."[61]

Such openness disappears in the later documents. The Habakkuk *pesher* equates the non-Qumran members of the parent group with the other (wicked) Jews. They are enemies to be treated with contempt: "[Interpreted, this concerns] those who were unfaithful together with the man of lies, since they [did] not [listen to the word received by] the teacher of righteousness from the mouth of God. (And it concerns) the unfaithful of the new [covenant] since they did not believe in the covenant of God [and profaned] his holy name" (1QpHab 2:1-4).

61. Davies, *Damascus Covenant*, 193.

"Absalom" becomes the new label of the traitors: "O traitors, 'why do you stare and stay silent when the wicked swallows up one more righteous than he?' [[= Hab 1:13b]]. Interpreted, this concerns the house of Absalom and the members of its council who were silent at the time of the reproach of the teacher of righteousness and did not help him against the man of lies who flouted the law in the midst of their whole [congregation]" (1QpHab 5:8-12). Like Peleg, and even more than Peleg, Absalom is a symbol of internal division; Absalom is the unfaithful son of David who betrayed the unity of his family and plotted against the legitimate leadership.

The growing hostility that the teacher of righteousness met within and outside his own movement was probably the most immediate cause of the phenomenon we now call Qumran. The followers of the teacher of righteousness abandoned (and were forced to abandon) his initial attempt to gain the leadership of the movement. In a dramatic move they decided to leave for the desert and form a settlement of their own. The founding manifesto is in the Rule of the Community: "When these form a community in Israel, they shall be separated from the midst of the men of iniquity to go to the desert, to prepare there the way of the Lord, as it is written, 'In the desert prepare the way of the Lord, straighten in the wilderness a highway for our God' [[Isa 40:3]]. This is the interpretation of the torah wh[ic]h he commanded through Moses to observe, according to everything that has been revealed (from) time to time, and as the prophets have revealed by his holy spirit" (1QS 8:12-16).

On the ideological level, dualism was the answer of the Qumran community to their progressive alienation from Jewish society and from their Enochic parent movement. The experience of rejection reinforced the self-consciousness of the followers of the teacher of righteousness that membership was based exclusively on an individual call by God ("called by name," CD 4:4). Now, as the book of Jubilees had already understood, predestination was the only way to secure the righteousness of the chosen in this world, a world full of evil and impurity. Hence God created the angel of darkness and the children of deceit, as well as the prince of light and the children of righteousness.

The progression toward a more and more pronounced dualism is apparent not only in the systemic analysis of the Dead Sea Scrolls, where dualism appears to be the culmination of centuries of intellectual reflection on the problem of evil within the Enochian tradition, but also in the redactional history of the sectarian documents, where dualism goes along with the abandonment of the Enochic myth of the fallen angels and of any reference to the freedom of the human will.[62]

The schism away from the parent movement also affected the eschatological ideas of the group.[63] While the Damascus Document had tried to define the new community (Heb. *yḥd*) in relation to the wider set of Enochic communities, now the rules that apply to the entire people of Israel (Heb. *'dh,* "congregation") are transferred to the future, to the end of days. The War Scroll (1QM) and the Rule of the Congregation (1QSa) are not pre-Qumranic texts[64] but sectarian documents envisaging a post-Qumranic eschatological scenario, when the hope was that all Israel would eventually join the Qumran community and accept its leadership. The War Scroll expresses the sect's belief that at the end of time God would reunite them with the rest of Israel, "when the exiled sons of light return from the desert of the peoples to camp in the desert of Jerusalem" (1QM 1:3). The endorsement of the temple and the reestablishment of family ties must be seen as part of this eschatological scenario, not as reflecting the actual way of life of the sect. The Rule of the Congregation is not the rule of the *yahad* but "the rule for all the congregation of Israel in the end of days, when they gather [in community to wa]lk in accordance with the regulation of the sons of Zadok, the priests, and the men of their covenant who have tu[rned away from walking in the] way of the people. These [[= the priests and the men of their covenant]] are the men of his [[= God's]] counsel who have kept the covenant in the midst of wickedness to ato[ne for the lan]d [[= the members of the Qumran *yahad*]]. When they [[= the entire congregation of Israel]] come, they [[= the members of the *yahad*]] shall assemble all those who enter, (including) children and women" (1QSa 1:1-4). Only in the *eschaton* would the concept of an ethnic Israel make sense again. "And this is the rule for all the hosts of the congregation, for all native Israelites" (1:6).

As Charlotte Hempel has recently shown, "the core of the Rule of

---

62. J. Duhaime, "Dualistic Reworking in the Scrolls from Qumran," *CBQ* 49 (1987) 32-56.

63. Collins, "The Eschatological War," in *Apocalypticism in the Dead Sea Scrolls,* 91-109.

64. This claim has been made by H. Stegemann, *Die Essener, Qumran, Johannes der Täufer und Jesus* (Freiburg: Herder, 1993).

the Congregation consists of a piece of communal legislation that goes back to the . . . parent movement of the Qumran community."[65] While developing a special legislation for themselves, the community of the Dead Sea Scrolls had no need to create new rules for the *eschaton*. The actual way of life of mainstream Enochians provided an effective prophecy for Israel in the messianic age. Until that time, the sectarians claimed that they were the only holy remnant and that all the attributes of the chosen people applied to them exclusively.

The Qumran community offers the first example of the notorious "theology of supersession" that the Church would often use in order to define itself in relation to the Synagogue.[66] The sectarians believed that they had superseded Israel in this world as the "eternal planting" celebrated in Enochic literature. "It shall be an eternal planting, a house of holiness for Israel, an assembly of supreme holiness for Aaron. They shall be witnesses to the truth at the judgment and shall be the elect of good will who shall atone for the land and pay to the wicked their reward. They shall be that tried wall, that precious cornerstone [[= Isa 28:16]], whose foundations shall neither rock nor sway in their place" (1QS 8:4-10). The supersessionist approach and the self-consciousness of being individually chosen led the sectarians to a path of complete segregation from the rest of humankind (including their fellow Jews). Each new member was asked to "swear by the covenant to be segregated from all the men of sin who walk along paths of irreverence. For they are not included in his covenant" (1QS 5:10-11).

In the face of the harshness of this evil world, concepts such as dualism, individual predestination, and self-segregation strengthened the identity and unity of the group, provided a way of explaining the suffering of the chosen and the opposition of outsiders, and targeted the adversaries as the devil's party according to a pattern that would be repeated often with tragic results in the history of religion.[67]

At the root of the Qumran community was a double frustration. In the aftermath of the Maccabean revolt, the Qumranites' parent movement failed

65. C. Hempel, "The Earthly Essene Nucleus of 1QSa," *DSD* 3 (1996) 253-69.

66. J. W. Parkes, *The Conflict of the Church and the Synagogue: A Study in the Origin of Antisemitism* (London: Soncino, 1934; repr. Cleveland: World, 1961).

67. E. H. Pagels, *The Origin of Satan* (New York: Random House, 1995); idem, "The Social History of Satan, the 'Intimate Enemy': A Preliminary Sketch," *HTR* 84 (1991) 105-28; cf. P. Sacchi, "The Devil in Jewish Traditions of the Second Temple Period (c. 500 BCE–100 CE)," in *Jewish Apocalyptic,* 211-32.

in its political attempt to replace the Zadokite leadership. Internally, the followers of the teacher of righteousness failed to gain the leadership of their movement. The double experience of failure brought about, along with a sense of impotence, an outburst of fanaticism. The chosen among the chosen, whom the Proto-Epistle of Enoch announced as a blessing for all Israel, were now the accusers of their people. In their view, Jews and Gentiles alike were under the dominion of Belial, and there was neither atonement for evil nor purification of impurity except for those individuals whom God had selected to step aside and enter the new community. "Anyone who declines to enter [the covenant of Go]d in order to walk in the stubbornness of his heart shall not [enter the com]munity of his truth. . . . He shall not be justified. . . . Defiled, defiled shall he be" (1QS 2:25–3:5).

No doubt the sectarians spoke out; but to what extent did people listen to their voice? The existence of a large body of non-Qumranic documents of Enochic Judaism and the many references to "traitors" in the literature of Qumran testify that the sectarians did not achieve what they sought; their call for leadership was fiercely challenged. Under these circumstances, the parting of Qumran from its parent movement was a bad bet; withdrawing to the wilderness, the community may have still hoped to become the headquarters of a larger movement, but it was just as likely to turn itself into a marginal fringe. The faith they had in predestination probably made them totally indifferent to such an alternative; they simply did what they believed God had preordained them to do. Their salvation did not depend on their being the majority or the minority. For an historical understanding of ancient Jewish thought, however, the question of the actual balance of power between these two Enochic branches is a fundamental and inescapable issue.

5. Missing Texts (II): Sectarian Documents outside Qumran

After examining the absence of nonsectarian texts from the Qumran library, we must now turn to another significant category of missing texts. These are the sectarian documents in the "virtual library" of middle Jewish literature.

No text that we have classified as written by the Qumran community appears to have had any significant impact in the development of middle Jewish thought. In vain one searches for a quotation in any of the ancient documents of Judaisms, other than Qumranic, or for a translation in Greek, Syriac, or any other ancient language. "None of the works connected to the Qumran Community was transmitted by other channels."[68]

Outside the Qumran caves, the only places in which copies of the sectarian scrolls have been found are the ruins of Masada and the Cairo Genizah. In the fragments found at Masada, archaeologists have identified, besides several "biblical" documents, a copy of the Hebrew Sirach identical to the text preserved at Qumran, and, notably, fragments of the book of Jubilees and of a sectarian text also well known from cave 4, the Songs of the Sabbath Sacrifice (4QShirShab).[69] The connection of these texts with the Qumran scrolls is stressed by the fact that they appear to have been written by some of the same scribes who copied the Qumran scrolls. Iin addition to some copies of an identical Hebrew Sirach, the Cairo Genizah yielded two large fragments of the Damascus Document. The connection of these texts with the Qumran scrolls is less direct but not less impressive; these are the only medieval copies we have of Qumran documents.

How these texts survived is a mystery, but there is an intriguing possibility that in both cases we can trace a direct connection with the community of the Dead Sea Scrolls. The presence of Qumran texts at Masada may well be explained by the arrival of some refugees from Qumran in the final years of the Jewish War, between 68 CE, when archaeology reveals that the settlement of Qumran was destroyed by the Romans and turned into a small military encampment for their own troops (cf. Josephus, *Ant.* 4.440-90), and 74 CE, when the Romans finally took the fortress of Masada and the Jewish War was brought to a final end (see *J.W.*

---

68. D. Dimant, "The Qumran Manuscripts: Contents and Significance," in Dimant and L. H. Schiffman, eds., *Time to Prepare the Way in the Wilderness: Papers on the Qumran Scrolls by Fellows of the Institute for Advanced Studies of the Hebrew University, Jerusalem, 1989-90,* STDJ 16 (Leiden: Brill, 1995) 23-58 (quotation on p. 32).

69. On Sirach see Y. Yadin, *The Ben Sira Scroll from Masada: With Introduction, Emendations and Commentary* (Jerusalem: Israel Exploration Society, 1965). On the other texts see E. Puech, "Notes sur les manuscrits des Cantiques du Sacrifice du Sabbat trouvés à Masada," *RevQ* 12 (1987) 575-83; C. Newsom, *Songs of the Sabbath Sacrifice: A Critical Edition,* HTS 27 (Atlanta: Scholars Press, 1985) 167-84, plate 16; C. A. Newsom and Y. Yadin, "The Masada Fragments of the Sabbath Sacrifice," *IEJ* 34 (1984) 77-88; Y. Yadin, "The Excavation of Masada," *IEJ* 15 (1965) 105-8. Cf. also idem, *Masada: Herod's Fortress and the Zealots' Last Stand,* trans. M. Pearlman (New York: Random House, 1966) 173-74; R. de Vaux, *Archaeology and the Dead Sea Scrolls,* rev. ed. (London: Oxford University Press, 1973) 121-22.

7.252-406). Masada is not far from Qumran, and with the Romans converging simultaneously from east and west at Jericho, so that Jerusalem was isolated "round about on all sides" (*Ant.* 4.490), the only way out was south. Along this road, the fortress held by the Sicarii was the natural and safest refuge.[70]

The circumstances that brought the manuscripts from Qumran to the Cairo Genizah may have been even more adventurous. In a letter written around 796, the Nestorian patriarch of Seleucia, Timothy I, informs his colleague of Elam, Sergius, that "ten years ago books were found in a cave in the vicinity of Jericho . . . books of the Old Testament as well as others written in Hebrew."[71] Timothy's testimony is supported by other ancient authors, notably the Karaite scholar Ja'qub al-Qirqisani (tenth century), and the Muslim authors Shahrastani (1076-1153) and al-Biruni (973-c. 1050). Some scholars hypothesize that these manuscripts may have been discovered in one of the Qumran caves and come into the possession of the Jewish sect of the Karaites, who copied and preserved them. Some of those copies were eventually crammed into the Cairo Genizah together with thousands of other manuscripts from many lands.[72] The 1947 discovery of the Dead Sea Scrolls may not have been the first time that a shepherd found manuscripts in the caves surrounding Qumran. The ancient discovery of some "Dead Sea Scrolls" might well explain the recognized influence of Qumran sectarian ideas in the development of Karaism, notably in authors such as Daniel al-Qumisi and Yefeth ben 'Ali.[73] The Qumran texts, however, had no significant impact on mainstream Rabbinic Judaism.

The chance circumstances through which the scrolls found their way to Masada and Cairo are evidence that we face the classical exceptions that prove the general rule: too little and too late to claim any significant and

70. See P. Vidal-Naquet, "Flavius Josèphe et Masada," *RH* 260 (1978) 3-21.

71. O. Braun, "Ein Brief des Katholikos Timotheos I über biblische Studien des 9 Jahrhunderts," *OrChr* 1 (1901) 299-313.

72. A. A. Di Lella, *The Hebrew Text of Sirach: A Text-Critical and Historical Study* (The Hague: Mouton, 1966); P. E. Kahle, *The Cairo Geniza*, 2nd ed. (Oxford: Blackwell, 1959); H. H. Rowley, *The Zadokite Fragments and the Dead Sea Scrolls* (Oxford: Blackwell, 1952); R. de Vaux, "A propos des manuscrits de la Mer Morte," *RB* 57 (1950) 417-29.

73. H. Bardtke, "Einige Erwägungen zum Problem 'Qumran und Karaismus,'" *Hen* 10 (1988) 259-70; A. Paul, *Écrits de Qumrân et sectes juives aux premiers siècles de l'Islam: Recherches sur l'origine du qaraïsme* (Paris: Letouzey et Ané, 1969); N. Wieder, *The Judean Scrolls and Karaism* (London: East and West Library, 1962).

lasting impact on ancient Jewish thought. This phenomenon is more striking when one considers the success that the Enochic texts enjoyed even outside their original context, not only among the Christians, who were the most direct heirs of Enochic Judaism, but also among the rabbis, who fiercely opposed it. The countless quotations from and allusions to Enochic literature and the richness of ancient versions stand as witnesses of the enduring fortune of this literature in antiquity.[74]

Of the documents that belong to the formative period of the Qumran community, only a few have enjoyed some popularity. It cannot be accidental that the best known is the least sectarian of all, Jubilees, while the Proto-Epistle of Enoch, including the Apocalypse of Weeks, owes its survival outside Qumran only to its being enclosed in the Epistle of Enoch. Of the others, the Temple Scroll and the Halakhic Letter, we would know nothing without the discovery of the Qumran library.

That the ancient popularity of the Dead Sea Scrolls is in inverse proportion to their proximity to the Qumran community is further evidence of the isolationism of the sect. While Enochic Judaism never lost contact with the broader Jewish society, the Qumran community withdrew into itself. Speaking about the Testaments of the Twelve Patriarchs, David Flusser attributes its composition to a group of "heretics" who rejected the sect's idea of predestination and its doctrine of hatred.[75] In view of the popularity of this group and the isolationism of the sectarian literature, I would rather argue that the "heretics" were the people of Qumran. A community that lives isolated in the desert and over two centuries neither imports nor exports a single document can hardly be considered a leading group.

---

74. For an overview of the fortune of Enochic literature in Christianity and Rabbinic Judaism, see J. C. VanderKam, "1 Enoch, Enochic Mofits, and Enoch in Early Christian Literature," in J. C. VanderKam and W. Adler, eds., *The Jewish Apocalyptic Heritage in Early Christianity*, CRINT 3/4 (Assen: Van Gorcum; Minneapolis: Fortress, 1995) 33-101; J. C. Reeves, ed., *Tracing the Threads: Studies in the Vitality of Jewish Pseudepigrapha*, SBLEJL 6 (Atlanta: Scholars Press, 1994); M. M. Witte, *Elias und Henoch als Exempel, typologischer Figuren und apokalyptische Zeugen: Zu Verbindungen von Literatus und Theologie im Mittelalter* (Frankfurt am Main and New York: Lang, 1987); M. Himmelfarb, "A Report on Enoch in Rabbinic Literature," in *SBL Seminar Papers, 1978*, 259-69.

75. D. Flusser, "The Hatred Through the Love," in *Spiritual History*, 76-82.

6. Summary: A Bifurcation in the Chain
of Enochic Documents

Systemic analysis of the Dead Sea Scrolls reconstructs a single unbroken chain of related documents from the earliest Enochic literature to the sectarian literature of Qumran. The "Qumran chain" (see fig. 1) unfolds, link by link, from the Book of the Watchers, Aramaic Levi, and the Astronomical Book (fourth-third century BCE), to Dream Visions (at the time of the Maccabean revolt), to Jubilees and the Temple Scroll (immediately afterward), to the Proto-Epistle of Enoch and the Halakhic Letter (mid-second century BCE), to the Damascus Document and the sectarian literature (from the second half of the second century BCE to the first century CE).

By sharing the same generative idea of the superhuman origin of evil, this chain of documents gives evidence of the ideological continuity between Enochic Judaism and the Qumran community. The Dead Sea Scrolls tell us the history of a specific movement, from its Enochic roots in postexilic times (Book of the Watchers, Aramaic Levi, Astronomical Book, Dream Visions), to its gradual organizing in communities after the Maccabean crisis (Jubilees, Temple Scroll, Proto-Epistle of Enoch, Halakhic Letter), to the emergence of a distinct group under the leadership of the teacher of righteousness (Damascus Document) and its settlement at Qumran (the sectarian literature).

By the time of the composition of Jubilees and the Temple Scroll, the Qumran chain took in another chain of documents, that of Zadokite literature. Although having the common founding father in Ezekiel, the two priestly traditions of Enochic Judaism and Zadokite Judaism had developed autonomously and in reciprocal competition during the early second temple period. In the wake of the Maccabean revolt, with the end of Zadokite power, the Enochians recognized the Zadokite literature as part of the common Jewish religious heritage, while the mediation of the book of Daniel allowed it to be interpreted in light of the Enochic principles.

The ideological consistency of the tradition preserved in the Dead Sea Scrolls confirms that it was the same community which wrote the sectarian documents and preserved in its "library" the other documents that testified to the prehistory of the group. The scrolls were not randomly collected, but consciously selected. "One cannot . . . escape the conclusion that the collection was intentional and not a haphazard assemblage of

disparate works. . . . The Qumran library . . . [contains] the specific literature produced by the community together with a body of literary works
which they took over from their parent group."[76]

The earliest documents, both Enochic and Zadokite, provided the
legitimacy of the sectarian group, its link with the past. Thus they could
not be rejected. Exegetical interpretation allowed the group to consider
themselves as the fulfillment of the prophecies contained in the ancient
literature, more or less the same as the Christians would do, preserving
the documents of the "old" covenant along with those of the "new"
covenant.

When analysis of the Qumran library is carried out within the broader
context of the entire middle Jewish literature, it becomes apparent that the
sectarians consciously ignored any documents that did not fit into their
worldview or their ideological reconstruction of the past. Apart from the
sectarian literature, no document whatsoever, written after the end of the
second century BCE, managed to find its way into the Qumran library. The
outside world repaid them in the same coin; no sectarian document whatsoever managed to find its way out of Qumran.

Systemic analysis shows that the Enochic chain of documents split
immediately before the composition of the Qumran sectarian texts. A group
of first-century-BCE documents (Epistle of Enoch, Testaments of the Twelve
Patriarchs, and Similitudes of Enoch) continued the same Enochic heritage
according to a different trajectory. The schism would neither be absorbed
nor overcome; from this point of bifurcation the literature of the two groups
proceeds on parallel lines. After the first polemical phase, the two branches
ignored each other; the Qumran stream became more and more predeter-
ministic in its approach to the problem of evil and salvation, while the
Enochic stream staged the drama of responsible human beings torn between
divine deliverance and the temptation of Satan. Literary evidence does not
leave any doubt about which branch was more successful: the popularity

76. Dimant, "Qumran Manuscripts," 32-33, 36. See the same conclusion in
F. García Martínez and A. S. van der Woude, "A Groningen Hypothesis of Qumran
Origins and Early History," *RevQ* 14 (1990) 526: "All the works found in Qumran that
cannot be classified as strictly sectarian must have been composed *before* the split that
gave rise to the Qumran group, because otherwise they would never have been accepted
by the sect." Cf. Shavit, "Qumran Library," 300: "The DSS are indeed a diverse corpus,
but . . . it was collected and preserved by a defined group espousing a clear world
outlook."

of the Enochic stream shines in comparison with the grim isolation of the Qumran stream.

In short, systemic analysis leads to the overall conclusion that the community of the Dead Sea Scrolls was a radical and minority group within Enochic Judaism.

PART III

COMPARATIVE ANALYSIS

CHAPTER 6

Conclusion:
The Enochic/Essene Hypothesis

1. Enochic Judaism and Essene Judaism

Both historiographical analysis and systemic analysis show a relationship
between a mainstream movement and a minority group with more radical
positions and a clearly defined identity. In ancient historiography this
pattern functions to regulate the relationship between "mainstream Essenism" and the "Essene community of the Dead Sea." Systemic analysis
of middle Jewish documents reveals a strikingly similar pattern between
"mainstream Enochic Judaism" and the "Enochic community of the Dead
Sea Scrolls."

Since the dawn of Qumran studies, literary and archaeological evidence has led scholars to conclude that the "community of the Dead Sea"
(described by Pliny and Dio), the "community of the Dead Sea Scrolls"
(to whose existence the sectarian writings testify), and the "Qumran community" (whose ruins have been excavated on the western shore of the
Dead Sea) are one and the same community. I am not going to repeat here
the traditional arguments of the "Essene hypothesis"; I consider them
compelling and conclusive. My goal is to move forward. What the Essene
hypothesis has not clarified is the relationship between "the Qumran community" (= the Essene community of the Dead Sea = the Enochic community of the Dead Sea Scrolls) and "mainstream Essenism" (as described
by Philo and Josephus). The Essene hypothesis has failed to identify autonomously the broader Essene movement and its literature.

A comparison between historiographical analysis and systemic analysis implies that what the ancients called "Essenism" embraces both the religious phenomena we modern interpreters label "Qumran Judaism" and "Enochic Judaism." The identification of the "Essene community of the Dead Sea" with the "Enochic community of the Dead Sea Scrolls" suggests a connection also between "mainstream Essenism" and mainstream Enochic Judaism." In other words, while Pliny and Dio describe the particular Enochic/Essene community at Qumran that wrote the sectarian scrolls, Enochic literature gives the context within which the descriptions offered by Philo and Josephus fit perfectly.

A major problem is given by the absence in Enochic literature of any detailed reference to the communal life of the Enochians. The only extant documents are books of vision and moral teaching attributed to ancient patriarchs, whereas Philo and Josephus focus almost entirely on the way of life of the Essenes. However, the ideology and sociology of the Essene movement as provided by first-century Jewish sources present conspicuous similarities with the ideology and sociology of mainstream Enochic Judaism. In particular, Josephus and Philo agree with non-Qumranic Enochic literature every time they disagree with the sectarian literature of Qumran.

In order to verify the connection between Enochians and non-Qumran Essenes, we cannot be content with the discovery of random parallels. A holistic comparison of systems of thought has to address the substance, not the accidents; it has to establish that the roots, the ideology, and the sociology of the two movements are identical.

2. Common Roots: Both Moses and Enoch

Josephus and Philo say that the Essenes honored Moses, "the lawgiver" (Gk. *ho nomothetēs*). Philo claims that the teachings of Moses are the foundation of the Essene way of life: "Our lawgiver encouraged the multitude of his disciples to live in community: these are called the Essenes" (*Apol.* 1). Josephus agrees: "The name of the lawgiver is, after God, a great object of veneration among them, and if any man blasphemes against the lawgiver he is punished with death. . . . During the war against the Romans . . . they were subjected to every instrument of torture to compel them to blaspheme against the lawgiver . . . but they refused to do it" (*J.W.* 2.145, 153).

The honor given to Moses does not contradict the association of the Essenes with Enochic Judaism. The Mosaic torah is conspicuously absent from the earlier Enochic literature, up to and including Dream Visions, but this situation changed in post-Maccabean times. Thanks to Jubilees, Moses became an important figure in the Enochic movement, if not as important as Enoch. In their attitudes toward Moses, the Essenes and the later Enochians do not differ.

But what about Enoch? Neither in their description of the Essenes nor elsewhere in their monumental works do Philo and Josephus mention the Enochic literature explicitly. In their interpretation of Gen 6:1-4 they do not connect the story of "the giants" with the antediluvian patriarch or take it as an explanation of the origin of evil. Philo and Josephus's own Judaism was far removed from the principles of Enochic Judaism.[1]

When Philo and Josephus speak of the holy texts of the Essenes, however, they do not limit them to the Zadokite literature. Philo and Josephus agree that the Essene tradition was a written tradition based on "books" and that the study of this literature was essential in the Essenes' way of life. Josephus says that they were "zealous in the writings of the ancients" (*J.W.* 2.136) and "educated in holy books" (2.159). Philo confirms that they applied themselves with great industry to the study of "the laws of the fathers, laws that no human mind could have conceived without divine inspiration"; particularly on the seventh day they gathered together, listened to the reading of "the books," and were instructed in the interpretation that a learned person gave to "whatever is not easy to understand, most of the time by means of symbols in accordance with an ancient method of inquiry" (*Omn. Prob. Lib.* 80-82). Neither Philo nor Josephus names the books of the Essenes, but it is quite clear that the Essene sacred literature encompassed more books than those they would have recognized as part of the Jewish Bible. Josephus mentions explicitly the presence of "books of their sect" (Gk. *ta tēs haireseōs autōn biblia; J.W.* 2.142).

Are the secret books of the Essenes the books of Enochic Judaism? Two points strongly support this hypothesis. First, Essene Judaism is the only variety of second temple Judaism of which it is said that they had a written tradition of holy books other than the Zadokite. The testimony of Josephus is particularly significant inasmuch as he contrasts the Sadducean loyalty to the

---

1. See J. C. VanderKam, *Enoch: A Man for All Generations* (Columbia: University of South Carolina Press, 1995) 148-53.

Zadokite canon with the additional oral tradition of the Pharisees and the additional written tradition of the Essenes. The Sadducees "say that we are to esteem to be obligatory only those observances that are in the written word" (*Ant.* 13.297). "The Pharisees have delivered to the people a great many observances from their fathers that are not written in the law of Moses" (*Ant.* 13.297). The Essenes have "books" of their own (*J.W.* 2.142).

Enochic literature testifies to a tradition of documents that went back to the pre-Mosaic patriarchs and was independent of the Zadokite "canon." Since the book of Jubilees, this written tradition was viewed as a supplement to the Mosaic revelation. As late as the end of the first century CE, the followers of Enochic Judaism who wrote the book of 4 Ezra would attribute to the scribe Ezra not only the copying of the "twenty-four books" of the Zadokite (Sadducean and Pharisaic) tradition but also of "seventy" secret books. "The Most High spoke to me, saying, 'Make public the twenty-four books that you wrote first and let the worthy and the unworthy read them; but keep the seventy that were written last, in order to give them to the wise among your people. For in them is the spring of understanding, the fountain of wisdom, and the river of knowledge.' And I did so" (4 Ezra 14:45-48). As far as we know from the extant documents of second temple Judaism, no variety of Judaism other than the Enochic claimed to be the recipient of ancient secret books. Neither the Pharisees nor the Sadducees made this claim. Only the Enochians, that is, the Essenes, spoke of such a written tradition.

Second, according to Josephus the Essene books provided three teachings: prophecy, healing, and the names of angels. The capability of foretelling future events is an apocalyptic trait that books such as Daniel, Psalms of Solomon, and 2 Baruch show was not exclusive to Enochic Judaism, yet it fits well with the historical determinism of Enochic documents. "Now there are some among them who profess to foreknow the future, being educated in holy books and various rites of purification and sayings of prophets; and rarely, if ever, do they err in their predictions" (*J.W.* 2.159). From the Christian letter of Jude we know that Enoch was viewed as a "prophet," the quotation from the prologue of 1 Enoch (1:9) being introduced by the words: "It was also about these that Enoch, in the seventh generation from Adam, prophesied, saying" (Jude 14).[2]

2. C. D. Osburn, "The Christological Use of 1 Enoch 1,9 in Jude 14-15," *NTS* 23 (1977) 331-41; J. H. Charlesworth, *The Old Testament Pseudepigrapha and the New Testament,* SNTSMS 54 (Cambridge: Cambridge University Press, 1985).

The link with Enochic literature is even more apparent in the reference to healing and the names of angels. In these two cases, we have no parallel in Jewish literature other than Enochic. Josephus claims that "in the books, [the Essenes] search out medicinal roots and the properties of stones for the healing of diseases" (*J.W.* 2.136). The passage alludes to a doctrine well established in Enochic Judaism since its origin. According to the Book of the Watchers, after "taking wives unto themselves . . . [the fallen angels] taught them magical medicine, incantations, the cutting of roots, and taught them (about) plants" (1 En 7:1). The teaching of "incantations and the cutting of roots" is attributed specifically to the angel "Amasras" and listed among the secret knowledge that the angels made known, causing evil to spread on earth (8:3). Without an "antidote" human beings would be condemned to perish. This is the goal of the mission that God entrusted to an angel, Raphael, whose name is from the Hebrew root *rp'*, "to heal." "The Lord said to Raphael . . . 'Heal the earth that the angels have corrupted. And he will proclaim the healing of the earth: that he may heal the plague. And all the children of men will not perish through all the secrets (of the angels) which they taught to their sons' " (10:7).

According to the book of Jubilees this good medicine was taught by God's faithful angels to Noah, who wrote it "in a book" he gave to Seth and his descendants. "And [God] told one of us [[probably Raphael]] to teach Noah all of their healing because he knew that they would not walk uprightly and would not strive righteously. And we acted in accord with all his words. . . . And the healing of all their illnesses together with their seductions we told Noah so that he might heal by means of herbs of the earth. And Noah wrote everything in a book just as we taught him according to every kind of healing" (Jub 10:10-14). The later Enochic tradition would not be as confident as Jubilees that the Jews are fully protected,[3] but would never question that a "medicine" had been revealed to the chosen that helps them fight against the destructive influence of the evil spirits. The chosen would be defenseless if God had not provided them with some "antidote."

The teaching of the names of the angels is the other element that directly connects the books of the Essenes to the Enochic literature. Before entering the Essene community, the postulant had "to swear that he will transmit their teachings to no one in a way other than as he received them

---

3. See the discussion of the Epistle of Enoch in Ch. 5 above.

. . . and that he will preserve in like manner both the books of their sect and the names of the angels" (*J.W.* 2.142). Again, in no literature other than the Enochic do we find an equal emphasis on the role and names of the angels. Comparing the Qumran writings with the Book of the Watchers and the Epistle of Enoch, Maxwell J. Davidson has demonstrated the continuity between Qumran and the Enochic tradition.[4] The Book of the Similitudes of Enoch shows that the interest in the names of the angels remained an essential element in mainstream Enochic Judaism even after the breach with the sectarian Qumran community. For example, ch. 69 contains one of the most detailed lists of the names of the fallen angels provided in the entire Enochic tradition. The Essenes, that is, the Enochians, used the greatest care in transmitting the names of the angels.

In conclusion, whoever the Essenes were, they represent a variety of Judaism whose "canon" (exactly like the Enochic "canon") was broader than the Bible used by Philo and Josephus and encompassed books that were only their own. In light of the contents of these secret books, it is also likely that Josephus and Philo referred to the books of Enochic Judaism. If the Enochians were not Essenes, they were their twin.

3. Common Ideology: Rejection of Individual Predestination

The sectarian literature of Qumran gave a distinctive emphasis to the generative idea of Enochic Judaism, that is, the superhuman origin of evil. The concepts of cosmic dualism and individual predestination ultimately made God the origin of evil on both the cosmic and the individual level. The denial of angelic and human freedom became the main cause of disagreement between Qumran and the larger Enochic movement.

That the Qumran Essenes believed in the doctrine of individual predestination is confirmed by Solinus (3rd-4th cent. CE).[5] His *Collectanea*

---

4. M. J. Davidson, *Angels at Qumran: A Comparative Study of 1 Enoch 1–36, 72–108 and Sectarian Writings from Qumran,* JSPSup 11 (Sheffield: JSOT Press, 1992); cf. L. T. Stuckenbruck, *Angel Veneration and Christology: A Study in Early Judaism and in the Christology of the Apocalypse of John,* WUNT 2/70 (Tübingen: Mohr, 1995).

5. See M. Stern, *Greek and Latin Authors on Jews and Judaism,* vol. 2 (Jerusalem: Israel Academy of Sciences and Humanities, 1981) 416-22.

Rerum Memorabilium parallels Pliny's description of the Essenes virtually verbatim with one significant addition: Solinus states that the members of that community "have been destined for this way of life by divine providence" (34.9-12). Wherever Solinus took this strikingly accurate piece of information from, it shows that, despite the silence of Pliny and Dio, ancient historiography was aware of this distinctive trait of Qumran theology, which is clearly attested in the sectarian scrolls. But what do ancient sources tell us about the position of the non-Qumran Essenes?

According to Josephus, the three Jewish groups of Essenes, Sadducees, and Pharisees had "different opinions concerning human events [Gk. *peri tōn anthrōpinōn pragmatōn*]. . . . The race of the Essenes maintains that fate is ruler of all things [*pantōn*], and nothing happens [*apantaō*] to people except it be according to its decree" (*Ant.* 13.171-72). Elsewhere Josephus adds that "the Essenes like to teach that in all things [*ta panta*] one should rely on God" (*Ant.* 18.18).

Scholars usually connect these passages with the Qumran doctrine of predestination and quote them as evidence for the identification of the Essenes with the Qumran community.[6] The sectarians, however, went much further. Unlike Solinus and the sectarian scrolls, Josephus does not speak of individual predestination, but of the relationship between historical events (Gk. *pragmata*) and human behavior. He explores the connection between what humans do and what "happens" (Gk. *apantaō*) to them. In other words, while Qumran claims that what humans are and do is determined by God, Josephus simply argues that for the Essenes what "happens" to humans is determined by fate, that is, superhuman forces, either God or the angels. Then he adds that humans should always confidently rely on God.

The idea that the course of history is condemned to inexorable degeneration because of the sin of the angels, that humans can do nothing to change this situation of evil and decay, is exactly what makes Enochic Judaism different from any other variety of second temple Judaism. Josephus's description is perfectly consistent with what we know from systemic analysis of middle Jewish documents. In Enochic Judaism, however, historical determinism does not absolve humans of their wrongdoing. God was betrayed by the rebellious angels, and, as the supreme ruler of

6. J. C. VanderKam, *The Dead Sea Scrolls Today* (Grand Rapids: Eerdmans, 1994) 76-78.

the universe and the final judge, he will take revenge on them. At the end, everything will turn out well for those who rely on God and resist evil, while the sinners (angelic and human) will be punished.

While Josephus remains within the boundaries of Enochic theology, he does not tell us anything about the matter of disagreement between Enochic Judaism and Qumran. Philo is much more explicit and direct; the Essenes believe that "the Deity is the cause of all good, but of no evil" (*Omn. Prob. Lib.* 84). Strangely enough, scholars seldom mention this statement in discussions on the relationship between Qumran and the Essenes. It is perhaps the most striking piece of evidence of the discontinuity between the two movements. Philo's statement contradicts the teachings of the Qumran community, while it clearly reflects the teachings of Enochic Judaism, that is, of the non-Qumran Essenes. It confirms that individual predestination, which the sectarian scrolls and Solinus present as a distinctive trait of the Qumran community, was not representative of mainstream Essenism, which was characterized by a different approach to the issue. Although claiming the superhuman origin of evil and historical determinism, the Essenes of Josephus and Philo, that is, the Enochians, did not question the responsibility of angels and human beings and refused to make God the source of evil.

This may not be the only case in which the description of the Essenes offered by Philo and Josephus alludes to some Enochic doctrines that were fully developed only in mainstream Enochic Judaism and not at Qumran. Indeed, a reading of Philo and Josephus in light of mainstream Enochic Judaism provides some striking surprises.

As we have seen, at Qumran the myth of the fallen angels was silenced, inasmuch as it reveals the angels' freedom of will; it has no impact whatsoever on individuals, whose destiny has been preordained by God since the beginning. For exactly the opposite reason, the Similitudes of Enoch gave new emphasis to this traditional Enochic teaching. The spread of secret knowledge by the fallen angels was something against which people had to be warned.

In the Essene attitude toward oaths, it is possible to recognize the influence of such a doctrine. Philo says that the Essenes demonstrated their love for God "by rejection of oaths" (*Omn. Prob. Lib.* 84). According to Josephus (*Ant.* 15.371), Herod the Great exempted the Essenes from taking the oath of allegiance that he imposed on his Jewish subjects. No further explanation is given about this Essene custom.

Enochic literature provides the setting. According to the Book of the Watchers, at the beginning of the angelic sin an oath sealed their rebellion. "They all responded to [their leader, Semyaz], 'Let us swear an oath and bind everyone among us by a curse not to abandon this suggestion but to do the deed.' Then they all swore together and bound one another by (the curse)" (1 En 6:4-5). Similitudes took up this ancient myth and gave it a broader, cosmic dimension. The entire universe is sustained by an oath. God sent an angel to reveal the oath to his fellow angels and to Michael. "By it the earth is founded upon the water . . . and forever! By that oath, the sea was created . . . and forever! And by that oath the depths are made firm . . . and forever! By the same oath the sun and the moon complete their courses of travel . . . and forever! And by the same oath the stars complete their courses of travel . . . and forever! . . . This oath has become dominant over them; they are preserved by it and their paths are preserved by it (so that) their courses of travel do not perish" (69:16-26). Unfortunately, the same angel who was "the chief executor of the oath" (69:13) sinned, went to earth among the fallen angels and "revealed . . . to the children of the people . . . all the hidden things and this power of the oath" (69:15). It is no surprise that the Essenes, that is, the Enochians, restrained themselves from using "the power of this oath." Any oath of allegiance with any authority other than God would weaken the solidity and stability of the universe by challenging the "oath" by which the world is sustained.

Philo may allude yet again to the doctrine of the fallen angels. He says that the Essenes did not want to be involved in the making of instruments of war. "In vain would one look among them for makers of arrows, or javelins, or swords, or helmets, or breastplates, or shields; in short, for makers of arms, or military machines, or any instrument of war, or even of peaceful objects which might be turned to evil purpose" (*Omn. Prob. Lib.* 78). The explanation Philo provides, that the Essenes were a group of pacifists, is vague and contradicts the testimony of Josephus about their involvement in the Jewish war.

A reading of Philo in light of Enochic literature is, once again, enlightening. The Book of the Watchers attributed the making of war instruments to a chief of the fallen angels: "And Azaz'el taught the people (the art of) making swords and knives, and shields, and breastplates" (1 En 8:1). In the Similitudes Azaz'el is replaced by another angel, Gader'el; he is also the one who is blamed for tempting Eve. "The third [evil angel] was named Gader'el; this one is he who showed the children of the people

173

all the blows of death, who misled Eve, who showed the children of the people (how to make) the instruments of death (such as) the shield, the breastplate, and the sword for warfare, and all (the other) instruments of death to the children of the people" (69:6). By contrast, the eschatological era would be a time in which "there shall be no iron for war, nor shall anyone wear a breastplate" (52:8). Strikingly, both the Book of the Watchers and the Similitudes have a list of war instruments that parallels the Philonic text and, as in Philo, includes "sword, . . . breastplate, . . . and shield." The Enochians/Essenes had a good reason not to fabricate instruments of war; they did not want to be involved in crafts that were taught by the evil angels.

Finally, as Pierre Grelot already noticed in the 1950s, Enochic literature provides the way to explain one of the most obscure aspects of Essene theology: their view of the afterlife.[7] Josephus establishes a direct parallel between the Essene and the Greek beliefs in the afterlife. He ascribes to the Essenes the doctrine that "the souls are immortal and continue forever" (*J.W.* 2.154); immediately after death, each individual would be either rewarded or punished for what each had done in this world. "Agreeing with the sons of the Greeks, [the Essenes] declare that an abode is reserved beyond the ocean for the souls of the just; a place oppressed neither by rain nor snow nor torrid heat, but always refreshed by the gentle breeze blowing from the ocean. But they relegate evil souls to a dark pit shaken by storms, full of unending chastisement" (*J.W.* 2.155).

Some have suggested that Josephus replaced the belief in bodily resurrection with the Greek doctrine of the immortality of the soul on behalf of his Gentile readers. There is evidence that he did so with the Pharisees. Unlike the Sadducees (cf. Acts 23:8), the Pharisees certainly believed in the resurrection of the body, yet Josephus ascribed the doctrine of the immortality of the soul to them too (*Ant.* 18.14; *J.W.* 2.163).[8]

Is the case of the Essenes identical to that of the Pharisees? Paolo Sacchi has shown that in Enochic Judaism the doctrine of the immortality of the soul

7. P. Grelot, "L'eschatologie des Esséniens et le livre d'Hénoch," *RevQ* 1 (1958) 113-31.

8. On Jewish expectations in the afterlife, see G. W. E. Nickelsburg, *Resurrection, Immortality, and Eternal Life in Intertestamental Judaism,* HTS 26 (Cambridge: Harvard University Press, 1977); H. C. Cavallin, *Life After Death: Paul's Argument for the Resurrection of the Dead in I Cor 15. Part 1: An Inquiry into the Jewish Background,* ConBNT 7/1 (Lund: Gleerup, 1974).

is very ancient and precedes that of resurrection.[9] The Book of the Watchers already presents a sophisticated doctrine of the immortal soul that resembles that of the Greeks and parallels Josephus's narrative. In his journey to the extreme western boundaries of the earth, Enoch was "lifted up unto the waters of life [[=Josephus's ocean]], unto the occidental fire which receives every setting of the sun" (1 En 17:4; cf. 67:4). There, the angel Rufael showed him the dwelling places of "the spirits of the souls of the dead" (22:3, 9), the righteous souls being separated from the wicked ones. The Ethiopic text of ch. 22 is occasionally obscure (esp. v. 2), but with the help of the Greek version and the Aramaic fragments (4Q206 [4QEn^e ar]) it is possible to have a clear picture of what Enoch saw: "a great and high mountain of hard rock and inside it four <hollow>[10] corners . . . <three of them being dark and one bright, and there was a fountain of water in the middle of it.> . . .[11] These <hollow> corners (are here) in order that the spirits of the souls of the dead should assemble into them — they are created so that the souls of the children of the people should gather here.[12] Thus these are the wells that function as a prison for them. They are made in this way up to the day on which they will be judged, up to the instant of the last day on which the Great Judge will deal with them" (22:2-5).

After listening to the crying "spirit which had left Abel," Enoch asks the angel for what reason the souls of the righteous are separated from the souls of the wicked. Rufael answers that the punishment (the "pain") of the wicked begins immediately after death and is forever. "These three (corners) have been made in order that the spirits of the dead might be separated (by) this spring of water with light upon it; in like manner, the sinners are set apart when they die and are buried in the earth and judgment has not been executed upon them in their lifetime, upon this great pain, until the great day of judgment. . . . The souls of the people who are not righteous . . . shall be together with criminals who are like them; they will not be killed on the day of judgment but will not rise from there" (22:9-13).

9. P. Sacchi, "La vita oltre la morte: anima immortale e risurrezione dei corpi," in *Storia del Secondo Tempio* (Turin: Società Editrice Internazionale, 1994) 402-14.

10. Here, as later in 1 En 22:3, the Ethiopic misread the Greek *koiloi* ("hollow") as *kaloi* ("beautiful").

11. The phrase, missing in the Ethiopic text, is preserved in the Greek version. The reference to the "three corners" and the "spring of water" in the Ethiopic text of 1 En 22:9 confirms that the phrase was part of the original text.

12. From this point onward, my translation follows the extant Aramaic text.

Josephus's narrative was not an outline of Greek beliefs in the afterlife but a Hellenistic-style reworking of the Book of the Watchers.

In ancient Judaism the doctrine of the immortality of the soul was not shared outside Enochic circles. Any possibility of life after death was explicitly denied (Job 14), with the general conception being of a shadowy existence for the dead in "sheol" (Ps 49:14 [MT 15]; Prov 9:18). Enochic Jews, not elusive Greek philosophers preaching in Jerusalem, were the target of the ironical words of the book of Ecclesiastes against those who believe that "the life-breath of the children of men goes upward, [while] the life-breath of animals goes earthward." Instead, Qohelet claims, "the lot of man and of animals is one lot; the one dies as well as the other. Both have the same life-breath, and man has no advantage over the animals. . . . Both go to the same place; both were made from the dust, and to the dust they both return" (Qoh 3:19-21).[13] As late as the beginning of the second century BCE, Sirach would peremptorily repeat that from death "there is no return . . . once the life-breath has left" (Sir 38:16-23).[14]

While Zadokite Judaism knew the language of resurrection as a metaphor for national revival (Ezek 37:1-14; Sir 46:11-12; 49:10), only in the wake of the Maccabean crisis would the doctrine of bodily resurrection flourish in (Pharisaic?) Judaism (Dan 12:2; 2 Macc 7:1-41; 12:38-45; PssSol 3:12). Enochic Judaism was progressively influenced by this idea. While maintaining the traditional doctrine of the immortal soul and the belief in the reward or punishment of souls in the afterlife before the final judgment (Jub 23:31; 1 En 103:3-8; TAsh 6:5), Enochic Judaism clearly tended toward assimilating also the doctrine of resurrection. The ambiguity of Enochic literature in the second century BCE (1 En 90:33; Jub 23:30) leaves room for the more explicit statements of the first century BCE (TJud 25:4; TBenj 10:6-8), culminating in the unambiguous stance of Similitudes, in which resurrection plays an important role in emphasizing human responsibility before God's judgment: "In those days, sheol will return all the deposits which she had received and hell will give back all that which it owes. And [the Elect One] shall choose the righteous and the holy ones from among (the risen dead), for the day when they shall be selected and saved has arrived" (1 En 51:1-2; cf. 61:1-13).

---

13. See L. Rosso-Ubigli, "Qohelet di fronte all' apocalittica," *Hen* 5 (1983) 209-34.

14. See G. Boccaccini, "Death and Beyond Death," in *Middle Judaism: Jewish Thought, 300 B.C.E. to 200 C.E.* (Minneapolis: Fortress, 1991) 119-24.

When describing the afterlife beliefs of the Essenes, Hippolytus says that they believed also in the resurrection of the dead in the final judgment. "The doctrine of the resurrection has also derived support among them, for they acknowledge both that the flesh will rise again, and that it will be immortal, in the same manner as the soul is already unperishable . . . for they affirm that there will be both a judgment and a conflagration of the universe, and that the wicked will be eternally punished" (*Ref.* 27). Hippolytus's portrayal is closer to our literary sources than Josephus's parallel description. The combination of the concepts of bodily resurrection and immortality of the soul was a unique mark of later Enochic literature.

Compared with this development in Enochic Judaism, the sectarian literature of Qumran testifies to a more conservative approach. In the sectarian scrolls one searches in vain for either a reference to the immortal soul as explicit as in the earlier Enochic tradition (and Josephus), or a reference to the resurrection of the dead as explicit as in the later Enochic literature (and Hippolytus).[15] In the sectarian scrolls, we find the same ambiguity typical of Enochic Judaism in the transitional period immediately following the Maccabean crisis, which was also the formative period of the sect. Émile Puech ascribes the conservatism of the Qumranites to "the attachment of the disciples to the instruction and revelations of the teacher [of righteousness]."[16] This is actually just another clue to the isolation of the sect from the later development of mainstream Essenism. The emphasis on individual predestination and inaugurated eschatology prevented the doctrine of resurrection from evolving at Qumran as much as in Enochic Judaism.

We now have a better picture of what Josephus did. As attested by his treatment of the Pharisees, Josephus did have an interest in censuring the reference to such a non-Greek concept as bodily resurrection. But Enochic literature and Hippolytus show that, when describing the Essenes, Josephus did not replace the idea of resurrection with the idea of immortality of the soul, as he did regarding the Pharisees. In the case of the

15. E. Puech, "Messianism, Resurrection, and Eschatology at Qumran and in the New Testament," in E. C. Ulrich and J. C. VanderKam, eds., *The Community of the Renewed Covenant: The Notre Dame Symposium on the Dead Sea Scrolls* (Notre Dame: University of Notre Dame Press, 1994) 235-56; cf. idem, *La croyance des Esséniens en la vie future: Immortalité, résurrection, vie éternelle? Histoire d'une croyance dans le Judaïsme ancien,* 2 vols. (Paris: Gabalda, 1993).

16. Puech, "Messianism," 254.

Essenes, it was enough for him to pick up one aspect of Enochic theology and emphasize it over the other, eliminating the reference to the resurrection, which would have sounded odd to his Gentile readers. As witnessed by Hippolytus and the Enochic literature, both the immortality of the soul and the resurrection of the dead were parts of Essene beliefs in the afterlife.

In conclusion, Philo and Josephus (or the sources they used) show their familiarity with the major doctrines of Enochic Judaism, while they pass over in silence the particularities of Qumran thought. Mainstream Enochic literature offers a much better setting for the ideology of the mainstream Essene movement described by Philo and Josephus than the sectarian literature of Qumran.

4. Common Sociology: Diverse People, Yet Not Set Apart

Enochic literature is the literature of a group of people who, like the Essenes described by Philo and Josephus, had a distinct identity within the Jewish people and were proud of following their own path of life, and yet did not live in isolation. The Enochians/Essenes had serious reservations about marriage and the social and religious institutions of Israel, yet they had families, worked, and attended the Jerusalem temple. The sociology of the Essenes living in villages and towns fits much better with the sociology of the Enochic movement than with the sociology of the people who wrote the sectarian literature of Qumran. A comparison between Philo and Josephus on one hand, and the Enochic literature on the other, allows a solution to many of the problems that plague the traditional Essene hypothesis.

(a) *Family life.* The words of Philo and Josephus about the Essenes' marital life have their best parallel not in the sectarian literature of Qumran but in the documents of mainstream Enochic Judaism. In the Dead Sea Scrolls, references to women and children are confined to pre-Qumranic texts, up to and including the Damascus Document, or to sectarian texts envisaging the messianic age, such as the War Scroll (1QM), the Rule of the Congregation (1QSa), and perhaps 4Q502. The text of 4Q502 is too fragmentary to be interpreted as evidence that "women had an integral role in the communal life of the Qumran sect," as Joseph M. Baumgarten has claimed.[17] Most of the arguments of Baumgarten actually apply to the larger Essene movement. The sectarian literature as well as the architectural structure of the Qumran settlement and its cemetery betrays a manifest disregard for the institution of the family.[18]

The Enochic literature is more consistent in testifying to the lives of people who considered sexuality a major source of impurity and evil,[19] yet "it is not that they abolish marriage, or the propagation of the species resulting from it" (Josephus, *J.W.* 2.120-21). The Enochians/ Essenes were people for whom sexuality, women, and parental responsibilities were everyday concerns, not problems they had put behind them. When Josephus speaks of the licentiousness of women (*J.W.* 2.121), and Philo warns the husband against becoming a "slave" (*Apol.* 14-17), they repeat almost verbatim the Testament of Reuben.

> Do not devote your attention to the beauty of women, my children, nor occupy your minds with their activities. . . . For women are evil, my children, and by reason of their lacking authority or power over man, they scheme treacherously how they might entice him to themselves by means of their looks. And whomever they cannot enchant by their appearance they conquer by a stratagem. Indeed, the angel of the Lord told me and instructed me that women are more easily overcome by the spirit of fornication [Gk. *porneia*] than are men. They contrive in their hearts against men, then by decking themselves out they lead men's minds astray, by a look they implant their poison, and finally in the act itself they take them captive. For a woman is not able to coerce a man overtly, but by a harlot's manner she accomplishes her villainy. (TReu 4:1; 5:1-4)

Significantly, these words are pronounced not by a virgin but by an ancient patriarch famous for being a husband and father of many children (Gen 46:9) and the ancestor of one of the tribes of Israel. Moreover, these words are addressed not to virgins or former husbands who have broken

---

17. J. M. Baumgarten, "The Qumran-Essene Restraints on Marriage," in L. H. Schiffman, ed., *Archaeology and History in the Dead Sea Scrolls* (Sheffield: Sheffield Academic Press, 1990) 13-24 (quotation on p. 13).

18. See the discussion in Ch. 2 above.

19. L. Rosso-Ubigli, "Alcuni aspetti della concezione della porneia nel tardo-giudaismo," *Hen* 1 (1979) 201-45.

all relations with their families, as the Qumran sectarians did, but to males who, even while embracing a celibate life, continued to fulfill the social obligations of matrimony in relation to their wives and children, as the Essenes living in towns and villages did.

The members of the Enochic community addressed by the Testaments of the Twelve Patriarchs were taught that "fornication" [Gk. *porneia* = Heb *znwt*] was evil, but were not relieved from exercising their marital and paternal authority and duties. As young adults, they were advised to live a life of continence: "Live in integrity of heart in the fear of the Lord, and weary yourself in good deeds, in learning, and in tending your flocks, until the Lord gives you the mate whom he wills" (TReu 4:1). As husbands and fathers, they also were expected to "flee from fornication [Gk. *porneia*] and order [their] wives and daughters not to adorn their heads and their appearances so as to deceive men's sound minds" (5:5). The celibate life of the Enochians/Essenes had rules that did not exclude social contact with wives and children or marriage before joining the community. Was it not what the holy patriarchs and matriarchs had done? They "despised [sexual] intercourse," yet they married and mated "for the sake of children and not for fondness for pleasure" (TIss 2:1-3; cf. Josephus, *J.W.* 2.120-21).

Enochic literature gives us the underlying reasons for the Essene attitude toward sexuality, whereas Philo and Josephus merely articulate the attitude itself. Just as the making of war instruments was taught by the chief of the fallen angels, Azaz'el, so also was the art of seduction. "And Azaz'el . . . showed . . . bracelets, decorations, (shadowing of the eye) with antimony, ornamentation, the beautifying of the eyelids, all kinds of precious stones, and all coloring tinctures and alchemy" (1 En 8:1). The Testaments of the Twelve Patriarchs further assert that "fornication" is the grossest sin inasmuch as it affects the integrity of the human heart and gives room to the duplicity of Belial. "Guard yourselves from fornicating [Gk. *porneuō*], because fornication [Gk. *porneia*] is the mother of all wicked deeds; it separates from God and leads men to Belial" (TSim 5:3; cf. TReu 1:6, et passim; TLevi 9:9; 14:6; 17:11; TIss 4:4; 7:2; TJud 11:1-5, et passim). Enochic literature confirms that at the roots of the Essene attitude toward women was not a generic misogyny but purity concerns, related directly to the spread of evil.

(b) *Social life.* After "fornication" the major concern of Enochic Judaism was the "love of money." According to the Testaments of the

Twelve Patriarchs, Judah read "in the books of Enoch" that his children had to "guard themselves against fornication and love of money" (TJud 18:1-2). Consistently, Josephus and Philo speak of sexual abstinence and voluntary poverty as the two essential features of the Essene movement.

The Epistle of Enoch, the Testaments of the Twelve Patriarchs, and the Similitudes of Enoch identify the righteous with the poor and the sinners with the well-to-do. Without reticence the Enochic literature condemns "those who amass gold and silver" (1 En 94:7), those who "desire gold, . . . defraud [their] neighbor, . . . long for fancy foods, . . . want fine clothes" (TIss 4:2), "the governors, kings, high officials, and landlords" (1 En 63:12). Similitudes affirms that "the power [of the sinners] (depends) on their wealth," and with TJud 19:1 equates "love of money" and "idolatry" (1 En 46:7). A radical opposition divides the poor and the well-to-do in this world, and in the world to come whoever does not repent of the deeds of oppression would be destroyed without pity.

On these foundations the Testaments of the Twelve Patriarchs endorse an ethic based on love and "compassion toward poverty and sickness" (TIss 5:2), an ethic whose central feature is sharing of goods. "Being compassionate," the fisherman Zebulon "gave some of his catch to every stranger. If anyone were a traveler, or sick, or aged, I cooked the fish, prepared it well, and offered it to each person according to his need. . . . Therefore, the Lord made my catch to be an abundance of fish, for whoever shares with his neighbor receives multifold from the Lord. I fished for five years, sharing with every person whom I saw, and sufficing for my father's household" (TZeb 6:1-8). Issachar also is a model of virtue: "I shared my bread with the poor; I did not eat alone" (TIss 7:5). These passages are particularly significant when compared to Philo and Josephus's passages on the Essenes. We find the same emphasis on the value of communal meals and on the sharing of goods, including the explicit reference to those categories of people who directly received Essene charity: travelers, the sick, and the aged. The emphasis that the sharing of goods was without detriment to the needs of Zebulon's household confirms that the Essenes did not disregard social responsibilities toward their relatives and did have control over the fruits of their work.

By listing the evil crafts taught by the fallen angels (1 En 8; 69), Enochic literature also warns against some activities that are not rightfully permitted to human beings, first of all, as we have seen, the making of war instruments. But the list of forbidden activities is much broader. By putting the love of money, oppression, and idolatry on an equal level (46:7), Enochic Judaism denies any legitimacy to an economy of profit; instead it favors an economy of mere subsistence, which is exactly what Philo says when he claims that the Essenes "reject everything that might excite them to cupidity" (*Omn. Prob. Lib.* 79). It is no surprise that the Essenes looked at farming, fishing, and raising livestock as the ideal and, ultimately, only legitimate activities.

The lives of the twelve patriarchs offered an authoritative model for the Essene way of life. As Zebulon during the summer "sailed along the shores, catching fish for [his] father's household," and "in winter tended the flock of [his] brothers" (TZeb 6:1-8), so did the Essenes, who were "shepherds leading every sort of flock" (Philo, *Apol.* 6). As Issachar "became a farmer for the benefit of [his] father and [his] brothers" (TIss 3:1), so did "the Essenes [who] work in the field . . . for the benefit of themselves and their neighbors" (Philo, *Omn. Prob. Lib.* 76). The same patriarch invites his readers to "bend your back in farming, (and) perform the tasks of the soil in every kind of agriculture" (TIss 5:3; cf. Josephus, *Ant.* 18.19), while reminding them about the moral danger of following a different path, as many "in the last times will do, abandoning sincerity and aligning themselves with insatiable desire. . . . Abandoning the commands of the Lord, they ally themselves with Belial. Giving up agriculture, they pursue their own evil schemes" (TIss 6:1-2).

Enochic social criticism had great potential to be subversive. The present order was corrupt and needed to be "reversed." Nonetheless, mainstream Enochic Judaism avoided the extremes of physical and geographical isolation from the corrupt society and did not follow the Qumran community in their move to the desert. The Enochic texts addressed people who lived among the sinners and were constantly subjected to their oppression. Philo and Josephus also agree that the ideal of a flight from this evil world did not belong to the ideological horizon of the Essenes. Besides, the Essenes were asked to "swear constant loyalty to all, but above all to those in power, for authority never falls to a man without the will of God" (Josephus, *J.W.* 2.140). The contradiction between the Essene social criticism and their loyalty to the authorities is only apparent. In Enochic Judaism the superhuman origin of evil makes the powerful of this world the instruments of rebellious angelic forces that humans cannot defeat. Only God (and in Similitudes, God's messiah) has the authority and strength to triumph. Thus the Essenes' answer to the corruption of this world avoided also the extreme of too transformational an approach; they were content to form their separated society within the wider Jewish society and live their own way of life among people with different ways of life. They had no doubts about who was right and who was wrong, and aggressively called for repentance and foretold the destruction of the sinners. The "reversal" that Enochic Judaism announced, however, was not expected to occur in this world but only in the world to come.

(c) *Religious life.* The attitude toward the temple represents one of the deepest differences between the Qumran community and mainstream Essenes. The Qumran community claimed to have replaced the temple: "When, according to all these norms, these (men) become in Israel a foundation of the Holy Spirit in eternal truth, they shall atone for iniquitous guilt and for sinful unfaithfulness, so that (God's) favor for the land (is obtained) without the flesh of burnt offerings and without the fat of sacrifices" (1QS 9:4-5).[20]

Both Philo and Josephus bear witness that the Essenes also had some reservations about the legitimacy of the temple. Philo claims that "they are men utterly dedicated to the service of God; they do not offer animal sacrifices, judging it more fitting to render their minds truly holy" (*Omn. Prob. Lib.* 75). Josephus, however, clarifies that the Essenes still looked at the Jerusalem temple as the center of Jewish religious life. "Sending offerings to the temple, they <do not>[21] offer sacrifices since the purifications to which they are accustomed are different. For this reason, they are barred from entering into the common enclosure, and offer their sacrifices among themselves" (*Ant.* 18.19).

Josephus presents the picture of a group that did offer sacrifices, although with a great concern for ritual purity in the process. What the Essenes thought made them pure, apparently made them impure in the eyes

---

20. On the community of Qumran as the new temple, see B. E. Gartner, *The Temple and the Community in Qumran and the New Testament*, SNTSMS 1 (Cambridge: Cambridge University Press, 1965); G. Bissoli, "Gli scritti di Qumran," in *Il tempio nella letteratura giudaica e neotestamentaria. Studio sulla corrispondenza fra tempio celeste e tempio terrestre* (Jerusalem: Franciscan Printing Press, 1995) 34-55.

21. The Greek text is restored according to the Latin and Paleo-Slavonic translations. See E. Lupieri, "La purità impura: Giuseppe Flavio e le purificazioni degli Esseni," *Hen* 7 (1985) 15-43; J. Nolland, "A Misleading Statement of the Essene Attitude to the Temple," *RevQ* 9 (1978) 555-62; D. Wallace, "The Essenes and Temple Sacrifice," *TZ* 13 (1957) 335-38.

of the authorities of the temple. In the matter of sacrifices, the Essenes followed special rules; hence the Jerusalem priests excluded them from the common court and treated them as Gentiles.[22]

No matter how deep their disagreement was about the purity laws and the religious practices of the temple, the Essenes attended the sanctuary. No sign is given that they shared the radical supersessionist theology of Qumran. Josephus introduces Judas the Essene preaching to his disciples in the court of the Jerusalem temple (*J.W.* 1.78), and apparently it did not bother John the Essene to be appointed governor at a public meeting in the temple by the same religious authorities whose halakhah the Essenes so strongly opposed (*J.W.* 2.562-67).

The same attitude toward the Jerusalem temple is manifest in Enochic literature. The second temple was for the Enochians a largely impure temple, led by a sinful priesthood; but while criticizing the actual functioning of the temple and awaiting its future restoration, they never questioned its existence and centrality.

Some evidence even suggests that to a certain extent the later Enochic literature softened its opposition to the temple. Robert A. Kugler has noticed in the Testament of Levi "a general reduction of interest in purity issues over against Aramaic Levi."[23] He goes too far, however, when he makes the Testament of Levi "a legitimation document for Hasmonean princely and priestly rule."[24] The Testaments of the Twelve Patriarchs maintain the Enochic, and anti-Hasmonean, concept that the real restoration of the temple never occurred.[25]

The polemical setting of the parting of the ways between Qumran and Enochic Judaism offers a much better explanation for the diminished attention to purity. For the same reason, the later Enochic documents were much less interested in calendrical discussions. This point allows a solution to yet another predicament of the Essene hypothesis: why neither Philo nor Josephus mentions the solar calendar, which was preeminent at Qumran. The Essenes/Enochians were jealous of their own way of life, yet they

---

22. Lupieri, "La purità impura."

23. R. A. Kugler, *From Patriarch to Priest: The Levi-Priestly Tradition from Aramaic Levi to Testament of Levi,* SBLEJL 9 (Atlanta: Scholars Press, 1996) 218; cf. 222.

24. Ibid., 218.

25. See the discussion in Ch. 5 above.

continued to consider themselves part of the same religious community of Israel, which they summoned to repentance. They continued to use the solar calendar as their liturgical calendar, as they did with their different purity laws, even though this barred them from many rituals of the temple. But they did not regard the adoption of the lunar calendar, as well as the enforcement of purity rules they held illegitimate, as sufficient reasons to dismiss the entire cult of the Jerusalem temple and break the religious unity of Israel. Had the Similitudes of Enoch not reminded them that the sinners "like to congregate in [God's] houses and (with) the faithful ones who cling to the Lord of the Spirits" (1 En 46:8)? Whether they liked it or not, the non-Qumran Essenes knew that in this evil and impure world they had no other choice than to live side by side with the unfaithful; the separation between the righteous and the sinners would belong only to the future in the world to come.

5. A Composite Picture of the Enochic/Essene Movement

The connection between "mainstream Enochic Judaism" and "mainstream Essenism" allows one to draw a composite picture of the Essene movement that benefits from the data of both historiographical analysis and systemic analysis. The history of Essene Judaism is one and the same with the history of Enochic Judaism, and in the broader context of second temple Judaism (see fig. 2, p. xxii) it can be outlined as follows.

(a) *The Enochian roots of the Essene movement.* The roots of the Essene movement (and therefore of the Qumran community) are in a priestly anti-Zadokite tradition of the second temple period that expressed itself in the earliest Enochic literature (Book of the Watchers, Aramaic Levi, Astronomical Book). The generative idea of this dissident movement was that the good universe created by God was no longer such, since it had been corrupted by the sin of rebellious angels. Claiming to represent a competing (and more ancient) priestly line than that of the ruling Zadokite priesthood, the Enochians did not recognize the legitimacy of the second temple and maintained that Israel was still living in exile.

The view that Essenism was a Zadokite reaction following the Maccabean crisis has no foundation in our sources. After the death of Onias III, the strictly Zadokite party fled to Egypt, and the closest heirs of Zadokite

Judaism, the Sadducees, accepted the Hasmonean rule and priesthood. The Essenes had many reasons to oppose the Hasmoneans, but their Enochic genetic code never made them miss the Zadokite high priests.

(b) *From Enochic Judaism to Essene Judaism.* Ancient historiography and literary evidence point to the mid-second century BCE as the age in which Enochic Judaism turned into a larger movement. What in the early second temple period was probably only a minority phenomenon of some priestly families spread and won adherents during the Maccabean crisis. The end of the Zadokite priesthood gave confidence to the group, while the harshness of the struggle seemed to prove the soundness of their ideas about the spread of evil and the degeneration of history.

The Enochians contributed to the coalition of groups (the Hasidim) that supported the Maccabees against the high priest Menelaus and King Antiochus IV (Dream Visions). The success of the uprising opened new horizons. A group of documents expressed dissatisfaction with the earlier Enochic concept that all human beings, including the Jews, were affected by evil. God's historical determinism restored the foundations of Israel's election and gave sense to a concrete political and religious agenda for the chosen people even in this corrupted world. The inclusive theology of Jubilees and the Temple Scroll suggests that the Enochians became the center of a vast and composite movement that aimed to replace the Zadokite leadership.

In the pluralistic context of the newly independent Israel ruled by the Hasmoneans, this ambitious program turned out quite disappointingly to be the platform of an influential yet minority party. The self-consciousness of the Enochians as the chosen among the chosen and as having a message significant for the entirety of Israel gave to their party a clear and distinct identity and led them to seek a certain degree of separation from the rest of the people (Proto-Epistle of Enoch, Halakhic Letter). It is probably at this point that the Enochians (or part of the movement they initiated) became the "Essenes" of Philo and Josephus, with the establishment of communities in towns and villages. This may explain why ancient historiography presented the Essene movement as both a new phenomenon and a venerable movement. The many similarities between the life of the Essene communities in Palestine and the life of the Qumran community show that the structure of the Essene communities was already formed in its basic lines before the emergence of the Qumran community.

(c) *The Qumran schism.* In the turmoil of those years, a group of

Essenes led by a charismatic figure, "the teacher of righteousness," preached that the Essenes had to separate from the entire Jewish society in even more radical terms (Damascus Document). They believed that the non-Essene Jews were under the dominion of Belial, and looked at themselves as the only holy remnant of Israel. The move was highly controversial, both outside and inside the Essene party. While some joined the community of the teacher of righteousness, the majority of the Essenes did not accept the call, and even fewer followed the sectarians when they decided to move in a voluntary exile to the desert and cut off all relations with the religious and political institutions of Israel. As a result, the separation of the Qumran community from Israel meant also an increasing separation from their parent movement.

Both Enochic literature and the sectarian literature of Qumran testify to a period of internal confrontation within the Essene movement. The traditional Enochic principle of the superhuman origin of evil was subjected to a process of scrutiny and reassessment that resulted in the emergence of two distinct and divergent systems of thought, the one pointing to individual predestination (1QS, 1QH), the other to human responsibility (Epistle of Enoch, Testaments of the Twelve Patriarchs).

(d) *Qumran: A marginal community.* After the polemical phase of the parting of the ways between Enochic Judaism and Qumranic Judaism at the beginning of the first century BCE, the Qumran community remained marginal to the ideological debate that saw Essene Judaism still competing with the other varieties of middle Judaism. The Qumran sectarians implemented and strengthened their own separate identity within the Essene movement, and built on individual predestination and a dualistic worldview that made God the source of both good and evil. It is likely that the Qumranites continued to have contacts with the other Essenes on an individual level, and many people living in Essene communities outside Qumran may have looked at them with admiration and respect. After all, the Qumran sectarians continued to recruit members and managed to prosper for two centuries thanks to the continuous coming of new members. David Flusser has effectively caught the paradox of the sectarian life, which in relation to outsiders was subjected to the opposing needs of keeping them out and bringing them in. "On the one hand, [the sectarians] thought they had to isolate themselves from others because they were the true Israel, and they sentenced the rest of Israel to damnation; but on the other hand they were interested in attracting as many people as possible, so that they should accept their ideas, join the sect and live with them their peculiar, isolated life, different from that of the rest of Israel, in both its ideological collectivism and its organization."[26]

Since the emphasis was on individual call, however, the Qumran sectarians did not seek an organized relationship with the Essene communities or any other group. The analysis of the Qumran library within the broader context of middle Jewish literature demonstrates clearly that the community of the Dead Sea Scrolls virtually ignored other groups, including its parent movement, and received from them an equally open disdain. While quite marginal in the development of Jewish thought, the Qumran sect's distinctive and unique way of life attracted the curiosity of non-Jewish authors, such as Pliny and Dio of Prusa.

(e) *The impact of mainstream Essenism.* Mainstream Essenes maintained a more moderate approach that led them to reject the doctrine of individual predestination held by their sibling movement. The religious and social sources of disagreement with the Jewish society of the time were not pushed so hard as to justify a complete separation. The non-Qumran Essenes stood as champions of "the poor" of this world and bearers of a heroic morality, which allowed them to continue to play a recognized, influential role as one of the major Jewish movements of their time (Josephus and Philo).

Although in a theological context in which evil was still seen as having a superhuman origin, the principle of human responsibility was saved and hence the possibility for the individual to stand against Belial and Belial's temptations. Out of Qumran, the Essene movement focused on a message of salvation for the end of time. The notion of reversal envisaged an era in which the oppressed (the poor) would triumph over their oppressors (the well-to-do) and a superhuman messiah, the Son of Man, would defeat the rebellious angelic forces (Similitudes of Enoch). Mainstream Essenism provides a much more intriguing context for Christian origins than that offered by the sectarian literature of Qumran. John the Baptist called for repentance as a way to "force" the merciful God to forgiveness before the manifestation of the eschatological judge. The early followers of Jesus believed their teacher to be the new Adam, who would reverse the fall of the first Adam (Paul), or the heavenly Son of Man, who first came as a savior to bring forgiveness through his death and would

26. D. Flusser, *The Spiritual History of the Dead Sea Sect* (Tel Aviv: MOD Books, 1989) 35.

then return as the final judge (Mark). The clear distinction between mainstream Essenism and Qumran calls for an urgent reassessment of the Essene contribution to Christian origins.

(f) *The decline of the Essene movement.* Neither the destruction of the Qumran community in 68 CE nor the growth of Christianity as an autonomous movement meant the sudden death of Essenism. The presence of an ancient, first-century-CE interpolation in Similitudes, claiming that Enoch is the Son of Man (1 En 71:14), shows that mainstream Essenism reacted vigorously against the Christian identification of Jesus as the Son of Man.[27] The composition of texts such as the Apocalypse of Abraham and 4 Ezra bears witness that the Essene party was still active in the period between the Jewish war and the Bar-Kokhba revolt. The lack of an effective doctrine of salvation condemned the movement to a slow and painful agony of frustration and disillusionment, however, an agony that Jacob Neusner has effectively depicted: "The response of the visionaries [to the catastrophe was] . . . essentially negative. All they had to say is that God is just and Israel has sinned, but, in the end of time, there will be redemption. What to do in the meantime? Merely wait. Not much of an answer."[28]

(g) *The Essene legacy.* The Essenes' system of thought survived their decline as an organized movement. The Christian claim to be the "new Israel" against the parallel claim of Rabbinic Judaism to be the "one eternal Israel" outshone even the memory of the pluralistic environment from which both the Church and the Synagogue emerged.[29] The Essene legacy, however, never dried up in either Christianity or Rabbinic Judaism.

27. J. J. Collins, *The Scepter and the Star: The Messiahs of the Dead Sea Scrolls and Other Ancient Literature* (New York: Doubleday, 1995) 178-81; J. H. Charlesworth, *The Old Testament Pseudepigrapha and the New Testament,* SNTSMS 54 (Cambridge: Cambridge University Press, 1985) 18; P. Sacchi, ed., *Apocrifi dell'Antico Testamento,* 2 vols. (Turin: Unione Tipografica-Editrice Torinese, 1981-89) 1.571-72.

28. J. Neusner, "Judaism in a Time of Crisis: Four Responses to the Destruction of the Second Temple," *Judaism* 21 (1972) 314-27 (quotation on p. 317); cf. G. Boccaccini, "Testi apocalittici coevi all'Apocalisse di Giovanni," *RSB* 7/2 (1995) 151-61.

29. On the parallel origins of Christianity and Rabbinic Judaism, see H. Shanks, ed., *Christianity and Rabbinic Judaism: A Parallel History of Their Origins and Early Development* (Washington, D.C.: Biblical Archaeology Society, 1992); J. D. G. Dunn, *The Partings of the Ways between Christianity and Judaism and Their Significance for the Character of Christianity* (Philadelphia: Trinity Press International, 1991); A. F. Segal, *Rebecca's Children: Judaism and Christianity in the Roman World* (Cambridge: Harvard University Press, 1986).

The polemical arrows of Bereshit Rabbah against the wicked and hypocritical Enoch (GenR 25:1) and the dethronement of Enoch-Metatron in 3 Enoch (ch. 16) show that the rabbis had to fight for centuries to silence those who claimed the existence of "two powers in heaven."[30] The victory of Rabbinic Judaism over Enochic Judaism, however, was never complete. Enochic traditions remained alive in Jewish mysticism, and they managed to survive even in more orthodox settings under the guise of harmless folkloric tales.[31]

In Christianity the ancient Essene documents were initially preserved with the care due a precious family heritage and for some time were held as a legitimate source of authority.[32] If most Churches gradually rejected those documents from their canons, it was because the Church's confrontation with Rabbinic Judaism did not encourage a relation with a movement that the Church's direct competitors considered only a nest of heretics. It is not accidental that 1 Enoch has remained canonical in the Ethiopian Church — a Church that lived isolated from the other Christian Churches and had contact only with a nonrabbinical form of Judaism (the Falashas).[33]

30. A. F. Segal, *Two Powers in Heaven: Early Rabbinic Reports about Christianity and Gnosticism,* SJLA 25 (Leiden: Brill, 1977). On Bereshit Rabbah see M. Margulies, *Midrash Haggadol on the Pentateuch: Genesis* (Jerusalem: Mosad ha-Rav, 1967); J. Neusner, *Genesis Rabbah: The Judaic Commentary to the Book of Genesis,* BJS 104-6 (Atlanta: Scholars Press, 1985). On 3 Enoch see P. Alexander, "3 (Hebrew Apocalypse of) Enoch," in *OTP* 1.223-315.

31. On the former see I. Gruenwald, *Apocalyptic and Merkavah Mysticism,* AGJU 14 (Leiden: Brill, 1980). On the latter see L. Ginzberg, *The Legends of the Jews,* 7 vols. (Philadephia: Jewish Publication Society of America, 1910-38).

32. J. C. Vanderkam, "1 Enoch, Enochic Motifs, and Enoch in Early Christian Literature," in J. C. Vanderkam and W. Adler, eds., *The Jewish Apocalyptic Heritage in Early Christianity,* CRINT 3/4 (Assen: Van Gorcum; Minneapolis: Fortress, 1995) 33-101.

33. R. T. Beckwith, "The Canon in the Early Ethiopian Church," in *The Old Testament of the New Testament Church and Its Background in Early Judaism* (Grand Rapids: Eerdmans, 1985) 478-505. On the nonrabbinical character of the Judaism of the Falashas, see D. Kessler, *The Falashas: A Short History of the Ethiopian Jews,* 3rd rev. ed. (London: F. Cass; Portland: International Specialized Book Services, 1996); S. Kaplan, *The Beta Israel (Falasha) in Ethiopia: From Earliest Times to the Twentieth Century* (New York: New York University Press, 1992); J. A. Quirin, *The Evolution of the Ethiopian Jews: A History of the Beta Israel (Falasha) to 1920* (Philadelphia: University of Pennsylvania Press, 1992).

Essene ideas proved to be far more lasting than Essene literature. Concepts we consider typically Christian, such as original sin, the primeval war between Michael and the devil, the corruption and degeneration of history, and the apocalypse at the end of time, were Essene before being Christian. The Old Testament contains only a few, scattered allusions to these ancient Enochic doctrines, yet Christians read the entire Old Testament in light of those concepts. Without Essenism we simply could not understand the history and splendor of Christian liturgy, theology, and art — the debate of Augustine vs. Pelagius, the Reformation, as well as literary masterpieces such as Dante's *Divine Comedy,* Milton's *Paradise Lost,* the baroque religious poem *La Gerusalemme liberata* by Torquato Tasso, and the American epic novel *Moby Dick* by Herman Melville. Without Essenism and its drifting tendencies that led to the emergence of the Qumran community, we simply could not understand the "dark side" of Christianity, its drifting tendencies toward exclusivism, that over the centuries have fostered fringe phenomena of religious sectarianism and fanaticism — from medieval millenarianism to the deadly apocalypse of the Branch Davidians at Waco, Texas, as well as the mass suicide of the alien "sons of light" of Heaven's Gate at Rancho Santa Fe, California.[34] We may not be aware of it, but Essenism is still one of the most powerful and influential underlying components of Western civilization. We are Essene no less than Greek.

6. Summary: The Enochic/Essene Hypothesis and Its Implications

Since the Dead Sea Scrolls were discovered, many attempts have been made to overthrow the Essene hypothesis. None has overcome the burden of proof. The Essene hypothesis remains the most likely explanation of the evidence and the most solid starting point for any discussion of the material. Nonetheless, the development of research has pointed to some serious

34. N. R. C. Cohn, *The Pursuit of the Millennium: Revolutionary Messianism in Medieval and Reformation Europe and Its Bearing on Modern Totalitarian Movements,* 2nd ed. (New York: Harper, 1961); T. Robbins and S. J. Palmer, eds., *Millennium, Messiahs, and Mayhem: Contemporary Apocalyptic Movements* (New York: Routledge, 1997).

contradictions in the classical formulation of the Essene hypothesis. We are urged to go beyond, to build up a more refined Essene hypothesis, one that first of all clarifies the relationship between Qumran and the larger Essene movement. While the evidence shows overwhelmingly that the Qumran community was an Essene community, the terms "Essene" and "Qumran" have too often been taken as if they were identical and interchangeable, with the result of confusing two overlapping yet distinct historical phenomena.

The advantage of the Enochic/Essene hypothesis is that it provides an answer to the predicaments of the classical Essene hypothesis without requiring the rejection of all that has been thought in fifty years of research in the Dead Sea Scrolls. It also offers a comprehensive and flexible framework that makes sense out of apparently diverging hypotheses.

The Enochic/Essene hypothesis confirms the most important tenets of the Essene hypothesis: Qumran was "an Essene community in the wilderness" that owned the scrolls and authored some of them.[35] Against the repeated assaults of revisionistic hypotheses, it recognizes the existence of an organized community at Qumran that had a distinct identity, a sophisticated theology, and a marvelous library. We can now accept this view without reducing the Essenes to a Qumran-dependent sect. On the contrary, the Enochic literature proves that the Qumran community, a radical outgrowth of Enochic Judaism, depended on Essenism.

The Enochic/Essene hypothesis confirms and clarifies the "Groningen hypothesis" that Qumran and Essenism must be treated as two distinct phenomena. "Essenism is a widespread national movement which covers the whole country and its members do not at all consider themselves separate from the rest of the people of Israel. The Qumran community, instead, is a marginal phenomenon, a closed and isolated group, which deliberately lives apart from the rest of Judaism."[36] We can now accept this view without relying only on the vague and ambiguous indications contained in the sectarian literature of Qumran. The Enochic literature

35. F. M. Cross, *The Ancient Library of Qumran,* 3rd ed. (Sheffield: Sheffield Academic Press, 1995); cf. VanderKam, *Dead Sea Scrolls Today.*

36. F. García Martínez, "The Dead Sea Scrolls," in García Martínez and J. Trebolle Barrera, *The People of the Dead Sea Scrolls,* trans. W. G. E. Watson (Leiden: Brill, 1995) 3-16 (quotation on p. 11); cf. P. R. Davies, *Behind the Essenes: History and Theology in the Dead Sea Scrolls,* BJS 94 (Atlanta: Scholars Press, 1987).

provides additional and solid evidence of the schism between Qumran and mainstream Essene Judaism.

The Enochic/Essene hypothesis confirms the intuitions of Ben Zion Wacholder and Shemaryahu Talmon that the roots of the Qumran community are in the anti-Zadokite movements of the early second temple period.

> The roots of the *yaḥad*'s prophetically inspired belief-system, as that of the nascent rationalistic stream, reach down into the period of the Return from the Babylonian Exile, *viz.,* into the fifth, possibly even into the sixth century BCE. At that time a bifurcation in the Jewish body politic appears to have set in. Led by rival priestly houses, two major strands emerged which were divided on a variety of tenets pertaining to belief and ritual. In the course of their subsequent development, both movements experienced internal diversifications. . . . In both movements this diversification generated new schismatic groups. At the turn of the era, the process culminated in the distinct pluriformity of Judaism, to which the classical sources give witness.[37]

We can now share this view without being forced to rewrite the entire chronology of the documents or of the Qumran sect. The anti-Zadokite character of the Enochic literature gives us no reason to question that "the community of the renewed covenant" was the community of Qumran.

The Enochic/Essene hypothesis confirms Hartmut Stegemann's claim that the Essenes were indeed a mainstream movement, or, as he says, "the main Jewish Union of late Second Temple times," that in the aftermath of the Maccabean crisis aimed to gain, and almost gained, the leadership of the entire Jewish people.[38] We can now share this view without denying the very existence of the Qumran community with its separate identity, and

---

37. S. Talmon, "The Community of the Renewed Covenant: Between Judaism and Christianity," in Ulrich and VanderKam, eds., *Community of the Renewed Covenant*, 3-24 (quotation on pp. 22-23). Cf. B. Z. Wacholder, *The Dawn of Qumran: The Sectarian Torah and the Teacher of Righteousness* (Cincinnati: Hebrew Union College Press, 1983).

38. H. Stegemann, "The Qumran Essenes — Local Members of the Main Jewish Union in Late Second Temple Times," in J. Trebolle Barrera and L. Vegas Montaner, eds., *The Madrid Qumran Congress: Proceedings of the International Congress on the Dead Sea Scrolls, Madrid, 18-21 March, 1991,* STDJ 11/1-2 (Leiden: Brill, 1992) 1.83-166 (quotation on p. 165).

without dismissing the sectarian and intolerant character of its literature. The popularity of the Enochic literature proves that Stegemann's words apply to the non-Qumran Essenes, who were certainly an influential and highly regarded movement.

The Enochic/Essene hypothesis confirms Lawrence H. Schiffman's understanding of the similarities between Sadducean halakhah and Qumran halakhah.[39] We can now share this view without jumping to an unlikely identification between the Qumranites and the Sadducees. The ancient Enochians, of whom the Essenes were the most direct heirs, had common priestly roots with the Zadokites, of whom the Sadducees were the most direct heirs.

The Enochic/Essene hypothesis confirms the intuition of David Flusser about the pluralism of the Essene movement, even after the establishment of the Qumran community.[40] We can now share this view without reducing the post-Qumran Essenes to a small group of post-Essene dissidents. On the contrary, the terms of the relation between Qumran and the other Essenes must be overturned. What is post-Qumran is not necessarily post-Essene. The Enochic literature proves that the "heretic Essenes" were rather the Qumranites.

The Enochic/Essene hypothesis confirms the work of New Testament scholars who recognize a close relationship between Essenism and Christianity but also see many major differences between the New Testament and the sectarian literature of Qumran.[41] We can now share this view without speculative hypotheses, such as John the Baptist and Jesus visiting Qumran, or groundless tales about their being involved in secret Essene conspiracies. There was no need to go to Qumran in order to be familiar with the principles of Essenism. The Enochic literature provides a mainstream Essene context that is much closer to the early Christian theology than the Qumran dualism and predestination. "Jesus was closer to the non-Qumran Essenes than to the strict and withdrawn Essenes living in the desert of Judah."[42]

39. L. H. Schiffman, *Reclaiming the Dead Sea Scrolls* (Philadelphia and Jerusalem: Jewish Publication Society, 1994).

40. Flusser, *Spiritual History;* cf. F. M. Cross, *The Ancient Library of Qumran and Modern Biblical Studies* (New York: Doubleday, 1958) 150-51 (3rd ed., pp. 146-47).

41. See J. H. Charlesworth, ed., *Jesus and the Dead Sea Scrolls* (New York: Doubleday, 1992).

42. Idem, "The Dead Sea Scrolls and the Historical Jesus," in ibid., 1-74 (quotation on p. 40).

Finally, the Enochic/Essene hypothesis confirms what the specialists in Enoch literature have been saying for some time: 1 Enoch is the core of a distinct variety of second temple Judaism that played an essential role in Qumran (and Christian) origins. As Frank M. Cross already noticed in 1958, "the concrete contacts in theology, terminology, calendrical peculiarities, and priestly interests, between the editions of [1] Enoch, Jubilees, and the Testaments of Levi and Naphtali found at Qumrân on the one hand, and the demonstrably sectarian works of Qumrân on the other, are so systematic and detailed that we must place the composition of these works within a single line of tradition."[43] We can now share this view without bearing the paradox of a strong and influential group that went completely unnoticed in ancient historiography. Thanks to the Enochic/Essene hypothesis, Enochic Judaism, which scholars such as Paolo Sacchi and James C. VanderKam have identified and described exclusively on the basis of its literature,[44] ceases to be a mere intellectual phenomenon, an ingenious yet monstrously bodiless soul, and becomes flesh and blood in the sociology of the Essene group, a group that has left substantial evidence in ancient historiography.

The destiny of the Essenes is paradoxical. For centuries their existence was obscured by the extraordinary success of a small messianic group whose first steps they fostered and that later would be known as Christianity. Although many of the Essene ideas and documents would be preserved in Christianity, the memory of the Essenes was soon upstaged in the two-actor drama that mutually opposed the Church with the Synagogue.[45]

When the Dead Sea Scrolls were discovered, history repeated itself. This time the voice of the Essenes was obscured by the voice of another dissident group, a small group but one with a large and outstanding library. It has taken some time to realize that the Qumran library comprised not

43. Cross, *Ancient Library,* 148 (3rd ed., p. 144).

44. P. Sacchi, *Jewish Apocalyptic and Its History,* trans. W. J. Short, JSPSup 20 (Sheffield: Sheffield Academic Press, 1997); VanderKam, *Enoch: A Man for All Generations;* idem, *Enoch and the Growth of an Apocalyptic Tradition,* CBQMS 16 (Washington, D.C.: Catholic Biblical Association of America, 1984); cf. M. Barker, *The Lost Prophet: The Book of Enoch and Its Influence on Christianity* (Nashville: Abingdon, 1988).

45. G. Boccaccini, *Portraits of Middle Judaism in Scholarship and Arts: A Multimedia Catalog from Flavius Josephus to 1991* (Turin: Zamorani, 1992).

only the documents of a marginal sectarian community but also a substantial body of Essene literature from the second temple period, independent of Qumran. "Their Qumran secessionists have in one way given the Essenes a sectarian reputation, but they have also, it seems, redeemed themselves somewhat by handing over to us the means to rediscover a mainstream Jewish movement."[46]

Thanks to the Enochic/Essene hypothesis, we need no longer face the mystery of four thousand Essenes, creative and strong-minded, yet vanishing like the lady in the Hitchcock movie,[47] disappearing as though they had never been. Thanks to the Enochic/Essene hypothesis, those four thousand Essenes, forgotten and neglected, may come back to life and, through the Enochic literature, speak again.

46. P. R. Davies, *Behind the Essenes: History and Ideology in the Dead Sea Scrolls,* BJS 94 (Atlanta: Scholars Press, 1987) 134.
47. A. Hitchcock (dir.), *The Lady Vanishes* (Great Britain, 1938).

Bibliography:
The Dead Sea Scrolls
and Second Temple Judaism

From Late Judaism to Middle Judaisms

In 1948, one year after the discovery of the first scrolls, photographs and transcriptions began making available the findings to scholars and the general public. It was clear from the beginning, however, that the publication of the Dead Sea Scrolls would be a very long and painful process. The objective difficulty of publishing fragmentary texts was complicated by the most diverse interests (religious, political, scholarly, economical, even military) and by an endless series of controversies, which now and then degenerated into rumors of conspiracy and deception. The battle for free access to the manuscripts progressively escalated in the media until fall 1991, when the Huntington Library, soon followed by other institutions, eventually released the complete set of photographs of the scrolls.

Despite the slow process of publication, the impact of the Dead Sea Scrolls on the study of second temple Judaism was immediately noticeable in scholarship. It took only a few years for the Dead Sea Scrolls to create a field of their own with scholars and research centers working full-time on the manuscripts.

The relevance of the Dead Sea Scrolls went far beyond the boundaries of Qumran studies. It changed forever the predominantly derogatory approach of Christian scholarship to the "age of Jesus Christ." In the same years in which the tragedy of the Holocaust was forcing the Church to rethink its relationship with the Synagogue, the discovery of the scrolls fostered a more appreciative view of ancient Jewish pluralism,

197

a renewed interest in apocryphal and pseudepigraphic literature, and a reappraisal of Christianity within its original Jewish environment. What once was viewed merely as the background of Christianity, a "late" and decadent period of religious stagnation "between the Old and the New Testaments," turned out to be a lively and dynamic age of spiritual creativity.

The Dead Sea Scrolls also opened a breach in the wall of indifference of Jewish scholarship toward an age "between the Bible and the Mishnah," in which Rabbinic Judaism was believed to be already so strong and normative as to make the influence of sectarianism negligible. Scholars became more sensitive to viewing Judaism as a developing religion that knew different stages in its evolution. The scrolls were "reclaimed" as witnesses of an "early" stage in Jewish history characterized by several competing approaches before mainstream Judaism found its natural course and the rabbis emerged as the leaders of ancient Jewish thought.

The more we learn from the Dead Sea Scrolls, however, the more we realize that studying Judaism means studying a plurality of autonomous groups, or Judaisms. Each of them needs to be examined diachronically in its evolution over time. All of them need to be examined synchronically in their complex dialectic relationship. Hence we need to discuss phenomena like apocalypticism and mysticism not only as intellectual categories of Judaism but also for the diverse role they played in each of the many Judaisms.

Thanks to the scrolls, we, Christian and Jewish scholars alike, are learning that the ideological differences of Judaisms can hardly be understood as nuances within a single normative system or as results of an evolutionary process that merely multiplied choices before selecting the predominant one. Thanks to the scrolls, we are learning that Judaism between the third century BCE and the second century CE was not the final, "late" period of Judaism before Jesus, nor the starting, "early" point of Rabbinic Judaism. It was the transitional, "middle" age of many competing Judaisms, including the Qumranic, from which both Christianity and Rabbinic Judaism would emerge as fraternal, not identical, twins.

The following bibliography aims to locate the Qumran research in the broader context of second temple studies and to emphasize the contribution that, methodologically and conceptually, the Dead Sea Scrolls have given to the rediscovery of the pluralism of middle Judaism. The listing, obviously selective, is limited to scholarly works published after the finding of the scrolls and, with a few exceptions, takes into account only the most significant monographs. The items are arranged under three headings: (1) general introductions to the history and religion of second temple Judaism, with special emphasis on studies in Jewish apocalypticism; (2) studies on the Old Testament Pseudepigrapha; and (3) studies on the Dead Sea Scrolls.

1. General Introductions to the History and Religion of Second Temple Judaism

a. Bibliographies

G. Boccaccini, *Portraits of Middle Judaism in Scholarship and Arts: A Multimedia Catalog from Flavius Josephus to 1991.* Turin: Zamorani, 1992.

D. R. Bourquin, *First-Century Palestinian Judaism: A Bibliography of Works in English.* San Bernardino: Borgo, 1990.

D. Dimant, *Bibliography of Works on Jewish History in the Persian, Hellenistic, and Roman Periods, 1981-85.* Jerusalem: Historical Society of Israel, 1987.

M. Mor and U. Rappaport, *Bibliography of Works on Jewish History in the Persian, Hellenistic, and Roman Periods, 1976-1980.* Jerusalem: Historical Society of Israel, 1982.

S. F. Noll, *The Intertestamental Period: A Study Guide.* Madison: Inter-Varsity Christian Fellowship of the U.S.A., 1985.

U. Rappaport, "Bibliography of Works on Jewish History in the Hellenistic and Roman Periods, 1946-1970," in B. Oded, et al., eds., *Studies in the History of the Jewish People and the Land of Israel* {Hebrew}. 5 vols. Haifa: University of Haifa, 1970-80. 2:247-321.

U. Rappaport and M. Mor, *Bibliography of Works on Jewish History in the Persian, Hellenistic, and Roman Periods, 1971-1975.* Jerusalem: Historical Society of Israel, 1977.

b. Specialized Journals

Journal for the Study of Judaism in the Persian, Hellenistic and Roman Period. Leiden: Brill, 1970-.

c. General Introductions

M. Avi-Yonah and Z. Baras, *Society and Religion in the Second Temple Period.* World History of the Jewish People 8. Jerusalem: Jewish Historical Publications and Massada, 1977.

G. Boccaccini, *Middle Judaism: Jewish Thought, 300 BCE–200 CE.* Minneapolis: Fortress, 1991.

————, *Il medio giudeismo.* Genoa: Marietti, 1993.

L. Bronner, *Sects and Separatism during the Second Jewish Commonwealth.* New York: Bloch, 1967.

S. J. D. Cohen, *From the Maccabees to the Mishnah.* Philadelphia: Westminster, 1987.

D. Flusser, *Judaism and the Origins of Christianity.* Jerusalem: Magnes and Hebrew University Press, 1988.

D. E. Gowan, *Bridge between the Testaments: A Reappraisal of Judaism from the Exile to the Birth of Christianity.* PTMS 14. Pittsburgh: Pickwick, 1976; 2nd ed. 1979; 3rd ed. 1986.

L. L. Grabbe, *Judaism from Cyrus to Hadrian.* 2 vols. Minneapolis: Fortress, 1992.

C. G. Howie, *The Creative Era Between the Testaments.* Richmond: John Knox, 1965.

M. S. Jaffee, *Early Judaism.* Upper Saddle River, N.J.: Prentice Hall, 1997.

H. Jagersma, *A History of Israel from Alexander the Great to Bar Kochba.* Trans. J. Bowden. London: SCM, 1985; Philadelphia: Fortress, 1986.

E. Lohse, *The New Testament Environment.* Trans. J. E. Steely. Nashville: Abingdon, 1976.

————, *Umwelt des Neuen Testaments.* Göttingen: Vandenhoeck & Ruprecht, 1971.

H. Maccoby, *Judaism in the First Century.* London: Sheldon, 1989.

J. Maier, *Zwischen den Testamenten: Geschichte und Religion in der Zeit des zweiten Tempels.* Würzburg: Echter, 1990.

F. J. Murphy, *The Religious World of Jesus: An Introduction to Second Temple Palestinian Judaism.* Nashville: Abingdon, 1991.

J. Neusner, *Judaism in the Beginning of Christianity.* Philadelphia: Fortress, 1984.

J. Neusner, ed., *Judaism in Late Antiquity.* 2 vols. Leiden: Brill, 1995.

J. D. Newsome, *Greek, Romans, Jews: Currents of Culture and Belief in the New Testament World.* Philadelphia: Trinity Press International, 1992.

E. Nodet, *A Search for the Origins of Judaism: From Joshua to the Mishnah.* Trans. E. Crowley. JSOTSup 248. Sheffield: JSOT Press, 1997.

B. Otzen, *Judaism in Antiquity: Political Development and Religious Currents from Alexander to Hadrian.* Trans. F. M. Cryer. Sheffield: JSOT Press, 1990.

C. F. Pfeiffer, *Between the Testaments.* Grand Rapids: Baker, 1959.

G. L. Prato, ed., *Israele alla ricerca di identità tra il III sec. a.C. e il I sec. d.C.* Ricerche storico-bibliche 1; Brescia: Assoc. Biblica Italiana, 1989.

B. Reicke, *Neutestamentliche Zeitgeschichte: Die biblische Welt 500 v.-100 n. Chr.* Berlin: Töpelmann, 1964.

————, *The New Testament Era: The World of the Bible from 500 B.C. to A.D. 100.* Trans. D. E. Green. Philadelphia: Fortress, 1968.

J. Riches, *The World of Jesus: First-Century Judaism in Crisis.* Cambridge: Cambridge University Press, 1990.

D. S. Russell, *Between the Testaments.* Philadelphia: Fortress, 1960.

P. Sacchi, *Storia del mondo giudaico.* Turin: Società Editrice Internazionale, 1976.

————, *Storia del Secondo Tempio: Israele tra VI secolo a.C. e I secolo d.C.* Turin: Società Editrice Internazionale, 1994.

S. Safrai and M. Stern, eds., *The Jewish People in the First Century: Historical Geography, Political History, Social, Cultural and Religious Life and Institutions.* CRINT 1/1. Assen: Van Gorcum; Philadelphia: Fortress, 1977.

A. J. Saldarini, *Pharisees, Scribes, and Sadducees in Palestinian Society: A Sociological Approach.* Wilmington, Del.: Glazier, 1988.

E. P. Sanders, *Judaism: Practice and Belief, 63 BCE–66 CE.* Philadelphia: Trinity Press International, 1992.

S. Sandmel, *Judaism and Christian Beginnings.* New York: Oxford University Press, 1978.

C. Saulnier with C. Perrot, *De la conquête d'Alexandre à la destruction du temple.* Paris: Cerf, 1985.

P. Schäfer, *Geschichte der Juden in der Antike: Die Juden Palästinas von Alexander dem Grossen bis zur arabischen Eroberung.* Stuttgart: Katholisches Bibelwerk, 1983.

————, *The History of the Jews in Antiquity: The Jews of Palestine from Alexander the Great to the Arab Conquest.* Trans. D. Chowcat. Luxembourg: Harwood Academic Publishers, 1995.

L. H. Schiffman, *From Text to Tradition: A History of Second Temple and Rabbinic Judaism.* Hoboken: Ktav, 1991.

E. Schürer, *The History of the Jewish People in the Age of Jesus Christ.* Rev. G. Vermes, et al. 3 vols. Edinburgh: T. & T. Clark, 1973-87.

J. J. Scott, *Customs and Controversies: Intertestamental Jewish Backgrounds of the New Testament.* Grand Rapids: Baker Books, 1995.

M. Simon, *Jewish Sects at the Time of Jesus.* Trans. J. H. Farley. Philadelphia: Fortress, 1967.

G. Stemberger, *Jewish Contemporaries of Jesus: Pharisees, Sadducees, Essenes.* Trans. A. W. Mahnke. Minneapolis: Fortress, 1995.

————, *Pharisäer, Sadduzäer, Essener.* Stuttgart: Katholisches Bibelwerk, 1991.

M. E. Stone, *Scriptures, Sects and Visions: A Profile of Judaism from Ezra to the Jewish Revolts*. Philadelphia: Fortress, 1980.

R. F. Surburg, *Introduction to the Intertestamental Period*. St. Louis: Concordia, 1975.

L. E. Toombs, *The Threshold of Christianity: Between the Testaments*. Philadelphia: Westminster, 1960.

L. T. Whitelocke, *The Development of Jewish Religious Thought in the Intertestamental Period*. New York: Vantage, 1976.

S. M. Wylen, *The Jews in the Time of Jesus: An Introduction*. New York: Paulist, 1996.

d. Studies on Jewish Apocalypticism

H. Althaus, ed., *Apokalyptik und Eschatologie: Sinn und Ziel der Geschichte*. Freiburg im Breisgau, Basel, and Vienna: Herder, 1987.

J. Bloch, *On the Apocalyptic in Judaism*. Philadelphia: Dropsie College, 1952.

J. J. Collins, *The Apocalyptic Imagination: An Introduction to the Jewish Matrix of Christianity*. New York: Crossroad, 1984.

———, *Apocalypticism in the Dead Sea Scrolls*. London and New York: Routledge, 1997.

———, *Daniel, with an Introduction to Apocalyptic Literature*. FOTL. Grand Rapids: Eerdmans, 1984.

J. J. Collins, ed., *Apocalypse: The Morphology of a Genre*. Semeia 14. Atlanta: Scholars Press, 1979.

J. J. Collins and J. H. Charlesworth, eds., *Mysteries and Revelations: Apocalyptic Studies since the Uppsala Colloquium*. JSPSup 9. Sheffield: JSOT Press, 1991.

S. L. Cook, *Prophecy and Apocalypticism: The Postexilic Social Setting*. Minneapolis: Fortress, 1995.

S. B. Frost, *Old Testament Apocalyptic: Its Origins and Growth*. London: Epworth, 1952.

R. W. Funk, ed., *Apocalypticism*. JTC 6. New York: Herder and Herder, 1969.

F. García Martínez, *Qumran and Apocalyptic: Studies on the Aramaic Texts from Qumran*. STDJ 9. Leiden: Brill, 1992.

I. Gruenwald, *Apocalyptic and Merkavah Mysticism*. AGJU 14. Leiden: Brill, 1980.

———, *From Apocalypticism to Gnosticism*. Frankfurt: Lang, 1988.

P. D. Hanson, *The Dawn of Apocalyptic*. Philadelphia: Fortress, 1975.

———, *Old Testament Apocalyptic*. Nashville: Abingdon, 1987.

P. D. Hanson, ed., *Visionaries and Their Apocalypses*. IRT 2. Philadelphia: Fortress, 1983.

D. Hellholm, ed., *Apocalypticism in the Mediterranean World and in the Near East: Proceedings of the International Colloquium on Apocalypticism, Uppsala, August 12-17, 1979*. Tübingen: Mohr, 1983.

M. Himmelfarb, *Ascent to Heaven in Jewish and Christian Apocalypses*. New York: Oxford University Press, 1993.

————, *Tours of Hell: An Apocalyptic Form in Jewish and Christian Literature*. Philadelphia: Fortress, 1983.

K. Jeppesen, et al., eds., *In the Last Days: On Jewish and Christian Apocalyptic and Its Period*. Aarhus: Aarhus University Press, 1994.

C. Kappler, ed., *Apocalypses et voyages dans l'au-delà*. Paris: Cerf, 1987.

K. Koch, *Ratlos vor der Apokalyptic*. Gütersloh: Gütersloher Verlaghaus, 1970.

————, *The Rediscovery of Apocalyptic*. Trans. M. Kohl. SBT 2/22. Naperville: Allenson, 1972.

W. G. Lambert, *The Background of Jewish Apocalyptic*. London: Athlone, 1978.

B. Marconcini, *Apocalittica*. Turin: Elle Di Ci, 1985.

L. Monloubou, et al., *Apocalypses et théologie de l'espérance*. LD 95. Paris: Cerf, 1977.

L. Morris, *Apocalyptic*. Grand Rapids: Eerdmans, 1972.

C. Münchow, *Ethik und Eschatologie: Ein Beitrag zum Verständnis der früh-jüdischen Apokalyptik*. Göttingen: Vandenhoeck & Ruprecht, 1981.

P. von der Osten-Sacken, *Die Apokalyptik in ihrem Verhältnis zu Prophetie und Weisheit*. Munich: C. Kaiser, 1969.

C. Rowland, *The Open Heaven: A Study of Apocalyptic in Judaism and Early Christianity*. New York: Crossroad, 1982.

H. H. Rowley, *Jewish Apocalyptic and the Dead Sea Scrolls*. London: Athlone, 1957.

————, *The Revelance of Apocalyptic: A Study of Jewish and Christian Apocalypses from Daniel to the Revelation*. Rev. ed. London: Lutterworth, 1955. Repr. Greenwood, S.C.: Attic, 1980.

D. S. Russell, *Apocalyptic, Ancient and Modern*. Philadelphia: Fortress, 1978.

————, *Divine Disclosure: An Introduction to Jewish Apocalyptic*. Minneapolis: Fortress, 1992.

————, *The Method and Message of Jewish Apocalyptic*. OTL. Philadelphia: Westminster, 1964.

P. Sacchi, *Jewish Apocalyptic and Its History*. Trans. W. J. Short. JSPSup 20. Sheffield: Sheffield Academic Press, 1997.

————, *L'apocalittica giudaica e la sua storia*. Brescia: Paideia, 1990.

J. M. Schmidt, *Die jüdische Apokalyptik: Die Geschichte ihrer Erforschung von den Anfängen bis zu den Textfunden von Qumran*. Neukirchen-Vluyn: Neukirchener, 1969.

W. Schmithals, *The Apocalyptic Movement: Introduction and Interpretation*. Trans. J. E. Steely. Nashville: Abingdon, 1975.

————, *Die Apokalyptik: Einführung und Deutung*. Göttingen: Vandenhoeck & Ruprecht, 1973.

J. Schreiner, *Alttestamentlich-jüdische Apocalyptik: Eine Einführung.* Munich: Kösel, 1969.

D. Sneen, *Visions of Hope: Apocalyptic Themes from Biblical Times.* Minneapolis: Augsburg, 1978.

J. C. Vanderkam and W. Adler, eds., *The Jewish Apocalyptic Heritage in Early Christianity.* CRINT 3/4. Minneapolis: Fortress, 1996.

A. Yarbro Collins, *Cosmology and Eschatology in Jewish and Christian Apocalypticism.* Leiden: Brill, 1996.

3. Studies on the Old Testament Pseudepigrapha

a. Bibliographies

J. H. Charlesworth, *The Pseudepigrapha and Modern Research, with a Supplement.* SBLSCS 7. Chico, Calif.: Scholars Press, 1981.

G. Delling and M. Maser, *Bibliographie zur judisch-hellenistischen Literatur 1900-1970.* 2nd ed. Berlin: Akademie, 1975.

L. Rosso-Ubigli, "Gli apocrifi (o pseudepigrafi) dell'Antico Testamento. Bibliografia 1979-1989," *Hen* 12 (1990) 259-321.

b. Specialized Journals

Journal for the Study of the Pseudepigrapha. Sheffield: Sheffield Academic Press, 1987-.

c. General Introductions

J. H. Charlesworth, *The Old Testament Pseudepigrapha and the New Testament.* SNTSMS 54. Cambridge: Cambridge University Press, 1985.

J. H. Charlesworth and C. A. Evans, eds., *The Pseudepigrapha and Early Biblical Interpretation.* JSPSup 14. Sheffield: JSOT Press, 1993.

M. Cimosa, *La letteratura intertestamentaria.* Bologna: Centro Editoriale Dehoniano, 1992.

A. M. Denis, *Introduction aux pseudépigraphes grecs d'Ancien Testament.* SVTP 1. Leiden: Brill, 1970.

O. Eissfeldt, *Einleitung in das Alte Testament.* 2nd ed. Tübingen: Mohr, 1956; 3rd ed. 1964.

————, *The Old Testament: An Introduction*. Trans. P. R. Ackroyd. New York: Harper & Row, 1965.

C. A. Evans, *Noncanonical Writings and New Testament Interpretation*. Peabody, Mass.: Hendrickson, 1992.

M. de Jonge, ed., *Outside the Old Testament*. Cambridge: Cambridge University Press, 1985.

R. A. Kraft and G. W. E. Nickelsburg, eds., *Early Judaism and Its Modern Interpreters*. Philadelphia: Fortress, 1986.

A. R. C. Leaney, *The Jewish and Christian World, 200 BC to AD 200*. Cambridge: Cambridge University Press, 1984.

M. McNamara, *Intertestamental Literature*. Wilmington, Del.: Glazier, 1983.

M. J. Mulder and H. Sysling, eds., *Mikra: Text, Translation, Reading, and Interpretation of the Hebrew Bible in Ancient Judaism and Early Christianity*. CRINT 2/1. Assen: Van Gorcum; Minneapolis: Fortress, 1988.

G. W. E. Nickelsburg, *Jewish Literature Between the Bible and the Mishnah*. Philadelphia: Fortress, 1981.

L. Rost, *Einleitung in die alttestamentlichen Apokryphen und Pseudepigraphen einschliesslich der grossen Qumran-Handschriften*. Heidelberg: Quelle & Meyer, 1971.

————, *Judaism Outside the Hebrew Canon: An Introduction to the Documents*. Trans. D. E. Green. Nashville: Abingdon, 1976.

D. S. Russell, *The Old Testament Pseudepigrapha: Patriarchs and Prophets in Early Judaism*. Philadelphia: Fortress, 1987.

M. E. Stone, ed., *Jewish Writings of the Second Temple Period: Apocrypha, Pseudepigrapha, Qumran Sectarian Writings, Philo, Josephus*. CRINT 2/2. Assen: Van Gorcum; Philadelphia: Fortress, 1984.

d. Collections in Modern Translation

J. H. Charlesworth, ed., *The Old Testament Pseudepigrapha*. 2 vols. Garden City, N.Y.: Doubleday, 1983-85.

A. Diez Macho, ed., *Apócrifos del Antiguo Testamento*. 5 vols. Madrid: Cristiadad, 1982-87.

A. Dupont-Sommer and M. Philonenko, eds., *La Bible: Ecrits intertestamentaires*. Paris: Gallimard, 1987.

W. G. Kummel and H. Lichtenberger, eds., *Jüdische Schriften aus hellenistisch-römischer Zeit*. Gütersloh: Mohn, 1973-.

P. Sacchi, ed., *Apocrifi dell'Antico Testamento*. 2 vols. Turin: Unione Tipografica-Editrice Torinese, 1981-89.

H. F. D. Sparks, ed., *The Apocryphal Old Testament*. Oxford: Clarendon, 1984.

e. First Book of Enoch

M. Albani, *Astronomie und Schöpfungsglaube: Untersuchungen zum astrono-mischen Henochbuch.* Neukirchen-Vluyn: Neukirchener, 1994.

C. P. van Andel, *De structuur van de Henoch traditie en het Nieuwe Testament/The Structure of the Enoch-Tradition and the New Testament* {Dutch with sum-mary in English}. Utrecht, 1955.

M. Barker, *The Lost Prophet: The Book of Enoch and Its Influence on Christianity.* London: SPCK, 1988.

M. Black with J. C. VanderKam and O. Neugebauer, *The Book of Enoch, or, I Enoch: A New English Edition with Commentary and Textual Notes.* SVTP 7. Leiden: Brill, 1985.

M. Black, *Apocalypsis Henochi Graece.* PVTG 3. Leiden: Brill, 1970.

S. Chialà, *Libro delle parabole di Enoc.* Brescia: Paideia, 1997.

F. Dexinger, *Henochs Zehnwochenapokalypse und offene Probleme der Apokalyp-tikforschung.* SPB 29. Leiden: Brill, 1977.

L. Hartman, *Asking for a Meaning: A Study of Enoch 1–5.* ConBNT 12. Lund: Gleerup, 1979.

M. A. Knibb with E. Ullendorf, *The Ethiopic Book of Enoch: A New Edition in the Light of the Aramaic Dead Sea Fragments.* 2 vols. Oxford: Clarendon, 1978.

H. S. Kvanvig, *Roots of Apocalyptic: The Mesopotamian Background of the Enoch Figure and of the Son of Man.* WMANT 61. Neukirchen-Vluyn: Neukirch-ener, 1988.

J. T. Milik with M. Black, *The Books of Enoch: Aramaic Fragments of Qumrân Cave 4.* Oxford: Clarendon, 1976.

E. Rau, *Kosmologie, Eschatologie und die Lehrautorität Henochs: Traditions- und formgeschichtliche Untersuchungen zum äthiopischen Henochbuch und zu verwandten Schriften.* Diss., Hamburg, 1974.

R. Rubinkiewicz, *Die Eschathologie von Henoch 9–11 und das Neue Testament.* Klosterneuburg: Osterreichisches Katholisches Bibelwerk, 1984.

D. W. Suter, *Tradition and Composition in the Parables of Enoch.* SBLDS 47. Missoula, Mont.: Scholars Press, 1979.

P. Tiller, *A Commentary on the Animal Apocalypse of 1 Enoch.* Atlanta: Scholars Press, 1993.

J. C. VanderKam, *Enoch: A Man for All Generations.* Columbia: University of South Carolina Press, 1995.

———, *Enoch and the Growth of an Apocalyptic Tradition.* CBQMS 16. Wash-ington, D.C.: Catholic Biblical Association of America, 1984.

M.-T. Wacker, *Weltordnung und Gericht: Studien zu 1 Henoch 22.* Würzburg: Echter, 1982.

f. Book of Jubilees

C. Endres, *Biblical Interpretation in the Book of Jubilees*. CBQMS 18. Washington, D.C.: Catholic Biblical Association of America, 1987.

G. L. Davenport, *The Eschatology of the Book of Jubilees*. SPB 20. Leiden: Brill, 1971.

A.-M. Denis, *Concordance latine du Liber Jubilaeorum sive parva Genesis*. Louvain: Louvain University Press, 1973.

M. A. Knibb, *Jubilees and the Origins of the Qumran Community: An Inaugural Lecture in the Dept. of Biblical Studies, King's College*. London: King's College, 1989.

M. Testuz, *Les idées religieuses du Livre des Jubilés*. Geneva: Druz; Paris: Minard, 1960.

J. C. VanderKam, *The Book of Jubilees*. 2 vols. CSCO 510-11. Louvain: Secrétariat du CSCO, 1989.

————, *Textual and Historical Studies in the Book of Jubilees*. HSM 14. Missoula, Mont.: Scholars Press, 1977.

W. Wirgin, *The Book of Jubilees and the Maccabean Era of Shmittah Cycles*. Leeds: Leeds University Oriental Society, 1964.

g. Testaments of the Twelve Patriarchs

J. Becker, *Die Testamente der zwölf Patriarchen*. JSHRZ 3/1. Gütersloh: Mohn, 1974.

————, *Untersuchungen zur Entstehungsgeschichte der Testamente der zwölf Patriarchen*. AGJU 8. Leiden: Brill, 1970.

C. Burchard, J. Jevell, and J. Thomas, *Studien zu den Testamenten der zwölf Patriarchen*. BZNW 36. Berlin: Töpelmann, 1969.

H. W. Hollander, *Joseph as an Ethical Model in the Testaments of the Twelve Patriarchs*. SVTP 6. Leiden: Brill, 1981.

H. W. Hollander and M. de Jonge, *The Testaments of the Twelve Patriarchs: A Commentary*. SVTP 8. Leiden: Brill, 1985.

A. Hultgård, *L'Eschatologie des Testaments des Douze Patriarches*. 2 vols. AUUHR 6-7. Uppsala: Almqvist & Wiksell, 1977-82.

M. de Jonge, *Jewish Eschatology, Early Christian Christology, and Testaments of the Twelve Patriarchs: Collected Essays*. NovTSup 63. Leiden: Brill, 1991.

————, *Testamenta XII Patriarcharum*. PVTG 1. Leiden: Brill, 1964; 2nd ed., 1970.

————, *The Testaments of the Twelve Patriarchs: A Study of Their Text, Composition, and Origin*. Assen: Van Gorcum, 1953.

M. de Jonge, ed., *Studies on the Testaments of the Twelve Patriarchs: Text and Interpretation.* SVTP 3. Leiden: Brill, 1975.

M. de Jonge, H. W. Hollander, H. J. de Jonge, and T. Korteweg, *The Testaments of the Twelve Patriarchs: A Critical Edition of the Greek Text.* PVTG 1/2. Leiden: Brill, 1978.

M. Philonenko, *Les interpolations chrétiennes des Testaments des Douze Patriarches et les manuscrits de Qoumrân.* Paris: Presses Universitaires, 1960.

H. D. Slingerland, *The Testaments of the Twelve Patriarchs: A Critical History of Research.* SBLMS 21. Missoula, Mont.: Scholars Press, 1977.

J. H. Ulrichsen, *Die Grundschrift der Testamente der zwölf Patriarchen: Eine Untersuchung zu Umfang, Inhalt und Eigenart der ursprünglichen Schrift.* AUUHR 10. Uppsala: Almqvist & Wiksell, 1991.

4. Studies on the Dead Sea Scrolls

a. Bibliographies

C. Burchard, *Bibliographie zu den Handschriften vom Toten Meer.* 2 vols. BZAW 76. Berlin: Töpelmann, 1957-65.

J. A. Fitzmyer, *The Dead Sea Scrolls: Major Publications and Tools for Study.* Rev. ed. SBLRBS 20. Atlanta: Scholars Press, 1990.

F. García Martínez and D. W. Parry, *A Bibliography of the Finds in the Desert of Judah 1970-95: Arranged by Author with Citation and Subject Indexes.* STDJ 19. Leiden: Brill, 1996.

B. Jongeling, *A Classified Bibliography of the Finds in the Desert of Judah, 1958-1969.* STDJ 7. Leiden: Brill, 1971.

C. Koester, "A Qumran Bibliography, 1974-1984," *BTB* 15 (1985) 110-20.

W. S. LaSor, *Bibliography of the Dead Dea Scrolls, 1948-1957.* Pasadena: Fuller Theological Seminary, 1958.

M. Yizhar, *Bibliography of Hebrew Publications on the Dead Sea Scrolls, 1948-1964.* HTS 23. Cambridge: Harvard University Press, 1967.

b. Specialized Journals

Dead Sea Discoveries. Leiden: Brill, 1994-.

The Qumran Chronicle. Cracow: Enigma, 1990-.

Revue de Qumran. Paris: Gabalda, 1958-.

c. General Introductions and Collections of Essays

J. M. Allegro, *The Dead Sea Scrolls*. Harmondsworth: Penguin, 1956.

————, *The Dead Sea Scrolls: A Reappraisal*. Baltimore: Penguin, 1964.

H. Bardtke, ed., *Qumran-Probleme*. Berlin: Akademie-Verlag, 1963.

J. M. Baumgarten, *Studies in Qumran Law*. SJLA 24. Leiden: Brill, 1977.

O. Betz and R. Riesner, *Jesus, Qumran and the Vatican: Clarifications*. Trans. J. Bowden. New York: Crossroad, 1994.

————, *Jesus, Qumran und der Vatikan: Klarstellungen*. Freiburg im Breisgau: Herder, 1993.

M. Black, *The Scrolls and Christian Origins: Studies in the Jewish Background of the New Testament*. New York: Scribner's, 1961.

M. Black, ed., *The Scrolls and Christianity: Historical and Theological Significance*. London: SPCK, 1969.

H. Braun, *Qumran und das Neue Testament*. 2 vols. Tübingen: Mohr, 1966.

G. J. Brooke, ed., *New Qumran Texts and Studies*. STDJ 15. Leiden: Brill, 1994.

F. F. Bruce, *Second Thoughts on the Dead Sea Scrolls*. Repr. Grand Rapids: Eerdmans, 1977.

P. R. Callaway, *The History of the Qumran Community: An Investigation*. JSPSup 3. Sheffield: JSOT Press, 1988.

L. Cansdale, *Qumran and the Essenes: A Re-Evaluation of the Evidence*. TSAJ 60. Tübingen: Mohr-Siebeck, 1997.

J. Carmignac, *Christ and the Teacher of Righteousness: The Evidence of the Dead Sea Scrolls*. Trans. K. G. Pedley. Baltimore: Helicon, 1962.

————, *Le Docteur de Justice et Jésus-Christ*. Paris: Éditions de l'Orante, 1957.

J. M. Casciaro, *Qumrán y el Nuevo Testamento*. Pamplona: Ediciones Universidad de Navarra, 1982.

J. H. Charlesworth, ed., *Jesus and the Dead Sea Scrolls*. New York: Doubleday, 1992.

J. H. Charlesworth, ed., *John and Qumran*. London: Chapman, 1972. Enlarged ed.: *John and the Dead Sea Scrolls*. New York: Crossroad, 1990.

E. M. Cook, *Solving the Mysteries of the Dead Sea Scrolls: New Light on the Bible*. Grand Rapids: Zondervan, 1994.

F. M. Cross, *The Ancient Library of Qumran*. Garden City, N.Y.: Doubleday, 1958. 2nd ed. 1961. 3rd ed. Sheffield: Sheffield Academic Press, 1995.

F. M. Cross and S. Talmon, eds., *Qumran and the History of the Biblical Text*. Cambridge: Harvard University Press, 1975.

J. Daniélou, *The Dead Sea Scrolls and Primitive Christianity*. Trans. S. Attanasio. Baltimore: Helicon, 1958.

————, *Les manuscrits de la Mer Morte et les origines du christianisme*. Paris: Editions de l'Orante, 1957.

A. P. Davies, *The Meaning of the Dead Sea Scrolls*. New York: New American Library, 1956.

P. R. Davies, *Behind the Essenes: History and Ideology in the Dead Sea Scrolls*. BJS 94. Atlanta: Scholars Press, 1987.

————, *Qumran*. Grand Rapids: Eerdmans, 1982.

————, *Sects and Scrolls: Essays on Qumran and Related Topics*. Atlanta: Scholars Press, 1996.

M. Delcor, ed., *Qumrân: Sa piété, sa théologie et son milieu*. BETL 46. Paris: Duculot, 1978.

D. Dimant and U. Rappaport, eds., *The Dead Sea Scrolls: Forty Years of Research*. STDJ 10. Leiden: Brill, 1992.

D. Dimant and L. H. Schiffman, eds., *Time To Prepare the Way in the Wilderness: Papers on the Qumran Scrolls by Fellows of the Institute for Advanced Studies of the Hebrew University, Jerusalem, 1989-90*. STDJ 16. Leiden: Brill, 1995.

G. R. Driver, *The Hebrew Scrolls from the Neighbourhood of Jericho and the Dead Sea*. London: Oxford University Press, 1951.

————, *The Judaean Scrolls: The Problem and a Solution*. Oxford: Blackwell, 1965.

A. Dupont-Sommer, *Aperçus préliminaires sur les manuscrits de la Mer Morte*. Paris: Maisonneuve, 1950.

————, *The Dead Sea Scrolls: A Preliminary Survey*. Trans. E. M. Rowley. New York: Macmillan, 1952.

————, *The Jewish Sect of Qumran and the Essenes: New Studies on the Dead Sea Scrolls*. Trans. R. D. Barnett. London: Vallentine, Mitchell & Co., 1954. Repr. New York: Macmillan, 1956.

————, *Noveau aperçus sur les manuscrits de la Mer Morte*. Paris: Maisonneuve, 1953.

J. A. Fitzmyer, *Responses to 101 Questions on the Dead Sea Scrolls*. New York and Mahwah, N.J.: Paulist, 1992.

D. Flusser, *The Spiritual History of the Dead Sea Sect*. Trans. C. Glucker. Tel Aviv, 1989.

C. T. Fritsch, *The Qumran Community: Its History and Its Scrolls*. New York: Macmillan, 1956.

N. S. Fujita, *A Crack in the Jar: What Ancient Jewish Documents Tell Us about the New Testament*. New York and Mahwah, N.J.: Paulist, 1986.

F. García Martínez and J. Trebolle Barrera, *Los Hombres de Qumrán*. Madrid: Trotta, 1993.

————, *The People of the Dead Sea Scrolls*. Trans. W. G. E. Watson. Leiden: Brill, 1995.

F. García Martínez and E. Puech, eds., *Hommage à Jozef T. Milik. RevQ* 17 (1996).

A. N. Gilkes, *The Impact of the Dead Sea Scrolls*. London: Macmillan, 1962.

N. Golb, *Who Wrote the Dead Sea Scrolls? The Search for the Secret of Qumran*. New York: Scribner, 1995.

A. Gonzalez Lamadrid, *Los descubrimientos del Mar Muerto*. Madrid: Catolica, 1971.

G. Graystone, *The Dead Sea Scrolls and the Originality of Christ*. New York: Sheed & Ward, 1956.

K. E. Grözinger, et al., *Qumran*. Darmstadt: Wissenschaftliche Buchgesellschaft, 1981.

G. Jeremias, *Die Lehrer der Gerechtigkeit*. Göttingen: Vandenhoeck & Ruprecht, 1963.

Z. J. Kapera, ed., *Mogilany 1989: Papers on the Dead Sea Scrolls*. Cracow: Enigma, 1991.

G. Lambert, *Le Maître de justice et la communauté de l'alliance*. Louvain: Louvain University Press, 1952.

W. S. LaSor, *The Dead Sea Scrolls and the New Testament*. Grand Rapids: Eerdmans, 1972.

J. McDonald, ed., *Dead Sea Scrolls Studies, 1969*. Leiden: Brill, 1969.

M. Mansoor, *The Dead Sea Scrolls: A College Text-Book and a Study-Guide*. Grand Rapids: Baker, 1964.

J. T. Milik, *Dix ans de découvertes dans le désert de Juda*. Paris: Cerf, 1957.

————, *Ten Years of Discovery in the Wilderness of Judaea*. Trans. J. Strugnell. SBT 1/26. Naperville: Allenson, 1959.

L. Mowry, *The Dead Sea Scrolls and the Early Church*. Chicago: University of Chicago Press, 1962.

J. Murphy-O'Connor, ed., *Paul and Qumran*. Chicago: Priory, 1968.

J. Murphy-O'Connor and J. H. Charlesworth, eds., *Paul and the Dead Sea Scrolls*. New York: Crossroad, 1990.

D. W. Parry and S. D. Ricks, eds., *Current Research and Technological Developments on the Dead Sea Scrolls: Conference on the Texts from the Judean Desert, Jerusalem, 30 April, 1995*. STDJ 20. Leiden: Brill, 1996.

M. Pearlman, *The Dead Sea Scrolls in the Shrine of the Book*. Jerusalem: Israel Museum, 1988.

C. F. Pfeiffer, *The Dead Sea Scrolls and the Bible*. Grand Rapids: Baker, 1969.

J. van der Ploeg, *The Excavations at Qumran: A Survey of the Judean Brotherwood and Its Ideas*. Trans. K. Smyth. New York: Longmans, Green, 1958.

————, *Vondsten in de Woestijn van Juda: De Rollen der Dode Zee*. Utrecht: Uitgeverij het Spectrum, 1957.

J. van der Ploeg, ed., *La secte de Qumrân et les origines du christianisme*. Bruges: Desclée du Brouwer, 1959.

C. Rabin, *Qumran Studies*. London: Oxford University Press, 1957. Repr. New York: Schocken, 1975.

C. Rabin and Y. Yadin, eds., *Aspects of the Dead Sea Scrolls*. ScrHier 4. Jerusalem: Magnes and Hebrew University Press, 1958; 2nd ed. 1965.

C. Roth, *The Historical Background of the Dead Sea Scrolls*. Oxford: Blackwell, 1958.

H. H. Rowley, *The Dead Sea Scrolls and Their Significance.* London: Independent Press, 1955.

————, *The Dead Sea Scrolls and the New Testament.* London: SPCK, 1957.

L. H. Schiffman, *Reclaiming the Dead Sea Scrolls: The History of Judaism, the Background of Christianity, the Lost Library of Qumran.* Philadelphia and Jerusalem: Jewish Publication Society, 1994.

L. H. Schiffman, ed., *Archaeology and History in the Dead Sea Scrolls: The New York University Conference in Memory of Yigael Yadin.* Sheffield: Sheffield Academic Press, 1990.

J. Schreiden, *Les énigmes des manuscrits de la Mer Morte.* Wetteren: Cultura, 1961.

H. Shanks, ed., *Understanding the Dead Sea Scrolls: A Reader from the Biblical Archaeology Review.* New York: Random House, 1992.

H. Shanks, et al., *The Dead Sea Scrolls After Forty Years: Symposium at the Smithsonian Institution, October 27, 1990.* Washington, D.C.: Biblical Archaeology Society, 1991.

J. A. Soggin, *I manoscritti del Mar Morto.* Rome: Newton, 1978.

H. Stegemann, *Die Enstehung der Qumrangemeinde.* Diss., Bonn, 1965; privately published, 1971.

————, *Die Essener, Qumran, Johannes der Täufer und Jesus.* Freiburg: Herder, 1993.

————, *The Library of Qumran: On the Essenes, Qumran, John the Baptist, and Jesus.* Trans Robert R. Barr. Grand Rapids: Eerdmans, 1998.

K. Stendhal, ed., *The Scrolls and the New Testament.* New York: Harper, 1957.

E. F. Sutcliffe, *The Monks of Qumran as Depicted in the Dead Sea Scrolls.* Westminster, Md.: Newman, 1960.

S. Talmon, *The Dead Sea Scrolls or the Community of the Renewed Covenant.* Tucson: University of Arizona Press, 1993.

————, *The World of Qumran from Within: Collected Studies.* Jerusalem: Magnes and Hebrew University Press; Leiden: Brill, 1989.

J. Trebolle Barrera and L. Vegas Montaner, eds., *The Madrid Qumran Congress: Proceedings of the International Congress on the Dead Sea Scrolls, Madrid, 18-21 March, 1991.* STDJ 11/1-2. Leiden: Brill, 1992.

J. C. Trever, *The Dead Sea Scrolls: A Personal Account.* Grand Rapids: Eerdmans, 1977.

————, *The Untold Story of Qumran.* Westwood, N.J.: Revell, 1965.

E. C. Ulrich and J. C. VanderKam, eds., *The Community of the Renewed Covenant: The Notre Dame Symposium on the Dead Sea Scrolls.* Notre Dame: University of Notre Dame Press, 1994.

J. C. VanderKam, *The Dead Sea Scrolls Today.* Grand Rapids: Eerdmans, 1994.

G. Vermes, *The Dead Sea Scrolls: Qumran in Perspective.* London: Collins, 1977. Repr. Philadelphia: Fortress, 1981. 3rd ed. London: SCM, 1994.

————, *Discovery in the Judaean Desert.* New York: Desclée, 1956.

————, *Les manuscrits du désert de Juda.* Tournai: Desclée, 1953.

212

J.-C. Violette, *Les esséniens de Qoumrân*. Paris: Lafont, 1983.

B. Z. Wacholder, *The Dawn of Qumran: The Sectarian Torah and the Teacher of Righteousness*. Cincinnati: Hebrew Union College Press, 1983.

Y. Yadin, *The Message of the Scrolls*. New York: Simon & Schuster, 1957. Repr. New York: Crossroad, 1991, with a preface by J. H. Charlesworth.

d. Collections of Texts

J. M. Allegro and A. Arnold, *Qumran Cave 4, I*. DJD 5. Oxford: Clarendon, 1968.

H. Attridge, et al., *Qumran Cave 4, VIII: Parabiblical Texts, Part 1*. DJD 13. Oxford: Clarendon, 1994.

M. Baillet, *Qumrân Grotte 4, III (4Q482–4Q520)*. DJD 7. Oxford: Clarendon, 1982.

M. Baillet, J. T. Milik, and R. de Vaux, *Les "petites grottes" de Qumrân*. DJD 3. 2 vols. Oxford: Clarendon, 1962.

D. Barthélemy and J. T. Milik, *Qumran Cave I*. DJD 1. Oxford: Clarendon, 1955.

K. Beyer, *Die aramäischen Texte vom Toten Meer*. Göttingen: Vandenhoeck & Ruprecht, 1984. *Ergänzungsband*. 1994.

M. Broshi, et al., *Qumran Cave 4, XIV: Parabiblical Texts, Part 2*. DJD 19. Oxford: Clarendon, 1995.

M. Burrows, J. C. Trever, and W. H. Brownlee, *The Dead Sea Scrolls of St. Mark's Monastery*. 2 vols. New Haven: American Schools of Oriental Research, 1950-51.

R. de Vaux and J. T. Milik, *Qumrân Grotte 4, II: I. Archéologie. II. Tefillin, Mezuzot et Targums (4Q128–4Q157)*. DJD 6. Oxford: Clarendon, 1977.

R. H. Eisenman and J. M. Robinson, *A Facsimile Edition of the Dead Sea Scrolls*. 2 vols. Washington, D.C.: Biblical Archaeology Society, 1991.

J. A. Fitzmyer and D. J. Harrington, *A Manual of Palestinian Aramaic Texts*. BibOr 34. Rome: Biblical Institute Press, 1978.

E. Qimron and J. Strugnell, *Qumran Cave 4, V: Miqṣat Maʿaśe ha-Torah*. DJD 10. Oxford: Clarendon, 1994.

S. A. Reed, *Dead Sea Scrolls Inventory Project: Lists of Documents, Photographs and Museum Plates*. 14 fascs. Claremont: Ancient Biblical Manuscript Center, 1992.

S. A. Reed, rev. and ed. M. J. Lundberg with M. B. Phelps, *The Dead Sea Scrolls Catalogue: Documents, Photographs and Museum Inventory Numbers*. SBLRBS 32. Atlanta: Scholars Press, 1994.

S. A. Reed, rev. and ed. M. J. Lundberg with M. B. Phelps, *The Dead Sea Scrolls on Microfiche*. Vol. 3: *Inventory Lists of Photographs*. Leiden: Brill, 1993.

J. A. Sanders, *The Psalms Scroll of Qumrân Cave 11*. DJD 4. Oxford: Clarendon, 1965.

P. W. Skehan, E. Ulrich, and J. E. Sanderson, *Qumran Cave 4, IV: Palaeo-Hebrew and Greek Biblical Manuscripts.* DJD 9. Oxford: Clarendon, 1992.

E. L. Sukenik, *Megillot Genuzot.* 2 vols. Jerusalem: Bialik Foundation, 1948-50.

E. L. Sukenik and N. Avigad, *The Dead Sea Scrolls of the Hebrew University.* Jerusalem: Hebrew University and Magnes Press, 1955. Modern Hebrew edition: Jerusalem: Bialik Foundation and the Hebrew University, 1954.

E. Tov and R. Kraft, *The Greek Minor Prophets Scroll from Naḥal Ḥever (8ḤevXI-Igr).* DJD 8. Oxford: Clarendon, 1990.

E. Tov with S. J. Pfann, *The Dead Sea Scrolls on Microfiche.* Vol. 1: *A Comprehensive Facsimile Edition of the Texts from the Judaean Desert.* Vol. 2: *Companion Volume.* Leiden: Brill, 1993; 2nd ed. 1995.

E. C. Ulrich and F. M. Cross, eds., *Qumran Cave 4, VII: Genesis to Numbers.* DJD 12. Oxford: Clarendon, 1994.

E. C. Ulrich, et al. *Qumran Cave 4, IX: Deuteronomy, Joshua, Judges, Kings.* DJD 14. Oxford: Clarendon, 1995.

B. Z. Wacholder and M. G. Abegg, *A Preliminary Edition of the Unpublished Dead Sea Scrolls: The Hebrew and Aramaic Texts from Cave Four.* 2 vols. Washington, D.C.: Biblical Archaeology Society, 1991-92.

e. Concordances

R. E. Brown, et al. *A Preliminary Concordance to the Hebrew and Aramaic Fragments from Qumran Caves II-X, Including Especially the Unpublished Material from Cave IV.* 5 vols. Göttingen: privately printed, 1988.

J. H. Charlesworth and R. E. Whitaker, *Graphic Concordance to the Dead Sea Scrolls.* Tübingen: Mohr; Louisville: Westminster/John Knox, 1991.

K. G. Kuhn, et al., *Konkordanz zu den Qumrantexten.* Göttingen: Vandenhoeck & Ruprecht, 1960.

f. Collections in Modern Translation

I. D. Amusin, *Teksty Kumrana.* Moscow: Akademia Nauk, 1971.

M. Berettas, *Ta cheirographa tēs Nakrēs Thalasson.* Athens: Dibres, 1978.

M. Burrows, *The Dead Sea Scrolls.* New York: Viking, 1955.

———, *More Light on the Dead Sea Scrolls.* New York: Viking, 1958.

J. Carmignac, et al. *Les textes de Qumrân traduits et annotés.* 2 vols. Paris: Letouzey et Ané, 1961-63.

J. H. Charlesworth, ed., *The Princeton Theological Seminary Dead Sea Scrolls Project,* 12 vols. Tübingen: Mohr; Louisville: Westminster/John Knox, 1994-.

A. Dupont-Sommer, *Les écrits esséniens découverts près de la Mer Morte.* Paris: Payot, 1959; 2nd ed. 1960; 3rd ed. 1964.

————, *The Essene Writings from Qumran.* Trans. G. Vermes. Oxford: Blackwell; 1961; Cleveland: World, 1962. Repr. Gloucester: Peter Smith, 1973.

A. Dupont-Sommer and M. Philonenko, eds., *La Bible: Écrits intertestamentaires.* Paris: Gallimard, 1987.

R. H. Eisenman and M. O. Wise, *The Dead Sea Scrolls Uncovered.* Rockport: Element, 1992.

F. García Martínez, *The Dead Sea Scrolls Translated.* Trans. W. G. E. Watson. Leiden: Brill; Grand Rapids: Eerdmans, 1994; 2nd ed. 1996.

————, *Textos de Qumrán.* Madrid: Trotta, 1992.

F. García Martínez and C. Martone, *Testi di Qumran.* Brescia: Paideia, 1996.

F. García Martínez and A. S. van der Woude, *De Rollen van de Dode Zee: Ingeleid en in het Nederlands vertaald.* 2 vols. Kampen: Kok Pharos, 1994-95.

T. H. Gaster, *The Dead Sea Scriptures in English Translation.* Garden City, N.Y.: Doubleday, 1956; 2nd ed. 1964; 3rd ed. 1976.

M. A. Knibb, *The Qumran Community.* Cambridge: Cambridge University Press, 1987.

E. Lohse, *Die Texte aus Qumran: Hebraisch und Deutsch.* Munich: Kösel; Darmstadt: Wissenschaftliche Buchgesellschaft, 1964; 2nd ed. 1971.

J. Maier and K. Schubert, *Die Qumran-Essener: Texte der Schriftrollen und Lebensbilder der Gemeinde.* Munich: Reinhardt, 1973.

F. Michelini-Tocci, *I manoscritti del Mar Morto.* Bari: Laterza, 1967.

G. Molin, *Die Sohne des Lichtes: Zeit und Stellung der Handschriften vom Toten Meer.* Vienna and Munich: Herold, 1954.

L. Moraldi, *I manoscritti di Qumran.* Turin: Unione Tipografica-Editrice Torinese, 1971; 2nd ed. 1986.

M. Sekine, ed., *Shikai-bunsho.* Tokyo: Yamomoto Shoten, 1963.

G. Vermes, *The Dead Sea Scrolls in English.* Baltimore: Penguin Books, 1962. 2nd ed. 1975. 3rd ed. 1987. 4th ed. Sheffield: Sheffield Academic Press, 1995.

A. L. Vincent, *Les manuscrits hébreux du désert de Juda.* Paris: A. Fayard, 1955.

M. O. Wise, M. Abegg, and E. Cook, *The Dead Sea Scrolls: A New Translation.* San Francisco: HarperSanFrancisco, 1996.

g. *The Temple Scroll (11QT)*

G. J. Brooke, ed., *Temple Scroll Studies: Papers Presented at the International Symposium on the Temple Scroll, Manchester, December 1987.* Sheffield: JSOT Press, 1989.

J. Maier, *Die Templerolle vom Toten Meer.* Munich: Reinhardt, 1978.

————, *The Temple Scroll.* Trans. R. T. White. JSOTSup 34. Sheffield: JSOT Press, 1985.

W. Nitsch, *Die Tempelrolle von Qumran: Vergleiche der Bibelzitate in den kultischen Gesetzen (Kolumnen 51,19-54) mit dem masoretischen Text, dem Targum Onkelos und der Septuaginta.* Giessen: Nebe, 1983.

E. Qimron, *The Temple Scroll: A Critical Edition with Extensive Reconstructions.* Beer-Sheva and Jerusalem: Israel Exploration Society, 1996.

D. D. Swanson, *The Temple Scroll and the Bible: The Methodology of 11QT.* STDJ 14. Leiden: Brill, 1995.

A. Vivian, ed., *Il Rotolo del Tempio.* Brescia: Paideia, 1990.

M. O. Wise, *A Critical Study of the Temple Scroll from Qumran Cave 11.* SAOC 49. Chicago: Oriental Institute, 1990.

Y. Yadin, *Megillat ha-miqdaš.* 3 vols. Jerusalem: Sifriyat maariv, 1977.

————, *The Temple Scroll.* 3 vols. Jerusalem: Israel Exploration Society, 1983.

————, *The Temple Scroll: The Hidden Law of the Dead Sea Sect.* New York: Random House, 1985.

h. The Halakhic Letter (4QMMT)

B. W. W. Dombrowski, *An Annotated Translation of Miqṣat Maʿaśeh ha-Tôrâ (4QMMT).* Cracow: Enigma, 1993.

J. Kampen and M. J. Bernstein, eds., *Reading 4QMMT: New Perspectives on Qumran Law and History.* Atlanta: Scholars Press, 1996.

Z. J. Kapera, ed., *Qumran Cave 4: Special Report on 4QMMT.* Cracow: Enigma, 1991.

i. The Damascus Document (CD)

M. Broshi, ed., *The Damascus Document Reconsidered.* Jerusalem: Israel Exploration Society, 1992.

P. R. Davies, *The Damascus Covenant: An Interpretation of the "Damascus Document."* JSOTSup 25. Sheffield: JSOT Press, 1983.

A.-M. Denis, *Les thèmes de connaissance dans le Document de Damas.* Louvain: Publications Universitaires, 1967.

C. Rabin, *The Zadokite Documents.* Oxford: Clarendon, 1954; 2nd ed. 1958.

H. H. Rowley, *The Zadokite Fragments and the Dead Sea Scrolls.* Oxford: Blackwell, 1952.

S. Zeitlin, *The Zadokite Fragments.* Philadelphia: Dropsie College, 1952.

j. The Rule of the Community (1QS)

W. H. Brownlee, *The Dead Sea Manual of Discipline: Translation and Notes.* BASORSupSt 10-12. New Haven: American Schools of Oriental Research, 1951.

A. R. C. Leaney, *The Rule of Qumran and Its Meaning.* London: SCM; Philadelphia: Westminster, 1966.

J. Licht, *The Rule Scroll* {Hebrew}. Jerusalem: Bialik, 1965.

C. Martone, *La "Regola della Comunità": Edizione critica.* Turin: Zamorani, 1995.

S. Metso, *The Textual Development of the Qumran Community Rule.* STDJ 21. Leiden: Brill, 1997.

J. Pouilly, *La Règle de la Communauté de Qumran: Son évolution littéraire.* Paris: Gabalda, 1976.

L. H. Schiffman, *The Eschatological Community of the Dead Sea Scrolls: A Study of the Rule of the Community.* SBLMS 38. Atlanta: Scholars Press, 1989.

P. Wernberg-Møller, *The Manual of Discipline.* STDJ 1. Leiden: Brill; Grand Rapids: Eerdmans, 1957.

k. The Thanksgiving Hymns (1QH)

M. Delcor, *Les hymnes de Qumrân (Hodayot).* Paris: Letouzey et Ané, 1962.

S. Holm-Nielsen, *Hodayot: Psalms from Qumran.* Aarhus: Universitetsforlaget, 1960.

B. P. Kittel, *The Hymns of Qumran: Translation and Commentary.* SBLDS 50. Chico, Calif.: Scholars Press, 1981.

J. Licht, *The Thanksgiving Scroll* {Hebrew}. Jerusalem: Bialik, 1957.

M. Mansoor, *The Thanksgiving Hymns.* STDJ 3. Leiden: Brill; Grand Rapids: Eerdmans, 1961.

E. H. Merrill, *Qumran and Predestination: A Theological Study of the Thanksgiving Hymns.* STDJ 8. Leiden: Brill, 1975.

l. The War Scroll (1QM)

J. Carmignac, *La règle de la guerre des fils de lumière contre les fils de ténèbres.* Paris: Letouzey et Ané, 1958.

P. R. Davies, *1QM, the War Scroll from Qumran: Its Structure and History.* BibOr 32. Rome: Biblical Institute Press, 1977.

R. G. Jones, *The Rules for the War of the Sons of Light with the Sons of Darkness.* New Haven: 1956.

B. Jongeling, *Le rouleau de la guerre des manuscrits de Qumrân.* Assen: Van Gorcum, 1962.

J. van der Ploeg, *Le rouleau de la guerre.* STDJ 2. Leiden: Brill, 1959.

Y. Yadin, *The Scroll of the War of the Sons of Light against the Sons of Darkness.* Trans. C. Rabin. Oxford: Oxford University Press, 1962.

m. The Pesharim

W. H. Brownlee, *The Midrash Pesher of Habakkuk.* SBLMS 24. Missoula, Mont.: Scholars Press, 1979.

K. Elliger, *Studien zum Habakkuk-Kommentar vom Toten Meer.* BHT 15. Tübingen: Mohr, 1953.

H. Feltes, *Die Gattung des Habakkukkommentars von Qumran (1QpHab).* FB 58. Würzburg: Echter, 1987.

M. P. Horgan, *Pesharim: Qumran Interpretation of Biblical Books.* CBQMS 8. Washington, D.C.: Catholic Biblical Association of America, 1979.

B. Nitzan, *Megillat Pesher Habakkuk.* Jerusalem: Bialik, 1986.

Index of Main Subjects

Index of Ancient Sources

Index of Modern Interpreters

TITLE 396

BEYOND THE ESSENE HYE

NAME

THEOLOGY

296 Bo